Lamar C

Barb Carruth

Lamar County Kin Volume One

Copyright © 2017 Barbara Carruth

All rights reserved.

ISBN-13: 978-1979047395

ISBN-10: 1979047391

LAMAR COUNTY KIN VOLUME ONE

This book contains stories collected or written by the author, Barb Carruth, unless otherwise notated. Barb is well known as a researcher of the early history of Lamar County Alabama as well as Fayette, Marion, Pickens, and Winston counties in Alabama and Monroe County, Mississippi for over twenty years.

FROM THE AUTHOR

It is my intent for this book to serve as an easy reference in the reader's search of Lamar County people. I focus on many who have been forgotten, bringing their stories to life again.

You will likewise read about the lives of present day Lamar people who have and are contributing to the preservation of our history or community.

I am not a writer but a COLLECTOR of local historical information which may be used in your research or enjoyed just by reading the interesting stories.

Local historical newspapers sited in this book were all printed in Vernon, Lamar County, Alabama unless sourced in the text.

You may visit me at https://walabamahistory.com/

Barb

DEDICATION

This book is dedicated to my husband Dewey and all my history friends who help me keep our history alive. My life is richer because of all of you.

CONTENTS

Lamar County People	1
Akens, J. J.	1
Allman, Minnie Lee Pennington	2
Anderson, Robert Houston	2
Armstrong Family	3
Armstrong Murder	3
Atkins, Spenser	5
Baines, Lona	5
Baines, Wayne & Kathleen	6
Bankhead Family	8
Bankhead, G. E.	8
Bankhead, John Hollis	9
Bankhead, Marion	10
Bardon, Betty Etma	10
Beard, Andy	11
Beard, Onay Ray	12
Black, Ralph	13
Blackwell, Levina Catharine	13
Blaylock, James David	14
Bobo, Raymond	14
Bobo, W. L.	15
Bolin, Nellie	15
Bolin, Robert Donathan	15
Bolin, R. D. Mrs.	17
Boman, Sammie Lee	17
Boman, Thos S.	19
Bonman, Egbert	19
Box, William Lyles MD	19
Bradley, Emma	20
Bradley, Robert Luther	21
Bridges, Francis R.	22
Brock, Berneal	22
Brock, Hubert	22
Brown, Burrell	22
Brown, David	23
Brown, James	23
Brown, J. W.	23
Brown, Rias	23
Brown, Watson	24
Buckley, Corky	24
Burnett, Robert A. and E. Loucinda Traylor	25

Burns, Samuel	25
Burrow, John T.	26
Burrow, Martha Caroline Terry	26
Burrow, Rube and Sim Green	27
Byrd, L. D. Killed	28
Caldwell Family	29
Cantrell Family Travel to Roots	31
Carden, Avist 95th Birthday	35
Carr, Jean Smith	36
Carruth, Robbie Omary	37
Christain, Loree Hankins Butler	39
Clark, Erah Burks	41
Cleveland, Dorothy Noe	41
Clouse, Jane	42
Cobb, R. W.	43
Coker, F. M.	43
Cole, Jesse Hollis and Eunice Tomlin	43
Cole, Nellie Price	47
Collins, James	48
Combs, P. C.	48
Cooper, W. T.	48
Cox, Diaderea	49
Cox, Will	49
Danner, Levi Mrs.	49
Darnel, G. B.	50
Davidson, Lillie Millican Evans	50
Draper, Isaiah	51
Duke, Mose	51
Edgeworth, Carolyn Black	52
Edgeworth, Clovis and Ola Robinson	52
Edwards, John Bankhead	55
Edwards Infant	55
Edwards, Henry Tracy	56
Elliott, Billie Brooks	57
Evans, Charles	59
Evans, Richard Green	61
Falkner, B. L.	62
Flinn, W. J.	63
Flynn, Erma Jaggers	63
Gibbs, Farmer	64
Gilmer, John Thompson Fraizer	64
Gilmer, Virginia Woods	65
Goodwin, S. P.	66

Gosa, Faustina Hankins	66
Guin, A. L.	66
Guthrie, D. R.	67
Guyton, John Strawbridge	67
Hale, Harrison and Abraham Murdock	68
Hamilton, W. F.	68
Hankins, Huse	68
Hankins, John Franklin	69
Hankins, Stephen	69
Hankins Thomas	69
Harris, Milas	70
Hayes, Maggie Lee Davis	71
Hays, Hilda	72
Hays, Paul	73
Henson, L. N.	73
Hocutt, Rose Marie Gardner Smith	73
Holladay, C. C.	74
Holladay, James	74
Holladay, John Daniel Sr.	74
Holliday, Joe Mrs.	75
Hollis Family	75
Hollis, Darling Jones Jr.	77
Hollis, D. U.	78
Homan Family	78
Ingle, Louise Bankhead	79
Irvin - Norton Family	80
Jaggers, Clytee Turman	81
Jones, Harold	81
Jones, Jim	82
Jordan, Hiram	82
Jordan, J. E.	83
Kabell, Cynthia Mary Jackson	83
King, Mary Lou Kinard	84
Kirk, Robert	85
Knight, Girthie Coker	85
Knight, James	87
Lamar, Lucius Quintius Curtius	88
Lawrence	88
Lowery, Anderson	89
Livington, Richard	89
Lusk and Pennington Family	90
Marchbanks Infant	91
Marler, Adine	92

McClung, Jim	92
McDaniel, Albritian	93
McGee, Peter	94
McKinney, Veneta Aldridge	94
McReynolds, Bobby	94
Metcalf Family	95
Middleton, James	97
Mixon, J. W.	97
Mixon, William Pierce	97
Molloy, Thomas	98
Moore, George	98
Moore, James Field	99
Moore, John T.	99
Moore, Thomas B.	99
Morris, Floyd Jr.	100
Morris, John	101
Morris, Ruby Cash	101
Morton, M. Dr.	102
Morton, James M.	102
Mose	103
Mozley, John Coleman and Mary Jane Evans	103
Nesmith, T. B.	104
Nixon, W. L. Dr.	104
Noe Family	105
Noe, Lockie Reese	105
Noe Murders	106
Nolen, Ellie Ester Birmingham	106
Nolen, George Washington	112
Norton, Elmer	112
Oakes, Evelyn Elliott	112
Odom, Renzo Franklin	114
Pearson, Green	115
Pennington Family of Lamar County	115
Pennington, Hugh	117
Pennington, Mollie	117
Pennington, Rena	125
Pennington, Richard	125
Pennington, Silas Filmore	127
Perkins, Laverne Cunningham	129
Perry, R. J.	130
Pinkerton, Austin	130
Pollard, Mr.	132
Rasbury, Elizabeth	132

Rasbury, Isaac	133
Rector, Charlie Franklin and Annie Lucas	133
Rector Kin – Digging Up	136
Redden Family	139
Reese	141
Reeves, Jimmy Paul	141
Revolutionary Patriot Dedication Held	142
Roberts	144
Roberts, John Monroe Dr.	144
Robertson, Fay Memories	145
Robertson, Tom	146
Rush	147
Sanders	147
Sanders, Bill	147
Shackelford, Thurman and Margaret McDill	148
Shaw, Peter	149
Shelton, Dr. L. F.	149
Shields, Captain	149
Smith, A. Q.	149
Smith, L. R.	157
Smith, Rube	157
Smithson, Claud	157
Springfield, E. M.	157
Springfield, Harriet	158
Stanford, Martha Brown Heirs	158
Stanford, Thomas	160
Stanford, William Estate	161
Stone, Commissioner	162
Sudberry, Sabra Newell	162
Tate, Alfred William	163
Taylor, Jesse	164
Terrell, John D. Jr.	165
Terrell, S. M. Mrs.	165
Thomas Family Reunion	165
Thomas, William Murray	166
Thornton, Annie Belle Flynn	166
Todd, Ruby	168
Trim, J. M.	170
Trimm, Eunice and Willie Mae Trimm Hamm	170
Turner, Joe and Sibbie	171
Vail, Jeremiah and John Michael	172
Veal, Laura	175
Vernon, Edmond	176

Waldrop, W. W.	178
Wall, A. A.	178
Wall - Summers Wedding	179
Ward Family	180
Webb, Dumas	180
Webb, Jack	181
Webb, Joseph and Lucinda Emiline Evans	181
Weeks	182
Wells, Dug	183
Wells, Susie Davis	183
Wheeler, A. J.	184
Wheeler, Andy	184
Wheeler, William Chester	185
White	187
Wilson, J. E. A. and Rody Pennington	187
Wimberly, L. M.	188
Woods, Jessie Woolbright	188
Woolbright, Lula King	192
Wright, Ellis Northington	193
Wright, Robert Green	193
Young, Alexander	195
Young, Dora	196
Young, Eddie	197
Young, J. P. & R. W.	197
Young, Judge Mrs.	198
Young Limited Partnership	198
Young, William A.	198

Lamar County Kin
Volume One

Lamar County People

Pioneer settlers came by covered wagon, many walked, rode horses, mules, oxen, bringing everything they owned with them on their backs or either in a wagon. Many left everything behind. They came with a dream, a dream of finding land, a better place, to build a future with hope for themselves and their family. Most came from Tennessee, North Carolina, South Carolina, Georgia and Virginia.

Many saw our area for the first time after the War of 1812 as soldiers returning back to Tennessee, recognized the potential, later coming back to claim land or work on the Military Road (Known as Andrew Jackson's Military Road) built after the war.

Some came with nothing more than determination and a desire for a better life. They built homes, worked the land growing their food and crops to sell, began traditions that we keep today.

Many have been forgotten, their footprints are gone, washed away by the rains of time. But their hardworking spirit and their pride in our land is not forgotten. This pioneer spirit is alive today in remnants of the past. We will not forget.

J. J. Akens

On the 25th, J. J. Akens, residing near Detroit, in this county, went out early in the morning coon hunting, about sun up. He cut a tree, which struck him senseless in which condition he died on the 29th ult. He leaves a wife to mourn his departure. Source: *The Vernon Clipper* October 10, 1879

Minnie Lee Pennington Allman

Daniel and Minnie Lee Pennington Allman

Minnie Lee Pennington daughter of Richard Pennington, married Daniel Allman September 18, 1904. Her father insisted that that Daniel built a separate household for her prior to marriage. Daniel at that time was living with his mother in the farm house on the Allman original tract of land. Source: Interview with Eugene Allman

Robert Houston Anderson

If you think Sheriff Anderson won't get your still, just let it stay where it is and you'll have another think coming. He took his deputies Monday and went over on, and across Buttahatchie, and took in one together with about ten barrels of beer, etc. They had a funny experience in the operation too. The still was across the river on an island, and the operators were over there and had the boat on that side of the river, and they waited for them to return, which they did pretty soon, and Sheriff Anderson took charge of them, and left one with his deputies on this side of the river, took the other one with him and deputy Wilson set sail for the other side of the river to get the still. About the middle of the river the boat turned turtle and spilled the whole bunch into the river.

Sheriff Anderson and Wilson managed to reach the shore on the side where the still was, but the other fellow turned for the bank from whence they started, and seemingly in need of help, Deputy Joe Weaver laid his gun down to assist him, and when the man they were guarding picked it up, and held his captors at bay until he backed off, when he turned and left taking the gun with him. These men are known to the sheriff and they will be apprehended and put in touch with the courts before long. Keep your stills out of Anderson's way if you want to make "cat". Source: *The Lamar Democrat* April 20, 1921

Armstrong Family

Ezekiel Armstrong and his two brothers were the first of the family to settle in Lamar County then Marion County around 1830. The story is told that their father John a soldier in the First Regiment of Tennessee Volunteers Mounted Gunman of Coffee's troops, saw the land of present Lamar County on his return from the Battle of New Orleans. John Armstrong who directed his family to settle in the area died before he left Tennessee.

Ezekial Armstrong was married to Melinda Marchbanks and their children were James A., Matilda and Winston. The E. K. Armstrong family settled in the Mulberry Springs Community or Moscow.

James Alexander the son of Ezekial and Melinda Armstrong married Ella Clifton and owned a store in Moscow where he was also a postmaster and farmer. The Armstrong's children were: Felix, a physician who practiced medicine in Texas; Emma E. married first to John L. Oldshue then to Green Bankhead; Joe Woods, lived in Moscow and Sulligent also a physician in Texas; and Angie who died in infancy. Source: Writings of Mrs. Virginia Woods Gilmer

Armstrong Murder

A terrible tragedy happened in the Moore Hill house in the old Moscow community near Sulligent owned by Ezekial Armstrong and his wife Malinda Marchbanks Armstrong about 1882. The Winston Armstrong family were living in the Moore house at this time. Wint's wife had a new baby. One chilly morning, Wint had gone to the next farm to help his brother-in-law John Burton Woods with hog killing. Cap Bankhead a trusted old Negro man was splitting wood in the back yard. He went in the house carrying the ax going into the bedroom where Eliza was lying in bed with her little baby. He stood there looking at mother and baby. There were three other people in the room: Mrs. Malinda Armstrong Eliza's mother-in-law, ten year old Emma Armstrong and Elvira Hill a neighbor.

Mrs. Armstrong thought he had come in to see the baby. She asked, "Well Cap what do you think of our baby?" Without a word he went beserk, took his ax and spit Eliza's head open. Cap hit Mrs. Malinda Armstrong with the ax but she evaded him. Elvira Hill slipped out of the house and ran on the path through the woods to the home of Burt Woods and told the terrible news.

Wint had brought his Winchester 38 rifle to kill the hog. He picked up the rifle and ran through the woods home. There in the back yard was a bloody Cap splitting wood with bloody clothes and bloody ax. Wint shot Cap on the spot and he fell lifeless beside his bloody ax.

The Armstrong family could not bear to live in the Moore house after that. The Armstrongs traded farms with Aaron Hill who lived just across Bogue Creek. Source: *Leroy Kennedy: Southern Patriot* by Mrs. Virginia Gilmer, pages 129-130.

Mrs. Beulah Hill previous owner of the Moore-Hill house also wrote her version of the murder: "In the front yard (Moore-Hill) house is the 'hanging tree', where a black man was hung in 1881 after he killed Mrs. Armstrong with a 'gantling' hook. Because of the killing and the uneasy aftermath, the Armstrong women no longer were comfortable living in the house, so a swap was made. Mr. A. A. Hill swapped houses with them in December 1881 for a like house across Bogue Creek. Mrs. Armstrong was killed by a black man with a 'gantling' hook on a chain. The cook ran out to the back of the house and to the men who were some distance away slaughtering hogs. They came and shot the crazed man and then hung him in the cedar tree out front."

One of the legends told of the Moore-Hill house is: "Nowadays on a dark still night when all is quiet, you can hear someone (Mrs. Armstrong) coming slowly down the steps rattling the chain. When she gets to the bottom of the steps the door slams shut and quietness settles over the house."

Spenser Atkins

Vernon, May 15 - (Special) - When Rube Burrow, the famous outlaw, started out with his band of desperadoes and train robbers, it was in Lamar County. This same county has given birth to another band which is equally as lawless as the famous Burrow gang.

At Vernon, a few nights ago, a band of white caps went to the house of Spenser Atkins, bound his hands, gagged him and marched him about 300 yards from his house and riddled his body with bullets. It is said that Atkins was an upholder of law and order and that this band would be safer if the county were rid of him. So on this account, according to the story, Atkins was finally murdered in cold blood.

On Sunday night Dre Nealands was arrested by Sheriff Pennington upon suspicion of being implicated in the murder of Atkins.

It seems that there had been an ironclad oath of allegiance to each other sworn by the band that attempted this outrage, and that if any member was caught the others were to rescue him.

Nealands spent Sunday and Monday nights in jail, and yesterday morning gave the whole methods of the band away and implicated Alex and Allen Jordan, nephews of Atkins, and another young man. The sheriff went at once and arrested these alleged outlaws and placed them in jail.

Owing to the alleged oath of the band and the fears that an attempt to release the prisoners would be made Sheriff Pennnington ordered out Company M of the Alabama state troops, which are now guarding Lamar county jail.

An attack was feared, but so far as is known nothing has transpired. Source: *The Hamilton Free Press*, May 17, 1894

Lona Baines

Baines, Lona   Kennedy, Ala - Jordan Baines, a poor though respectable farmer, living nine miles south of Kennedy, in Pickens county, on arising Sunday morning missed his eighteen year old daughter Lona but thought she had gone on a visit to neighbors. About the same time Andy Beard a negro, 22 years of age, employed by Mr. Baines, disappeared, which caused the parents to become suspicious, and a search was instigated, which raised the suspicion that Lona had eloped with the negro Beard. Parties were made up and are vigilantly searching for the pair, and doubtless, if caught Judge Lynch will pass sentence on Beard, and the girl will be severely dealt with. The pair were seen some time Sunday between Kennedy and Millport, going toward Columbus, Miss., the girl traveling half a mile in advance of the negro. It is supposed that a clandestine intimacy existing between the two is the cause of the elopement. (*Marion County News*, March 18, 1897)

Wayne & Kathleen Baines

Sun Fun And The Pea Patch

We all know our (Lamar County Genealogical & Historical Society) president and friend Wayne Baines. This is a tribute to his hard work, generosity, friendship and love. A thank you to his wife Kathleen for her patience, kindness, and friendship along with sharing Wayne with all the people who love and enjoy his involvements.

Before and after his retirement, Wayne found great enjoyment riding his tractor, plowing his fields, clearing his pine forest, and planting enormous gardens. His gardens are not just for Kathleen, Heath and himself. His plans are always to share with his friends.

Each year he invites friends to his corn fields, to pick corn and to his pea field (much too big for a patch) to pick peas. I have been a participant in the pea picking for a couple years since I moved back to Millport. Those of us who arise early in the morning and gather in Wayne's pea field have to derive fun and enjoyment from the event. I can't think of any other reason to get up so early and stay so long in the July heat. Of course, there are the peas, but then there are frozen peas to be bought in the grocery store. Some will say there is a great difference in fresh field peas and store frozen peas. Question, "Don't we bring them home and freeze them?"

This year some of us spent more than one day in the field. I picked two days. One for myself, which was pleasant from 6:30 a.m. to 7:30 a.m. hot from 7:30 a.m. to 8:30 a.m. and really hot by 9:30 a.m. none of us had any heat side effects that day. Wayne did tell me that I tried to stay in the shade. One day of peas was enough for me. My sister, Faye Bryant Walker, wanted peas, and we planned to go back on Monday. She got sick and ended up at the doctor's office so I decided I could stand one more day in the pea patch for my sister.

We started out early as usual. As we pick we go between two rows and pick each row, as we go. About two thirds of the way down my rows I got to feeling light headed, I thought "I can finish this." I told Tommy Cobb on the row beside me that I felt light headed, and she said she was also, and thought she would quit. I kept picking, then I became dizzy and sat down for a few minutes, then tried picking on my knees. Didn't work!! Wayne was coming down my row, I got up and told him I didn't think I could finish. He took my bucket and we started on down the row. All of a sudden, I thought I would faint, I said "Wayne, I think I'm going to faint." He came and took my arm, I got worse, by the time we came to a tree at the end of the field I told him to set me down and get my Jeep. As he drove the Jeep in near me, I stood up, I went left, then right, then forward on my face, the world had gone black. Wayne came got me to the Jeep and turned the air on real cold and got me across the road to the house. I got okay after sitting in the air; drinking a bottle of water, and eating a piece of watermelon. I wasn't the only one with bad effects that day. Tommy Cobb almost blacked out after she drove home and Martha Frakes got sick to her stomach. Wayne and another fellow finished the peas we hadn't picked and later he had leg cramps from the heat. He made Kathleen and me go to the house for a while before I went home. "Thanks for taking better care of me than yourself, my friend."

I'm not sure how many people have enjoyed peas from Wayne's fields in years past. This year some of us realized there were lots of folks who came and picked or Wayne picked, shelled and carried the peas to them. Yes, thank goodness he has a pea sheller. I actually enjoy picking the peas, shelling is for the birds. We asked Wayne to get us a head count. He came up with at least 50 people.

Some of the ladies decided we should do a "thank you" supper for Wayne and Kathleen. We made phone calls, asked for potluck and Wayne opened Bethel Church for us to gather. You might know God blessed us with a storm that night, the winds blew, trees fell over, and roofs came off. Despite Katrina we celebrated anyway. Some of us braved the storm and made the gathering. Martha Frakes' son, DeWayne Guyton gave a little talk about Wayne and Kathleen, and presented a plaque we had made for them. The plaque read "Certificate of appreciation, awarded to Wayne and Kathleen Baines August 27, 2005 for kindness and generosity as true friends to this community and Lamar County, from all your 'Pea Picking Friends'." Everyone enjoyed good food, fellowship, and made it home safely thru the storm.

Paul Hays, a special guest was down visiting from Washington DC, cataloging graveyards. Submitted and written by Flora Bryant McCool

Bankhead Family

The Bankhead family were early pioneers to the area and one of the first families to move in after the Jackson Military road was made from the wilderness of the Mississippi Territory after the War of 1812. In the 1820s, George Bankhead established a stage coach stop on the road. George's son, James built Bankhead house (standing today but in peril) about 1840 on part of a large plantation.

At the beginning of the Civil War, it is said James' son, John Hollis Bankhead, gathered Confederate troops in the house's front yard. John Hollis survived the war and was nominated to Congress at the Fayette County Courthouse in 1886. Captain Bankhead was elected and served from 1887 to 1907. He also served as a senator until his death in 1920.

His sons William B. and John Hollis Jr., born in the Sulligent house also served as distinguished public servants. William B. served as Speaker of the House from 1936 until his death in 1940. Before William's funeral at the First United Methodist Church in Jasper, the church had to build a special wheelchair ramp so that President Franklin Delano Roosevelt could attend.

G. E. Bankhead

G. E. Bankhead was in town (Vernon) Thursday of last week getting up a petition to the bosses of the K. C. M & B. R. R. for a depot at the entrance of the Buttahatchie swamp, just below his residence on the road. The site petitioned for is a beautiful and very convenient location for a depot. Source: *The Vernon Courier* December 3, 1886.

John Hollis Bankhead

John Hollis Bankhead and Sons

At the outbreak of the War Between the States, John Hollis Bankhead enlisted as a private in Co. K, 16th Alabama infantry regiment, J. B. Powers, as captain and Col. William B. Wood, of Florence, as regimental commander. He was in the conflict from the beginning to the end, and took part in the battles at Fishing Creek, Perryville, Murfreesboro, and all the battles of the Western Army, in which his command participated, except when disabled from wounds received in action.

After the battle of Fishing Creek he was promoted to third lieutenant and became captain after the battle of Shiloh. He led the 16th Alabama regiment in an impetuous and successful charge, at Chickamauga, where he was wounded. As he retired, with his wound, the sedge field on which a part of the battle had been fought, caught fire and burned rapidly. He stumbled upon the prostrate form of John Custer, a private, an elderly man who had fought the day through beside three sturdy sons, and who was now wounded by a gun shot through the hips and his life imperiled by the rapidly approaching fire. Captain Bankhead, with one arm useless, lifted himself from the ground with Custer clinging to his neck, and thus bore him to a spot of safety. The rescued man survived the war many years, and was always the devoted friend of his benefactor. Source: *History of Alabama and Dictionary of Alabama Biography* by Thomas McAdory Owen, Vol IV, Published by S. J. Clark Publishing Company, 1921 transcribed and submitted by Veneta A. McKinney

Marion Bankhead

Marion Bankhead, colored who killed Dug Wells on the evening of the 6th was put in jail here Monday. He was captured at Riverton, and Sheriff Haley went there after him. He claims to have been justifiable in the killing for he says he was running when he did the cutting and that Wells was trying to open his knife. He claims to have been afraid of Wells and that he was not at all mad when the deed was done.

DeWitt Flemings, who was with Bankhead, at the time of the killing was arrested last week, and charged with being an accomplice. He was tried before Squire D. W. Hollis and acquitted, but what statement he made as to the trouble is not known further than he, it is said, claims that Wells did not strike Bankhead at all. Source: *The Vernon Courier*, February 17, 1898

Marion Bankhead was indicted for the murder of Dug Wells. The charge was murder on the first degree, but an inquiring into the evidence, it was found that this could be sustained and the charge was reduced and he was granted bail in the sum of $500, which he made and was released from jail yesterday. Source: *The Vernon Courier*, March 10, 1898

Betty Etma Bardon

07-28-2004

Betty Etma Bardon, 100 years and nine months died Sunday July 25, 2004 in the hospital with granddaughter Amy Reeves Robinson by her side. Mrs. Bardon's daughter and son in- law Mattie and Truman Reeves have a peach farm that I visit quite frequently in the summer time. For several years, Truman has tried to get me to interview Mrs. Bardon because he knows how interested I am in the history of our county. She was a living history book, up until she fell about two years ago breaking her hip, she was very active and lived at her home independently. I never made the time to visit her, and I regret that.

Mrs. Bardon was born Oct. 23, 1903, to George and Viola Faulkner Mordecai. The Mordecais lived in the Bethlehem community of Lamar County, between Vernon and Millport. She was the oldest of eight children and out lived them all. Her grandfather Burrell L. Falkner was probate judge of Jones, Sanford and Lamar County 1867-1871 and 1873-1875. Her great-great-grandfather Moses Mordecai came to America from Germany in 1760.

On October 26, 2003 a 100th birthday celebration was held at the Star

Community clubhouse for her. Mrs. Bardon enjoyed everyone that came. She loved people and it is said that she never met a stranger. She loved her family and many friends. She leaves a legacy of being a true friend to many.

Mrs. Bardon was a member of Poplar Springs Primitive Baptist Church for 74 years, and attended church there until the end of May of this year. She loved gospel singing and Sacred Harp singing was her favorite. Wayne Baines, a friend of hers knows how much she loved the singing. She was an inspiration to those fortunate enough to be touched by her life.

She married Isaac Raymond Bardon on December 5, 1943. They were married 43 years when he died April 30, 1987. Murphy Bobo, Justice of the Peace, married them at his home four miles south of Vernon. Mrs. Bardon did not work away from home on a public job, until she was in her 60's. She took a job as nursing assistant at the local nursing home until mandatory retirement at age 70. She then did home care for the elderly for many years. She was remarkable. Her positive outlook will be missed. Many have eaten her chicken pies, enjoyed fruits of her canning, crocheting and growing plants. As a young girl she helped her mother with the cooking  and raising of her siblings so she knew how to manage a household, taking care of a husband and daughter was a joy to her.

Funeral services were held on Tuesday, July 27th, at Poplar Springs Primitive Baptist Church, where she had been a member for 74 years. The hymn "Amazing Grace" was sung by the congregation. Only a few weeks ago, this same hymn was sung at the funeral of president Ronald Reagan. "Amazing Grace" is said to be the most popular hymn ever.

Andy Beard

Kennedy, Ala - News reached here Monday afternoon that the negro, Andy Beard who eloped with the white girl, Lona Baines, who lived about ten miles south of this place, in Pickens county, was killed Saturday evening in the public highway, near Obney township in Pickens county. The couple were overtaken by a body of twenty-five mounted men, and as soon as they discovered that they were being pursued the negro began to run, whereupon the pursuers opened fire, killing him instantly. The girl Lona cried out to the slayers of her paramour to treat her in the same manner that they had him, but the body rode away, leaving her near the scene of the killing. Her father and brothers afterward took her back home, and it is not known in what manner her punishment was inflicted. Source: *The Marion County News,* March 25, 1897

Onay Ray Beard

9-15-2004

Mrs. Onay Ray Beard was born September 11, 1910 to Frances Marion and Adelena Arizona Irvin Ray. She celebrated her 94th birthday on Sunday, September 12, 2004 in the Fellowship Hall of Center Point Free Will Baptist Church with family and friends. I went by Sunday afternoon to wish her well and get a picture. I told her I was going to write about her this week. She told me if I wanted to tell her age, she didn't mind. She was having a good time visiting with everyone.

I have known Mrs. Onay for as long as I can remember. She lives "Just across the Line" in the Sipsey Fork Community, Monroe County Mississippi. I live near the Alabama/Mississippi line and we have always referred to folks living in the Sipsey Fork and Greenwood Springs communities as living "Just Across the Line."

Mrs. Onay's sisters are: Bertie May born 1902; Lola Grey born 1904; Mila Day born 1907 and Floree born 1912. Three of her sisters are deceased, Bertie May died 1966; Mila Day died 1991; Lola Grey died 1977.

Mrs. Onay has a sharp memory. She has seen many changes in her 94 years. She was married to John Wesley Beard who died in 1939 leaving her with two small daughters, Magdalene and Imogene. Imogene died in 1969. Mrs. Onay lives with Magdalene and her husband Charles Clifton in their home. She is interested in genealogy and has helped many who were researching their family history. She is a talking history book. It has been a delight for me to have the opportunity to know this woman. Happy Birthday Mrs. Onay!

Ralph Black

Lest We Forget- 2005

Mr. Ralph Black a long-time supporter and member of Lamar County Genealogical & Historical Society will not be with us at our meetings anymore. He will be missed and has been missed since his stroke a few months ago. Mr. Ralph did not talk much, but he was always listening and ready to offer a kind word and encouragement.

Ralph Black age 88 of Guin, AL died Thursday, September 22, 2005 in the Sunset Manor Nursing Home in Guin. Born in Guin, Alabama to James William and Lula Florence Weeks Black.

He was a Veteran of World War II having served in the US Air Force, a member of the VFW and the American Legion, a member of the Guin First United Methodist Church where he served as Sunday School Class Treasurer, a member of the Methodist Men, and a Trustee. He served on the Guin City Council, was a former member of the Guin Fire Department and was a member of the Marion County and Lamar County Genealogical Societies. He worked at Black's Hardware Store in Guin.

Services were held Sunday, September 25, 2005 at 3:30 PM from the Guin First United Methodist Church with burial in the Guin City Cemetery.

Levina Catharine Blackwell

Levina Catharine Blackwell was born in South Carolina, March 16, 1837, and departed this life June 15, 1886, aged forty-nine years and three months. She was married to James E. Blackwell, January 19, 1854, professed religion in 1856, and joined the M. E. Church South the same year. Since then she has lived a model Christian. She told her husband when he started to the late war that she would pray for him twice a day for him until he returned, and when he came back from the war she told him she had kept her promise.

She was the mother of seven children, all of whom except one have professed religion and are now members of the Methodist Church. She requested her husband, the night before her death, to tell all of her children that if she never saw them again on earth she would meet them at the pearly gates of heaven. She said there was not a shadow intervening between her and her Savior, and if it was God's will she had rather go than stay here and suffer as she had suffered for ten or twelve years. Sister Blackwell was a good woman —oved by all who knew her. I preached the last sermon that she heard on earth on Sunday afternoon at Free Hope Church. Wednesday following, a large congregation of weeping relatives and friends met at Walnut Grove Cemetery to pay the last tribute of respect to the remains of our departed sister. She has gone from us, but we mourn not as those who have no hope. She cannot come back to us, but we can go to her. May God bless the grief stricken ones, and my they all meet her in heaven. F. V. L. Finch Source: *The Lamar News*, September 9, 1886

James David Blaylock

James David Blalock Family
Standing in Front of House located Northwest of Sulligent

Left to right: Malinda L. Blalock, Ida Blalock, James David Blalock, William (Willie) Blalock, MaDora Leverett Blaylock.

The house, built in 1906, by Jim Blaylock's nephew Walter Evans, is standing today (2008) on the Jaggers' Farm. Source: Photo courtesy of Raburn Blaylock.

Raymond Bobo

Little Raymond Bobo son of Mr. & Mrs. Foss Bobo died September 5, 1916. Source: *The Lamar Democrat*, September 27, 1916

W. L. Bobo

Mr. W. L. Bobo, who lives on the road leading to Fayette Court House, eight miles west of the town told us one night last week that Judge Alex Cobb was the first man he ever voted for. He also told us there was a man residing in Lamar County, 32 years old, and who had never bought a pound of sugar nor borrowed a nickel. We really appreciate the hospitality of "Uncle Billie" Bobo, and enjoyed his war experience which he related to Sheriff Pennington and ye editor. Source: *The Vernon Courier*, November 19 1886

Nellie Bolin

Mrs. Nellie Bolin, wife of W. D. Bolin of Crews, died at her home last Thursday night. She has been a sufferer for a long while and all that could be done by the medical fraternity of this county to relieve her suffering was done. She was laid to rest in the cemetery at Crew Saturday morning. She was a daughter of Mr. and Mrs. R. E. Bradley. Source: *The Vernon Courier*, May 14, 1896

Robert Donathan Bolin

One of the pioneer settlers in Marion County, and what is now Lamar

County, was R. D. Bolin. In a memorial by Guin Lodge No. 478 it was stated that Robert Donathan Bolin was born in North Carolina August 16, 1822. He moved to Alabama in his early youth and lived for more than half a century in Marion and the adjoining county of Lamar. He died 28th of March 1899 at the home of his son Pleasant Bolin in Lamar County, surrounded by a host of relatives and friends. He died as he had lived, a man of God, a worthy member of the Masonic Order and a zealous worker in Christ's earthly kingdom. He was buried in the cemetery of the Mt. Hebron United Methodist Church at Crews, in Lamar County beside his wife, Nancy Edeline Cantrell Bolin, who preceded him in death. There was a granite marker some four feet tall inscribed with both R. D.'s name and that of his wife.

We do not know when he came to Marion County, but he purchased land there on January 04, 1844, per the book *First Land Settlers of Marion County 1820-1850* compiled by J. C. Lawler. This land was in Section 33, Township 11S, Range 14W. Later R. D. purchased more land in Marion County south and west of the earlier purchase and close to the Lamar County border near the Beaverton community. He was found in the 1840 United States census, so it is assumed he came to Marion County after 1840.

R. D. Bolin married Nancy Edeline Cantrell, daughter of Berry Cantrell and his first wife Malita, presumably in Marion County on December 25, 1843. Early Court House records were burned. Family oral history indicates that the couple's first child was born in November 1844 and died September 1845. Eleven or twelve other children were born to R. D. Bolin and wife. Nancy's date of birth is given as April 20, 1826 in Spartanburg County South Carolina where the Revolutionary War Soldier, John Cantrell settled after the War.

The most noticeful fact about R. D. Bolin is that he was a man of God. He was for many years a Methodist Circuit Rider preacher and performed many services for people in the area. He married many couples and has his name recorded as R. D. Bolin M. G. for Minister of the Gospel. Also he was a farmer and is listed as County Corner in the 1860 Marion County Census. He was fairly prosperous for the times according to census records.

Some additional facts concerning R. D. are as follows:

1. He gave all his children nicknames.
2. The Vernon Courier said of his passing that he was one of original settlers of this section of Alabama.
3. Most of his life was spent in the service of the Methodist Church.
4. During the events of 1863-64 Confederate and Union "outlaws" stole everything people had, and shot. Rev. Bob Bolin's oxen, just out in the road. This item is from *Memoirs of Miss Elliott Key* to her good friend William B. Ford.

5. He was also known as Robert and Bob.
6. Bolin was spelled several ways, Boling, Bolling, Bollen, Bolling, and Bowlen.
7. His first land purchase was close to Pikeville, which became the county seat in 1817 when Marion County was organized. Prior to that, the land was in the Cherokee Indian Territory.
8. He did not take part in the War Between the States nor did he own slaves.
9. Some of his sons moved to the Midwest and settled in Arkansas and Oklahoma.
10. Much of this information is taken from a paper, written by Mrs. Davis Doescher, a descendant, who lived in Panama City, FL and from recollection of my grandmother and mother, descendants of R. D. and Nancy Bolin.
11. The Mt. Hebron Cemetery marker for R. D. Bolin shows, born August 16, 1822 and died, March 28, 1899. For Nancy Edeline Cantrell Bolin's the dates are April 20, 1826 and January 06, 1893. Source: Alfred Tate to Barbara Carruth

Mrs. R. D. Bolin

Mrs. Bolin wife of Rev. R. D. Bolin died suddenly on the evening of the 6th. Source: *The Vernon Courier* dated January 12, 1893

Sammie Lee Chandler Boman

My Rich Granny Boman

I was just laying here thinking about my Granny Boman, Sammie Lee Chandler Boman, wife of William Lumpkin Boman. I always thought she was so rich. She had a grocery store truck come to her house. He had all kinds of things on it, from groceries to pots and pans. She picked me up and let me look inside.

She didn't need running water. She had her own well on her back porch. She even had a bucket with a dipper to drink out of there. I remember how cold the water was, no need to refrigerate it. It tasted better than any water I'd ever had. I probably drank more water at Granny's than anywhere else.

She had her own chickens, that kept her in fresh eggs. They even had their own house. Granny let me gather eggs when we came to visit. She did forget to tell me they would flog me if they were setting, and did that chicken ever flog me... Granny like to have never got all those tangles out of my hair.

One time when we came to visit her, she told me if I would go get a chicken we would have chicken for supper, I was going to make her so proud of me and get the biggest one.. I saw one and was going to get it... things took a turn for the bad, it chased me and bit me .. and it wasn't even a chicken it was a goose. The best I can remember I cried. She didn't even have to go get bacon... she had her own pigs, I can still smell it as she fried it.

There was a spring close by to play in, and look for mud puppies. Granny had a long beautiful table... no need for chairs, she had long benches. There wasn't a need for putting left over lunch in the refrigerator, she left it on the table with a cloth draped over it. Ready for supper ... when she would put her cloth over the food I would sneak under the table and reach under the cloth in the same place every time and get a hand full of green beans, and get the best biscuit and eat them ... I think granny knew I was doing that, because she was smiling while she was doing the dishes, and I was under the table eating... and somehow the beans and biscuits were always in the same place....

My granny even had an outhouse. I thought that was so grand. I always had to go. A whole room outside the house just to go "potty," I could even look through the cracks to the outside, no need for a window.

I remember how it sounded as I ran across her porch and through her house. One time Granny gave my sister and I a pie pan and a wire fly flap, if we could kill enough flies she promised to make us a fly pie, we spent a long time killing flies, it may be my memory failing me, but I don't remember a fly pie. I think Granny did that to keep us busy.

I can still see her brushing her beautiful long hair putting it up in a bun. I can still remember how she smelled as she hugged me up, how soft her cheek was against mine. Yes my granny was so rich, just the way I remember. Then we moved here from El Paso Texas, and we were rich too, we had an outhouse. It wasn't long before I found out that dogs falling in were not fun to get out.

Granny would come to visit us. one time she was in the bathroom, we decided to put an ironing board against the door and we ran and hid in our closet. We waited what seemed like forever and listened for it to fall... It didn't so we opened the closet door to go investigate and BAM!!!!!!!!!!!! there went the ironing board.. Granny had slipped out and put it against our closet door. Submitted and written by Liz Guyton

Thos. S. Boman

In the death of Mr. Thos. S. Boman, Lamar has lost a noble and good citizen. Source: *The Lamar News* September 23, 1886.

Egbert Bonman

The colored people will hold a camp meeting to being today, near "Uncle" EGBERT BONMAN'S. Hope they may accomplish great good. Source: *The Lamar News,* September 23, 1886

William Lyles Box

(1882-1958)

Dr. Box was born in the Bedford Community near Vernon. In researching Dr. Box, I read that in an attempt to save enough money to go to medical school, he taught school at Bedford. Finally giving up on this idea, he talked a Columbus, Mississippi banker into lending him money for medical school. He then attended the University of Alabama Medical School at Mobile. He graduated from medical school in a suit of clothes that cost him $6.00.

In 1906, Dr. Box married Josephine Lillian Woods (1888-1976) of the Shiloh Community in Lamar County. She was the daughter of Dr. Thomas Bailey Woods and Jane Elizabeth McCrary Woods. Her father was a country doctor so she was familiar with the lifestyle.

Practicing medicine as a country doctor wasn't easy, roads were either very bad or didn't exist. At first he had only a horse and saddlebags. Later he added a cart, then a buggy, later a Model T then a larger automobile. In the early days, Dr. Box often came home only long enough to change horses. A lap robe and lantern were necessary items.

Dr. Box's wife "Miss Josie" went with him on calls in all kinds of weather, at all hours and into all types of homes. People that couldn't pay received treatment and medicine just as if they had money. Dr. and Mrs. Box were known to supply food as well as clothing to families in need. While Dr. Box would be giving medicine to the sick, his wife would be offering words of encouragement to concerned family members. She was a wonderful helpmate and always tried to ease any hardship that she could for her husband.

Dr. Box practiced medicine for 53 years. In 1951, the townspeople of Vernon honored Dr. Box for his service with a testimonial dinner. Dr. J. M. Roberts was also honored on this night. In her tribute to the two doctors, Mrs. Lillie Mae Box said, "They not only cared for our ills, but they brought joy and cheers into our homes." It has been said that Dr. Box's jokes and stories did as much good for the sick as his medicine.

Dr. and Mrs. Box had two sons, Billy Burke and Joe. Dr. Box died in 1958 and Mrs. Box died in 1976. They are both buried in the New Hope Cemetery. Their grandson, W. C. Box who is a physician in Sulligent today is respected and possesses that concern for the people of Lamar County just as his granddaddy and grandmother did years ago. I know that they would be proud. Source: Mrs. Sarah Jo. Spearman Vernon, Alabama; *The Commercial Dispatch,* December 2, 1951 Columbus, Mississippi,

Emma Bradley

Elma (Bradley) Ward (descendant of Judge Bradley), wife of James V, (Veston) Ward, who is buried in row no. 16, plot 4 in Furnace Hill Cemetery near Vernon remembers when her sister Emma Bradley was buried in 1922, in row no. 9, plot no. 4 in the cemetery. They were carrying her by mule and wagon to the cemetery. A rain storm came up so they went by John W. Crowder's house, and unloaded the casket onto the front porch until the storm was over. They reloaded the casket back onto the wagon and went to the cemetery. There was no arbor, even at this time, they were still using the shade of the huge oak tree for the services. Burial services were held under this oak tree for years and years before the arbor was built. Source: *Furnace Hill Cemetery* book

Robert Luther Bradley

Born 1853-Died 1922
1898 Judge of Probate Lamar County, Alabama

Judge Robert Luther Bradley, dentist, State treasurer, probate judge, and State senator, was born October 8, 1853, at Palmetto, Pickens County; son of John and Barbara (Vail) Bradley, the former a native of Virginia; grandson of Hobbs Bradley, of Virginia, and of Jeremiah and Mary Vail natives of South Carolina who later located at Palmetto. Judge Bradley was educated at the Center Hill Academy Palmetto, where he was taught by A. M. Nuckels, Montgomery Bell and Miss Julia Propst. Later he attended the Vernon institute. He attended a school of dentistry in Chicago; entered upon the practice in 1874 at Vernon. Lamar County, and practiced that profession for twenty years.

In 1886 he was elected to the legislature from Lamar County, and again elected two years later. In 1890 he was elected to membership in the State senate. He served Lamar county as probate judge for eighteen consecutive years; captain, Thomas G. Jones riflemen State troops, for eight years; elected state treasurer, November 1918. He is a Democrat; chairman of Lamar County Democratic executive committee, of which he was a member for twenty-two years; and steward in the Methodist Church at Vernon for thirty years. He is a Mason and Odd Fellow. Married: in 1883, at Vernon, to Amanda Lee, daughter of Louis Monroe and Dorcas (Reynolds) Wimberly of that place. Although Judge and Mrs. Bradley have no children of their own they have raised six orphans who are now all married. Residence: Vernon. Source: *History of Alabama and Dictionary of Alabama Biography* by Thomas McAdory Owen, Vol III, Published by S. J. Clark Publishing Company, 1921. Source: Transcribed and submitted by Veneta McKinney

Francis R. Bridges

Possibly The Oldest In The County

On February 1st Mrs. Francis R. Bridges celebrated her 93rd birthday at the home of her son, Mr. D. G. Holcomb, of this county. She is yet able to walk about and only last week she made two of her own garments, with her own hands. Although somewhat feeble in memory, she converses readily, and has a vivid memory of her younger days. She is a native of South Carolina. Source: *The Vernon Courier*, February 14, 1895

Berneal Brock

Born 1922 - Died 1978

Married Bettye Ruth Falkner. Lamar County Judge of Probate Resigned due to health.

Hubert Brock

Editor Lamar News: On the 9th inst., Hubbert Brock, an old colored man, living near this place, while plowing for Mr. W. G. Hill, a farmer near Moscow, Hill seeing Hubbert's mule step, thought him drinking water, Mr. Hill walked up where this mule was standing and looking over behind a log - there lay Hubbert almost unconscious. Hill went and got four men and carried him to the house. Hubbert was sick with the colic from eating too much dinner. He ate 4 pones of bread, 16 biscuits, 1/2 gallon of milk, a quart of molasses, 4 pounds of meat, 1 pound of butter and one quart of peas. It is a wonder that Hubbert did not die. They carried him home in a wagon the next day. Source: *The Lamar News*, April 15, 1884

Burrell Brown

Mr. Burrell Brown, postmaster at Rias was stricken with pneumonia on last Thursday evening and died Monday morning. He was unconscious from the first. He was a young man the son of Mr. Rias Brown. He had been married for about two years previous to his death. Source: *The Vernon Courier*, December 19, 1895

David Brown

Mr. David Brown, who runs a gin at Hudson, Ala., had the misfortune to get his hand caught in the gin and badly mutilated last Friday. Drs. Barksdale and Seay amputated the two middle fingers of his left hand, and at last account was doing well. Source: *The Vernon Courier*, September 28, 1888

James Brown

James Adair, a young man from Mississippi, was traveling through the county last week, and stopped at Mr. James Brown's near Detroit to spend the night, and before leaving put on a pair of pants belonging to Mr. Brown's son, and then putting his own on top proceeded on his way. When young Brown discovered his loss himself and father started in pursuit of Adair, and came up with him near Vernon and found the pants on him. Adair was arrested and brought to jail Sunday to await trial, which was had before Judge Young Monday. Adair was fined $10 and the pants returned to Mr. Brown. Being unable to confess judgment went to jail, and will go to Pratt Mines long enough to work out the fine and cost. Source: *The Vernon Courier* November 28, 1889

J. W. Brown

Six-month-old baby of Mr. and Mrs. J. W. Brown, died at the family home, 4 miles west of Vernon last Sunday. The child had been ill for a few days and the death is a shock to the parents. The baby was buried at Wofford. Source: *The Lamar Democrat*, July 12, 1916

Rias Brown

There was a celebration of the "Glorious Fourth" of July, at Mr. Rias Brown's Mill on Monday last. Source: *The Lamar News*, July 7, 1887

Rias Brown-birthdate according to his grave marker is March 1832 with a death date of December 19, 1909. He married. Mary Ann Polly Hankins.

Watson Brown

Watson Brown of Beaverton called on us Saturday. Fresh he looked as a blooming sunflower. Into business again at Columbus soon he goes and his friends may then expect to hear from him through the Pioneer. *The Vernon Pioneer* July 16, 1875

Corky Buckley

April 8, 2009

My cousin Charles King had a friend Corky. They belonged to Alabama National Guard, and wore uniforms on occasions. They had haircuts called "crew cuts" smoked long and smelly cigars. They told me the cigars tasted fine. Now they were a couple of cool guys back in the late 1950's when Elvis was King and sang "Love Me Tender" and picture shows (movies) were shown at the Strand Theater in Sulligent.

I learned early that this Corky liked to play with words. As a young girl, I didn't always have a reply when approached with words from people I didn't know well. Corky always talked to me and said something funny and in the beginning, I didn't know how to respond. In my small world my uncles were the only ones who teased me with words.

My Aunt Mary Lou King lived in the Greenwood Springs community in Mississippi. I remember one hot summer Sunday afternoon my parents and I were visiting. Mother and daddy were inside the house talking and I was playing around outside. Charles and Corky arrived speeding up the driveway in Charles' red convertible jeep. They jumped out of the jeep running past me into the house. As I heard the screen door slam behind them, I knew they would not be in the house very long. They were always in a hurry. In a few minutes out of the house they came, Charles first and Corky right behind. I am standing there looking at them. Corky says to me "Is that your dog behind you?" When I looked around to see what dog, there was no dog to be found. When I turned back around they were jumping into the jeep and going down the dirt drive past the Magnolia tree and turning into the main gravel dirt road producing a cloud of dust as they headed toward someplace they had to be. As they were leaving I heard Corky laughing. After that I learned to be ready for Corky whenever I saw him and that tradition continued for about fifty years.

I was a grown woman before I learned Corky's legal name. He was born Martin Leon Buckley, the son of Horace Leon and Lorie Maddox Buckley, on September 26, 1929. Corky married Gwen Nolen before she graduated high school. He always said something like "I grew her up like I wanted her." But that is not true. Gwen was like he wanted her from the start. She is a wonderful person and I told Corky many times "I don't know why Gwen puts up with you," and he would laugh that famous Corky laugh. In reality they loved each other and had a good strong marriage.

Through the years I came to respect Corky as a man and for his integrity as he conducted farm business. He loved the farm and everything that went with it. Corky grew up attending First Baptist Church in Sulligent and was a member of the church and attended until he was not physically able. Corky didn't put his faith into words very much, I never heard him pray an eloquent prayer, but I witnessed him putting faith into action through the life he lived and things he did. He was full of fun and beneath all the jesting there was a caring loving heart for others.

On February 26, 2009 Corky took his last breath with Gwen holding his hand. Corky left a legacy of helping and encouraging others He touched many lives from his life-long commitment to the town of Sulligent as well as Lamar County. Corky had a rather large "network" as he branched out to other counties, towns, and states through Alabama National Guard, working with Liberty National Life Insurance Company and through the cattle business he shared with his brother Frank, making friends along the way.

Robert A. & E. Loucinda Traylor Burnett

Robert Augusta Burnett and Elizabeth Loucinda Traylor were married on October 8, 1875 at Samuel Miller's home. Born, August 8, 1857, Loucinda was the oldest child of William H. Traylor and Isabelle Miller Traylor.

Robert A. Burnett was born July 30, 1855, his parents were William P. and Elizabeth C. Burnett, who arrived in what was then Marion County, Alabama about 1854. Robert Burnett died September 3, 1935 and is buried in Providence Cemetery.

Loucinda Traylor Burnett died September 28, 1936 and she is buried in Providence Cemetery also. Source: Research of Fay Barnes

Samuel Burns

Mr. Samuel Burns has laid on our table the first cotton bloom of the season. "Sam" is an honest planter; different from a few other parties we know of who were going to present us with a hollyhock, passing it off on us as a cotton bloom, just because we were raised in a country where cotton cannot be grown and having, as a matter of course, never been introduced to these beautiful cotton blooms. Source: *The Vernon Pioneer* June 28, 1878

John T. Burrow

Live Oak Saloon. John T. Burrow & Co., Prop'r. Vernon, Alabama. Have in stock and will keep on hand a full assortment of whiskies, brandies, and wines, form the purest and best to cheapest grades. Tobaccos – chewing and smoking – cigars, snuts, etc. etc. While "warming up" the inner man, we will also keep on hand a full assortment of substantial such as: oysters, sardines, crackers, etc. Mr. L. S. Cash will be behind the counter and will attend to the wants of his many friends upon strictly Cash terms. Source: *The Vernon Pioneer*, June 28, 1878

Martha Caroline Terry Burrow

Rube Burrow's Mother Cures Rheumatism.
Margaret Garrie Marler Johnson, born in Lamar County, married, and moved to Mississippi. The Johnson's lived between Shannon and Nettleton. Mrs. Johnson known as "Grandma Johnson" (she lived to be 103) told a story that when she was young she had a bad case of rheumatism and couldn't even comb her hair. She heard of a woman in Alabama; a Mrs. "Barrow", who could cure rheumatism. One morning, Mrs. Johnson and an aunt got on their horses and took off to go find this woman.
They got to the area where Mrs. "Barrow" was supposed to live and saw an older woman walking up the road carrying a spinning wheel. They asked "Where does Mrs. Barrow live?" The woman said "What do you want her for?" Mrs. Johnson told her, that she had left her babies with her mother to come find the woman that could cure rheumatism and if she didn't find her soon she was going to have to go back home.
The woman said "get off your horse" and she rubbed different places on her neck and told her to go back home to her babies. Mrs. Johnson found out later, why the woman was so hesitant to tell her where she lived,

since she was Rube Barrows (Burrows) mother!! On Mrs. Johnson's 103 birthday, she said "I didn't have any more trouble with rheumatism until about age 98."

Rube Burrow's mother was Martha Caroline Terry, born 17 January, 1828; died 28 November 1912. She married Allen Burrow in August of 1848. Ruben Houston Burrow was born 12 December 1855.

Rube Burrow, the train robber, born in Lamar County, Alabama went to Texas in 1872 later robbed his first train with the help of brother, Jim Burrow and two cowboys on December 1, 1886 not in the dark of night, but day light.

Few bandits in the South or Southwest were so widely known from 1886-1890 as Rube Burrow. Source: *Cures Rheumatism* story written by Sandra Knight

Rube Burrow & Sim Green

Sim Green And The Train Robber

As told to me by my father, Jake (Monk) Green. Grandpa John C. Green somehow had become a friend of a notorious train robber by the name of Rube Burrow. Rube Burrow was about ten years younger than Grandpa, so it is not likely that he met him during the war of northern aggression. Rube's home was in Lamar County, Alabama, quite a distance from Lower Peach Tree so he was not a neighbor. Rube worked at sawmilling for a time in the Florida panhandle while he was hiding out from the law, so it is possible that they were acquainted through sawmill employment. In any case they were friends, maybe it's best that we don't know why.

Once, according to dad, they learned that Rube was going to pay them a visit and spend the night. This was big news as everyone at the time knew of Rube Burrow and what he was. Rube was considered a sort of Robin Hood in some circles, but his visit was "kept quiet" for obvious reasons.

Dad's older brother Sim had been given a nickel and, upon learning of the visit, was very concerned about Rube stealing his five cents - big money for a little fellow. Then he had an idea. The Greens had an old setting hen, as country folk did most of the time, and Sim thought of a perfect place for his money. He simply put it in the chicken house under the old setting hen for safe keeping for the duration of the visit by this famous outlaw. Word got out, of course, and Grandpa John shared it with his friend Rube. They both had a good laugh together about Sim's safe bank. Rube assured Sim that he would not steal his nickel. I wonder what Sim did spend that nickel on which he so carefully hid from the train robber.

Rube Burrow was killed after escaping from jail at Linden, Alabama, on October 7, 1890. He was returning home from Florida and passed through Repton, Alabama. He must have crossed the Alabama River somewhere near Packer's Bend and Lower Peach Tree and was spotted near Myrtlewood, Alabama, where he was captured in an abandoned house and taken to jail.

Is this the same trip when he spent the night with his friend, John Green, and family in Packers Bend and would not steal a little boy's money? Sim Green was born June 5, 1887 and this would have made him 3 years and 3 months old at the time. Pretty smart for a 3 year old.

Once, on a trip when I was small, my Dad took us to a country church in Lamar County to see the grave of Rube Burrow. The stone was chipped about half away by souvenir hunters. The story was that this was the third stone placed on his grave. Source: Written by Art Green

L. D. Byrd Killed

Early Thursday morning even before the sun had risen far above the eastern horizon, the alarm at the telephone rang out and "Hello what is wanted" went from the operator at this place. But how unexpected and how shocking was the reply which came from Sulligent. "Mr. Byrd was shot and instantly killed a moment ago by Burley Johnson of near this place."

It seems that an old grudge had been cherished between them for some time past, and they were evidently expecting trouble as both were armed and when the fatal combat occurred. It also seems from the best information we can get that Mr. Byrd was using every means possible to escape, when they met for the last time. Details are meager here, notwithstanding the affray occurred Thursday morning.

According to our information, Mr. Byrd, when seeing that he must meet Johnson, said to his nephue that Johnson was hunting trouble and so saying left the side-walk, giving to Johnson the right-of-way. They had not proceeded far when Johnson holding his pistol close to a shade tree took deliberate aim and fired. He continued to fire until he had fired five shots, four of which took effect, Mr. Byrd fired two shots, neither of which took effect. Johnson succeeded in making his escape. Source: *The Lamar Democrat* 07-23-1898

Caldwell Family

Thanks to the computer age genealogy research has been greatly enhanced. In our search for our ancestors much interesting information is found. Sometimes we are not sure about the connection or if there is a connection. When we go back to the fifteen, sixteen, and seventeen hundreds we have word of mouth and some written history. Sometimes written history has no verifiable connection to the verbal.

Chippewa Indians and Pelee Island

The following paragraph has no verifiable connection to the rest of this Caldwell story. It was of enough interest to be included in this narrative. The Caldwell band of Chippewa Indians in southern Ontario fought for their rights to land on Point Pelee and Pelee Island for over one hundred years. In the computer based history, there is no indication how the band came by the name of Caldwell. There was a Chief Robert Caldwell and his brother John Caldwell in the late 1800's. In 1778 Thomas McKee leased Pelee Island from the Chippewa's for three bushel of corn annually. The Caldwell Band never received anything. The McKee's sold the island in 1815, notice sold not released. In 1830 the Caldwell Nation pressed claim to the land. In the 1840's the Canadian Government decided, neither the Caldwells nor the claiming owners, were entitled to the land. Over the years, the Caldwell Band has corresponded with the government reaffirming their claim to the land. In 1922 the Island was made into a National Park. Another island, St. Ann was proposed by the government as a place of settlement for the Caldwell Band. The government then decided the cost was too prohibitive to prepare the island for habitation. Over the years the government and the Caldwell Band have gone back and forth. As of 1999 no settlement had been made. The matter is still under discussion.

There is much information on Caldwells on the computer. My thanks for information obtained to write this narrative to all the people who have contributed to various web sites. Also to my sister Faye Bryant Walker who did much of the computer research. She also put any information needed to complete our past and current ancestors in an understandable format, My thanks also goes to my mother Nell Vail Bryant and her cousin Mary Will Parker Mosley, who are our only living older connections, (that we are aware of.) They have answered many of my questions and supplied pictures, when I'm sure they wished I would just go away and not bother them, I love them both very much,

According to Legend, They Sailed With the Barbarossa Brothers

A story from the Caldwell historians is of three brothers who sailed for the Barbarossa Pirates. The Barbarossa brothers were of Algerian birth and were the dominant power (perhaps with the Turks) in the Mediterranean for 20 or more years after driving the Spanish from Algeria. After their downfall they returned to France and robbed King Frances I. They were run out of the country and settled in Scotland. There they obtained a Douglas Clan holding, which became known as Cauldewell. The spelling is an Anglo-Saxon word meaning "Well of Cold Water."

The French man known as French Caldwell, was probably born in the 1500's. His son Alexander was born about 1530. Hence the Caldwell name can be traced back to the 1500's. There is only one child traceable for the Caldwells for at least four generations. Alexander had William, and William had John. By the time John died in 1691/92 he was in Ireland. John had two sons Daniel and Joseph. Again Daniel only had one son and named him for himself; Daniel Caldwell. Daniel II had a son John H. John H. had a son William. Both John H, and his son William were born in Ireland. Both died in Spartanburg, S.C. John H. died in 1840 and William died in 1863.

William Served in Revolutionary War

William Caldwell served for his father John H in the Revolutionary War. One would assume because the father was too old.

William married Margaret Crawford in 1872 in Spartanburg, S.C. William and Margaret ended the chain of only one child for the Caldwell line. They had eleven children. Our line starts with their son William H. Caldwell, born 1804, married Elizabeth, born 1811, in South Carolina. Their first child St. John H. was born in South Carolina and died in Lamar County, Alabama. William H. and Elizabeth Caldwell had ten children. We know that two of their children, St. John's and his sister Mary J. stayed in Lamar County. Mary J. Caldwell married Rev, George L. Mouchette. They are buried in Andrews Chapel Cemetery in upper Pickens County, Alabama.

Branching from William and Margaret Crawford Caldwell, became numerous lines of Caldwell's and other lines from the daughter's marriages.

Several Caldwell men throughout history have been ministers of the gospel, mostly in the Presbyterian Faith. Another vocation that seems to have followed through the Caldwell men is that of barrister, or justice of the peace in our time. There is mention of various Caldwell men who went to college. The Caldwells were obviously very intelligent people and some used that intelligence to its best advantage. The Caldwell's amassed land and most seemed to have obtained a degree of wealth. Some served in government and most served in wars when called to do so. Our great-great grandfather St. John H. Caldwell was a private in the Civil War. He was in the Confederacy, Co. K. 41st AL Infantry.

Genetic Trait "Ole Malaise"

A genetic trait which some would propose to hide or deny follows a story about a Caldwell minister. He could no longer serve his Parrish because he had a mental disposition. He retired to his estate to recover, but was never of the health to return to his ministry. There are several notes of mental dispositions or nervousness. Those of us today know that trait still exist and do not deny it, where we came from is what we are. My grandfather used to call it his "ole malaise." Webster defines malaise as uneasy, disturbed or disordered.

Throughout history there seems to many Caldwell's who either died young or never married. Most of those who married only had one or two children. St. John H. Caldwell is my direct line. He married Annie Catherine B. They had thirteen children with nine living. Of the nine living to a marriageable age, only three had more than one or two children, Henrietta Caldwell Vail, my great grandmother, Andrew Jackson (Jack) Caldwell, and Sarah (Sally) E. Caldwell Parker.

A notable mention for great uncle George Caldwell, he farmed and was a justice of the peace. At the Vernon Court House in the records of deeds, there are many deeds signed by George Caldwell. St John H. and Annie Catherine Caldwell are both buried at Andrews Chapel in upper Pickens County, AL.

Andrew Jackson (Jack) Caldwell married twice, first to Mollie Ann Cook. They had seven children. He married second to Ida Parker and they had three children. Andrew Jackson Caldwell is buried in Springhill Cemetery between his wives.

Sarah (Sally) Caldwell married George William Parker. They had nine children. Their son Willie Roy Parker married Sarah Vera Byars, they are buried in Andrews Chapel Cemetery in upper Pickens Co. They had eight children and are the parents of my cousin, Mary Will Parker Mosley, who was much help in compiling the Sally Caldwell line.

Jacob Hiram and Henrietta Caldwell Vail

My great-great grandmother Henrietta Caldwell married Jacob Hiram (Jake) Vail. They had ten children. Their Vail home place today is owned by descendants of the family. They are buried in Springhill Cemetery in Lamar County. My grand-father William Walton Vail was their oldest son. My mother Nell Vail Bryant still lives on their home place just west of Millport Alabama. Written in 2004 and submitted by Flora Bryant McCool

Cantrell Family Travel to Their Roots

November 8, 2006

Ottis and Audra Fay Carrouth Cantrell returned to their roots and brought their family with them. Family members from Seattle, Washington, Washington D.C., Beauford, South Carolina and Nashville, Tennessee came to Alabama. On October 4, 2006 most of the family flew into Birmingham, Alabama, rented cars and came to Marion and Lamar counties, the homeland of Ottis and Audra, who married in 1947.

It was granddaughter Dana's idea for the family to visit Alabama. If I understood correctly, one grandson was left in Seattle taking care of the business and one granddaughter in college in Nashville, Tennessee was driving in that Friday afternoon.

Ottis is the son of John Thomas Cantrell and Pinkie Kirksy Cantrell. Audra Faye is the daughter of Londie and Ola Webb Carrouth.

Ottis and Audra Fay have six children, Dan, Mike who is deceased, Marce', Mark, Kim and Rob.

On Friday morning, the family and local relatives met for an adventure. A family legend, passed down to the descendants of John M. Cantrell that during the time of Civil War, while hiding for whatever reason, John M. carved his footprints, one handprint and several turkey prints into a large rock or boulder in Marion County.

According to the legend, one foot was larger than the other. As children, Ottis Cantrell and siblings played on the boulder with the carvings. Ottis moved away but never forgot about the rock.

Ottis' sister, Mrs. Elvie Cantrell Lacey passed the legend on to her granddaughters Mary and Samantha. I am sure the other siblings did the same. In the fall of 1998, current landowners gave permission to Ottis and his brother Bill Cantrell to search for the boulder. A group of about 30 people searched the woods and found the site. The rock was covered with a layer of moss and briers were growing all around, but the boulder was safe and the carvings visible.

On October 6, 2006, the family joined together, hiking into the woods, searching for the legendary rock again. Ottis' memory is good, because the large rock was found, covered with moss as in 1998, with underbrush all around, but it is still there and the carvings still visible, 140 years or so later. The family, excited to find the rock, cleaned the rock and made pictures for us to enjoy.

I learned more about the legend of John M. Cantrell. It seems that he hid in the woods in the daytime and came out working the crops in the field at night, wearing his wife's shoes, not leaving any evidence of a man around the farm. We don't know if he was hiding from the Union troops that came through the area, or if he was hiding from Confederate troops. Being curious as to how the prints were carved into the rock, I asked an expert in Indian relics and he told me the Indians used other stones to carve into stone.

Cantrell Family in Alabama
Front row, left to right: Noah Cantrell, and Ethan Cantrell
Second row, left to right: Marce' Shinall, Amy Cantrell, Audra Fay Cantrell, Ottis Cantrell, Anne Cantrell, and Barb Cantrell
Back row, left to right: Rob Cantrell, Gwen Howart, Kim Cantrell, Mark Cantrell, Dan Cantrell, Dana Rindall and Kevin Rindall

Cleaning the Rock

Left to right: Noah Cantrell, Katelyn Kostelc, Annia Belle Carruth

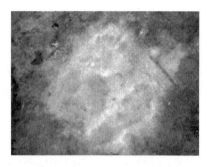

John M. Cantrell Footprints

John M. Cantrell Handprint

    I imagine Mr. Cantrell carved to pass time while hiding but do you think his intent was to leave something for his children and grandchildren to remember him?

    It was interesting talking to Anne Cantrell, Dan's wife, as we sat next to each other at lunch. Ann told me she has an ancestor, John Soule, who came to the United States on the ship Mayflower and stood up at the wedding of John and Priscilla Alden. Anne and her family are planning a trip to Portsmouth, Maine in another family history search. It was exciting afterward as I researched the Mayflower passenger list, finding George Soule listed as a passenger and in searching the site I found John Soule listed as his son.

    The Cantrell family visited in the area, most of them returning home on October 14th. It was an honor to visit with such a nice family and share their special time.

Avist Carden 95th Birthday

10-13-2004

    My neighbor, Mrs. Avist Carden, celebrated her 95th birthday recently. She has been my neighbor for as long as I can remember. She lives down the road, from the house where I grew up in the Lost Creek Community. If you know the location of the Shiloh North United Methodist Church, she lives near the church in a white house, sitting on a rise overlooking the highway. She has a front porch that is a favorite place of mine. She and I have spent time on that porch over the years talking and talking some more. She has always made me feel so welcome and loved, especially when I was a child visiting her. Time always passes fast when I visit, because we have so much to talk about. She has the most beautiful flowers, around and on the porch, there is always something in bloom.

    Mrs. Avist Blaylock Carden was born September 29, 1909 to Green Thomas and Effie Jane Knight Blaylock. Her parents had 12 children.

    She married Robert Matthew Carden at age 16. Her family was living with relatives in Sulligent, because the family's residence near Vernon had burned. They needed to relocate, when her father heard that Wash King needed workers at his saw mill in the Lost Creek Community, he thought this job might be more stable and stationary as he had been moving the family to where ever he could find work. King's mill operated daily except when the men were needed to plant and work the crops. The mill also shut down for harvest of corn. Mrs. Avist said the women and children harvested the cotton.

    Her parents made the decision to move to the Lost Creek, on the King place. Robert Carden, a nephew of the Kings, was sent to Sulligent to move the Blaylock family to Lost Creek by wagon and mules. When Robert arrived in town, he stopped where they were staying, Mrs. Avist as a young girl saw him for the first time sitting on the wagon. With a wistful look, she said to me "Robert had the prettiest eyes, I had ever seen."

    About 2 years later, on April 18, 1926, she married the "prettiest pair of eyes," the ceremony performed by Mr. Murff on the side of the road, which was not uncommon in that day, near Gattman, Mississippi. Robert's sister, Leona Carden and friend, Verlon Camp were their attendants. The Carden's three children are: Lavern, James and Gwyneth. Lavern is married to Gene Risner and they live near Mrs. Avist. James married Azell Christian and he lives near Amory, Mississippi. Gwyneth is married to Wayne Dalton and they live near Huntsville, Alabama.

    Robert and Avist had a good life together, living and working on the farm until he died in 1967, at age 70. He was a small man in stature, a honest dependable, trustworthy citizen of our Lamar county. Mrs. Avist, was a relatively young widow, in her fifties, after Robert died; she continued to live on the farm, in the house, where she and Robert lived, and she is still there today at age 95.

Mrs. Avist is a very kind, considerate loving person and I am a better for having known her all these years. Happy Birthday!

12-21-2005

Avist Blaylock Carden died December 12, 2005 at age 96. I have known her as long as I can remember. She always made me feel so loved and special. Mrs. Avist didn't drive an automobile so everywhere she went she walked or depepnded on someone to drive her. I grew up watching her walk to church. She was always at church, the weather never kept her away. When I got my driver's license, sometimes she rode with me.

I remember the pies and cakes she baked. When I visited she always gave me something to eat. After I married, she loved Dewey just as she loved me. When my son Barry was born, she cared for him. She loved Barry and made him feel special. She loved all the children that she cared for, they were all special to her.

Until a few months ago, Mrs. Avist lived in her own home. Her husband, Robert Carden died in 1967 and she lived alone in the house where she has lived in all her married life.

The afternoon of her death on my ride home from work, I was thinking of her. I know that she is in heaven, no doubt in my mind. As I reflected on her life, the life she lived before me, I noticed the most beautiful sunset. I felt God was letting me know that she was finally home. She told me many times how she knew she had to die and looked forward to dying because she knew it would be the beginning not the end. She was concerned about her two daughters, Laverne and Gwyneth, James her son, what they would do after she was gone. She didn't want them to be sad.

Mrs. Avist Carden leaves a legacy of hard work, perseverance, and love for her family, friends and her God. My life is richer because of her love.

Jean Smith Carr

November 15, 2006

Jean Carr is now doing genealogy in the great land beyond. I miss her. My emails from her have stopped. I received uncountable emails from her, and saved many. I find myself reading and re-reading those. She was a remarkable person. Always giving of self, and expecting nothing in return.

Jean befriended me, she encouraged me, she loved me. During the years,

I cared for my mother at night, Jean knew mother didn't sleep, and if Jean was awake, she emailed me. In the middle of so many nights, I got to know her. I will never forget the help she gave me in those difficult times. Even though her health was not good, she thought of me. The amazing thing is, I am not the only person whom she encouraged and helped through hard times. She lived her faith and made a difference in lives she touched.

Our Lamar County Genealogical & Historical Society was a dream of hers that became a reality. Janie Spencer said it well in her email telling us that Jean had died on October 11, 2006, "She will be missed by everyone who knew her and has benefited from her untiring support and seemingly unlimited resources."

Jean Smith Carr was born June 30, 1933 in Monroe County, Mississippi. Her parents were Roy Edward and Clarine Smith. She was a member of Vernon Church of Christ and a board member of Mary Wallace Cobb Memorial Library Museum and Art Council in Vernon, Alabama. She was a charter member of Lamar County Genealogical & Historical Society. She wrote the weekly column LINKS in *The Lamar Democrat* newspaper. Jean died October 11, 2006. A beautiful memorial service was held on Saturday, October 14th in Vernon, Alabama. She and husband A. C. Carr were married for 54 years.

Robbie Omary Carruth

On Wednesday, February 22nd, we buried my husband's mother Robbie Omary Carruth. Mrs. Carruth died Sunday, February 19, 2006 in Druid City Hospital in Tuscaloosa following a massive heart attack on the Friday before.

I have been in her family for almost 43 years. She was an ideal mother-in-law. She never interfered in my marriage to Dewey nor was she ever a "bother" to me. A quiet, most independent woman, she wanted to do things for herself. She lived alone and was happy. Having lost most of her eyesight because of diabetes, the last few years she didn't get out of her house very often. She spent much of her time listening to Christian music and ministers preaching the gospel on the radio or television. As long as I have known her she loved football. When her sons were in high school playing football, she was there to support and cheer for them. Mrs. Carruth has five sons: Dewey, James, Freddie, Larry, Don; and two daughters Linda and Deborah.

Mrs. Carruth's husband Cecil died August 16, 1982. They had a wonderful marriage and it seemed she missed him as much after 23 years as the day he died. In talking with her, she seldom failed to mention his name. Mrs. Carruth loved to quilt and most of us have a quilt handmade by her.

Born to George Washington and Laura Lindsey Omary on July 7, 1923, she was eighty-one when she died. The following poem was chosen by my husband Dewey and read during her funeral service which describes her well.

Mama's Bible, so ragged and worn,
Its pages are scribbled, ripped and torn.
Its been around for ages, she's had it for years,
Some pages smudged by rain and some by her tears

The name on the cover is faded, it's true.
There might be a page missing, or two.
To look at that book one might scoff and frown

They may say, "Why, there's no use in keeping it around.
"A new Bible, I'm certain, is what you must need,
With pages so perfect, and pictures indeed."
But friends, I know better and I tell you today
There's more in that book, more than I can say.

For she read it and held it so close to her heart,
Its Knowledge and Wisdom and Love to impart.
She held it so tightly, through storm and through chill,
But ever much closer when her children were ill.

Her faith can be seen on each page and each line,
Her writings of love time after time.
She carried it high through thick and through thin,
So proud of the holy scriptures contained within.

Of all of the treasures in this world we can hold,
The Bible of mother so ragged and old.
Is far more precious than silver or gold.
Author unknown.

Loree Christain

Loree Hankins

100 Years of All Day Decorating on the Ground in Song

Not many of us alive today can say that we have attended the same event every year for 100 years without missing a single time, but Mrs. Loree Christian can. This past Mother's Day, she attended her 100th Homecoming/Decoration Day service at Liberty Free Will Baptist Church in the Crossville Community. Mrs. Loree Hankins Butler Christian was born in February of 1918 to Thomas Jefferson and Cora Black Hankins, thus making her first Decoration Day attendance occurring before her first birthday. Although she now lives in Columbus, Mississippi, Mrs. Loree, has spent most of her life in Blooming Grove and Crossville Communities. Now the oldest member at Liberty, at the age of 17, she was the first Intermediate class teacher, when the church first formed a Sunday School in July 1935.

No one knows when Liberty had its first Decoration Sunday, or why they chose to have it on Mother's Day, but the custom of returning to one's "home" church one day each year, goes back to 16th century. The fourth Sunday of Lent, also known as Laetare (Rejoice) or Rose Sunday", was the day when worshipers were allowed to return to their "Mother" church. Servants, especially female were allowed to visit their mother, often gathering bouquets of flowers to present to her. Eventually this custom among others, help to inspire the idea of Mother's day.

The custom of decorating graves goes back to the Civil War days, perhaps even further. In most of the United States, the idea of decorating graves with flowers and flags is most commonly associated with Memorial Day. But many cultures and religions have had a history of decorating graves of loved ones and having feasts to celebrate. All Souls Day is one such day. It is celebrated each November 2 by Catholic, Orthodox and some Protestant Churches. It is more commonly known, in certain areas, as "Day of the Dead. A day celebrated in Mexico and other Latin American countries, where people clean off the graves of deceased family members and decorate them with flowers, food and other items.

Laetare Sunday, All Souls Day and Decoration Sundays all have various things in common, but one thing in particular, family reunions. It shouldn't come as a surprise that many families choose to have their reunions or family get together on Decoration Sundays. Cousins meet cousins every year to place flowers on the graves of their mutual relatives, who in their days decorated their ancestors' graves and so on.

Back in the days that Mrs. Loree was growing up, Decoration or Homecoming Sunday was usually preceded by the tag line: "All day singing and dinner on the ground." This literally meant having dinner on the ground, a la picnic style. Prior to outdoor picnic tables and the more modern fellowship halls, families would spread a blanket and eat the picnic lunch they had brought, often inviting another family to eat with them. This was before paper plates or plastic utensils, or Igloo coolers, and definitely before fellowship halls. After lunch everyone stayed to participate in the "all day singing part." Although one of the first documented singing convention was not until 1875, the custom of having singings at church predates the Civil War.

Sadly the time honored southern tradition of Homecoming/Decoration Sunday is apparently dying out. It may surprise people living here in this area of our state but there are people here in Alabama who have never even heard of this tradition. Many churches have fewer and fewer who come every year and some of those that do have it have stopped having the traditional afternoon singing because very few stay to listen or participate.

This past Mother's Day Sunday, Liberty Free Will Baptist Church held its 100+ Homecoming/ Decoration Day Service. The oldest in attendance was Mrs. Loree Christian, the youngest was John Ross Howell. Times have changed since Mrs. Loree's first "attended" Decoration Day at Liberty, from spreading dinner on the ground outside of a small one room church house to listening to singing while sitting inside an air-conditioned brick building. Only time will tell if young John Ross will one day attend his 100th consecutive Homecoming/Decoration Day at Liberty and the changes that will occur during those years.

Prologue: Sadly Mrs. Loree died less than a month after fulfilling this amazing milestone. When she was born World War I was still being fought, there was no minimum wage, a stamp cost $.03 and people still used mules and wagons.. When she died the world had changed drastically. Minimum wage was $7.25 per hour, a stamp cost $ .49, and the war to end all wars ended up leading to more wars. The small country school that she attended gave way to larger more consolidated ones. There were no standardized tests back then either, no ACTs to prepare for. Radio, tv's and the internet have all come into our lives, and we have had medical breakthroughs, and setbacks. The world has certainly changed in those 99 years since a baby girl was born to a couple in a small community in Lamar County Alabama. Source: Written and submitted by Stephanie Butler

Erah Burks Clark

01-22-2009
Mrs. Clark celebrates 90th Birthday

Mrs. Erah Clark celebrated her 90th birthday on Saturday, January 10th at the Sulligent Community Center. Family and friends gathered to honor Mrs. Clark. She has seen many changes in 90 years.

Mrs. Clark was married to James Clyde Clark until his death separated them. Mrs. Clark is a wonderful person, she has touched many lives through the years especially working in health care. I always thought there was something different about her, but in 1982 I had the privilege of getting to know her. She is a very kind and compassionate person who is an inspiration and friend to me. We both share a passion for reading. My life is richer because of knowing her.

Dorothy Noe Cleveland

11-07-2007
Mrs. Dorothy Cleveland Celebrates 86th Birthday

Country stores in local communities have all but passed away. Growing up in Lost Creek Community near Sulligent in the late 1950's, we had a small country store owned by Wilson and Dorothy Cleveland. Wilson was a master at repairing water well pumps and was gone from home much of the time working. Mrs. Dorothy took care of the children and the store, located in a room of their house. I cannot remember all the items she sold there, except gasoline, cokes and Nabs. The soft drinks or "Cokes" were in a big refrigerated box. Customers reached inside the drink box and selected a drink of choice. For those of you that don't know, "Nabs" were a package of crackers with peanut butter. If I remember correctly, there were four in a package and the package was not flat but tall.

The Cleveland store was a popular place to visit while catching up on all the happenings of the community On Sunday nights at our Shiloh North Methodist Church, we had MYF (Methodist Youth Fellowship) meetings. After MYF, we usually ended up at Cleveland's store. Mrs. Dorothy would open up so we could buy snacks and usually we stood around and talked for a while. The country store and her husband Wilson are gone now, but Mrs. Dorothy is still here and active in our community. She takes care of our community flower fund and we can always depend on her to let us know if there is a need in the community.

On Sunday, October 28, 2007, Mrs. Dorothy celebrated her 86th birthday with family and friends. A wonderful meal was shared and lots of reminiscing done. Mrs. Dorothy is the daughter of Green Claborne Noe and Mattie Emma Liza Comer Noe; and the granddaughter of Joseph Wilson Noe and Talitha E. Lewis.

Wilson L. Cleveland and Dorothy Noe married July 16, 1942. They were married for 51 years until his death in 1993.Their children are Billy, Janice, V.M., Grover, and Tommy. Their son Jacky died as a result of a car accident in 1969.

Family and friends sharing birthday lunch or just stopping by to wish Mrs. Dorothy "Happy Birthday" numbered close to a hundred. It was evident by the gathering of family members they share a special love for their mother, grandmother and aunt. "Mrs. Dorothy, thank you for all you do."

Jane Clouse

Over One Hundred Years.

Lamar County comes to the front with the oldest living person in the state.

Mrs. Jane Clouse, who lives on the Military road ten miles north of Crews, is now one hundred and five years of age. She has been very active until of late. For the last six months she has failed considerably and it is with difficulty that she does her house work. She says that she counts herself but a little over one hundred years old; but the record of her birth which is now in the possession of a well-known gentleman of Marion

County shows her to have been one hundred and five last autumn. The pure and wholesome air and water of this section, together with a plain and quiet life has produced this longevity. She was born in North Carolina, and is the mother of eight children. She has sided in this county for nearly fifty years. Source: *The Vernon Courier*, March 27, 1890

R. W. Cobb

R. W. Cobb has a fine lot of saddles and bridles which he is selling at a small advance above cost, for cash. Call and get supplied before they are all gone.

The new two-cent postal cards has made its appearance. It has two stamps – one at each end – and spaces for two messages. The sender occupies one of these and the return correspondent the other. It is expected that the cards will soon be in general circulation. Source: *The Vernon Clipper* October 10, 1879.

F. M. Coker

Old Soldier enjoys his 83rd Christmas. F. M. Coker of Detroit enjoyed his 83rd Christmas with his only daughter, Mr. J. C. Brown, his six grandchildren at his home Christmas Day. "Uncle Marvin", when at the age of 16 volunteered his services in the War Between the States. He fought through the entire war and was never wounded . Until a few years ago, he made his bale of cotton a year and is wonderfully nimble for a man of "83 wrinkles" The News wishes him many more years of happiness with his family. Source: *The Lamar Democrat* January 2, 1929.

Jesse Hollis & Eunice Tomlin Cole

They were born in Lamar County Alabama to John Cole and Ida Vernon Cole and Jacob Lafayette and Mary Emily (Molly) Tomlin. Both were reared on farms. The grandfathers of Jesse and Eunice were confederate soldiers. Jesse's formative years were spent in the Walnut Grove community while Eunice's were in the community between Mount

Olive and Kingsville.

Their courting began prior to World War I and were married before Jesse's entrance into the army. Jesse served with the infantry. His duties moved him rapidly and was unable to get mail from Eunice until he left the front line. Jesse was wounded, gassed, was blind and without food for seven days while serving in France. He served with a close friend and first cousin Edgar Louis Cole throughout his military career.

Upon being discharged from the Army they farmed on a farm adjoining Jacob Tomlin's farm until Jesse entered Mississippi A & M. His attention in college was studying raising and marketing poultry. Upon their leaving college they resumed fruits of his education as well as general farming. The depression soon terminated the growing of poultry because it was too difficult to protect the chickens from theft by people desperate for food.

Jesse and Eunice had six children. The three eldest were girls: Ratha, Christine and Jean. The boys Glen, Thad and Jake respectively.

The Coles continued on the farm near the Tomlin's homeplace. The farming experience included: cotton, corn, hay, truck farming (selling fruits and vegetables) and pure bred Guinea hogs. The marketing of these vegetables was a house to house approach in Kennedy and Fayette. The pigs were sold locally as well as advertised in farm publications and shipped throughout the America's farming communities. The hogs were famous for the large amount of lard they produced.

During Jesse's formative years he frequently attended singing schools during the summer months as did many of the other young people. It not only provided youngsters pastime activities, it also gave them skill. Jesse often used his knowledge of music as a means of earning money teaching music in the summer months. On one occasion he taught singing school for the Wilson community south of Kennedy and was paid with a model T Ford. On other occasions he was paid with products produced in the community.

During the years of rearing six children, Ida Vernon Cole, Jesse's mother came to live with them and remained through the remainder of her life. The town of Vernon was named after Ida Vernon Cole's father.

Jesse left the farm during World War II to work in a defense plant in Gadsden, Alabama. The three sons and Eunice remained on the farm until the end of the War. Upon Jesse's return to the community after the War he sold his farm and purchased a cafe in Millport from John Ed Ayres. The family moved to Millport and remained there until Jesse's retirement. After retirement they remodeled the house where Jacob and Minnie Tomlin had lived and moved there to live out their retirement years. After their move to Millport Eunice's father Jacob Lafayette Tomlin and her step-mother moved in with them due to her father's ill health and remained there until his death. After his death, his wife Minnie moved to Birmingham to live with her daughter and later a nursing home and remained there until her death.

Once the three girls graduated from Kennedy High School, they immediately left the community. Ratha and Jean came to Birmingham for employment. Ratha worked at the Tin Mill during the War. Jean worked for Western Union. Christine worked at Kennedy for a period of time. Ratha followed her dream in that she wanted to be a hair stylist of which she was trained and worked until her retirement. Jean later moved to California on a transfer from Western Union and while there met and married Robert C. Luftman, moved to Boston, Mass. upon his discharge. They have three daughters: Suzanne, Harriet and Robin. The daughters married and have eight children.

Ratha married Clint Fowler, recently discharged from the Army. They have two children: daughter Jackie and son David. Jackie has two children: Mark and Marty Payne. David's son is deceased.

Christine married Ray Max McGee of Vernon. Max, a veteran served as a Veteran instructor and later graduated from Mississippi State University majoring in agriculture and Christine also went to college where she majored in education. Both taught school for many years. They have one daughter, Karen, their daughter graduated from college and married Bobby Davis. They have three children: Mark, Shannon and Gary. They have three grandchildren.

Upon moving to Millport it was a completely different life style. We went from keeping fire and stove wood to coal for heating and cooking. Therefore our chores changed, but never the less we had responsibilities including washing dishes in the cafe.

About the time we arrived in Millport the Veterans began returning from World War II and they began to draw their 52-20, $20.00 per week for 52 weeks. This changed all rural communities. Actually the rural communities had not really gotten over the great depression and these dollars gave a big boost. Also, the veterans began their GI training in a broad variety of areas and this brought in more money. Therefore, the economy got a big lift.

Also changing from Kennedy school system to Millport was exciting, getting new friends, instead of riding the school bus (1st load in the morning and last load in the afternoon) to walking to school.

Sports quickly entered our life. Each of the boys participated in many of the high school sports. This is an identity that boys enjoy, one that gives more exposure. Each did very well, some excelled more than others of which is natural. Thad was truly a natural at center/linebacker. Some who had watched Millport sports for many years labeled Thad "pound for pound" the best linebacker they had ever seen. Thad possibly weighed in at about 150-160. Colleges were not looking for that size frame. Thad drove a school bus during his last year in school This provided him with an income. Thad was captain of the football team.

Jake, being slightly larger than the other boys gained notoriety at tackle and some colleges took notice to his skills. But, he chose not to go that direction. Jake and Billy Atkins were co-captains of the football team in 1954.

Thad decided Millport was too small for him, therefore he decided to enter the Navy during the Korean conflict.

Glen was captain of the football team his senior year and named to Lamar County's second team. He experienced injuries his senior year. Since his Dad did not especially care for football, he waited tables, washed dishes on Saturdays after spraining an ankle. It was not possible to evade responsibilities.

The restaurant created a different lifestyle for the family of which required many long hours. Our longer hours always occurred on weekends. During those days most people came to town on Saturdays to shop, visit friends as well as observe what is going on in the community. The busiest time usually came during the Nazarene Camp Ground Meeting of which lasted about 10 days. The cafe was rather busy for breakfast, lunch and very busy later in the day including after the evening services. We had a juke box of which played music and on occasions when they would play gospel music extreme excitement followed. The first time that occurred, the boys were especially excited in a different way. But, it also served as a degree of entertainment. After all, we had been to some of their services when this type excitement took place.

Thad decided he wanted a different type work to occupy him therefore, he bought a Service Cycle from Orville Biddle and along with the bike came a paper route. The paper route was the reason daddy agreed to the purchase, therefore this gave Thad an out from work at the cafe for a period of time. But, dad knew about how long it took and expected Thad to show up there for work as well

Jake decided he wanted to practice medicine while in school One of his classmates continued to solicit candy from Jake, therefore Jake substituted some ex-lax. After a short period of time his pal spent more time in the restroom than in class. Well, Mr. Kuykendall got into the picture soon and learned the source of his problem and brought Jake in for questioning. After this, Jake lost his desire to practice medicine.

After graduation Glen went to Birmingham and began working in the Steel Mill when he began his career in the electrical field. From Birmingham, he moved around a bit including Coyne Electrical School in Chicago where he also worked as a lab instructor. His career included two years in the Army Signal Corps, serving in Korea. Afterwards returning to the Steel Industry before going on staff with the AFL-CIO Human

Resources Department.

Thad spent four years in the navy during the Korean Conflict. Afterwards he was with the fire department in Birmingham as well as a variety of sales positions on a part-time basis. His most successful one being real estate.

Jake followed slightly later only he served in the air force. He also worked in the machine shop at ACIPCO and later utilizing his skills moving on to General Electric in their tool cutting division where he worked as a sales representative until his retirement. In school, Jake is also known for labeling his pals with nick-names of which all or most of them stuck with them until this day.

Glen is married to Millie Martha McDaniel and they have one daughter, Martha Ann. Martha Ann married Judd Conley Wilson and they have one son, Cole McDaniel Wilson.

Thad married Nan Richardson of New Hope Mississippi. They have two sons; Steve who is married to Betsey Whitten and Christopher Michael.

Jake is married to Nellie Jo Price of Reform and they have three living children: Kenneth Randall, Ronnie Kyle and Ronda Janelle. Randy is married to Sherry Farris and they have three sons: John, Jacob and Kenneth. Ronnie was married to Debra Cornelius (deceased) and they have one daughter, Stacy. He is now married to Kathy Rush and they have one daughter, Brittney. Ronda is married to James Fredrick Thomas and they have one son: Garett Cole Thomas.

Jake and Nellie have two deceased sons: John, Jr. and Roger buried at Christian Chapel on Alabama Highway 17 north of Millport . Source: Written by: Glen Cole in 2005. Submitted by John J. Cole 742 Narrows Point Circle Birmingham, AL 35242.

Nellie Price Cole

July 1, 1936 - February 11, 2014

We extend our heartfelt sympathy to Lamar County Genealogical & Historical Society member John J. Cole in the death of his beloved wife Nellie. Her niece Kelli Marlow wrote, "Nellie Jo Price Cole was an amazing woman - strong, smart, real, blunt, funny, wise, and witty. She was great at everything she did, whether it was golf, painting, sewing, bowling, cooking, or fishing. I will miss her very much, but treasure the memories I have of her."

Nellie was born in Pickens County, Alabama to parents, James and Elizabeth Price. She was a member of the Riverchase Church of Christ. As a former member of Woodward Golf and Country Club, she was an avid and accomplished golfer. She won the Ladies Club Championship in 1998, and again in 1999.

The funeral service was held in Ridout's Southern Heritage Chapel, Pelham on Saturday, February 15, 2014 at 11 a.m., followed by a brief, graveside service and interment at 2 p.m. at Christian Chapel Church of Christ Cemetery, located approximately seven miles north of Millport, Alabama on Alabama Highway 17. Active Pallbearers were John Cole, Andy Cole, Michael Cole, Cole Thomas, Freddy Thomas, Andrew Clark, Paul Moore, and Billy Barton. Honorary Pallbearers were The Ladies Birmingham Golf Association and Nellie's wonderful neighborhood friends.

James Collins

We regret to hear that Major Screws was quite sick on Saturday night and Sunday, having to lie over at Mr. James Collins' until Monday morning. Source: *The Vernon Pioneer* July 19, 1878

P. C. Combs

Mr. P. C. Combs who is now in his 84th year walks up to town occasionally and tells of things happening years ago. Mr. Combs framed the first house built in Aberdeen, Mississippi. Source: *The Vernon Courier*, April 27, 1888

W. T. Cooper

W. T. Cooper of Lamar County, Alabama with H. C. Goodrich, Dealer in all kinds of stoves, tables, tin and woodenware, china, glass, and crockery ware. Will sell cheaper than any house in the city. Mr. Cooper will be glad to have his friends to call on him at No. 59, Main Street, Columbus, Mississippi. Source: *The Vernon Pioneer*, October 31, 1877

Diaderea Cox

Notice – Probate Court
State of Alabama, Lamar County
Estate of Diaderea Cox, deceased.
Probate Court, Special Term, Sept. 24, 1877.

This day came G. G. Weir, a citizen of said County and filed in this court a paper purporting to be the last Will and Testament of Diadema Cox, late of said county, dec'd praying that said paper may be admitted to probate; when, It appearing from the Petition of the said G. G. Weir, herein filed with said paper, that the only heirs of said estate are Medora F. Weir, wife of G. G. Weir, Wm. P. Cox, Rebecca M. Albritton, wife of William Albritton, Julia F. Cox and Richard F. Cox, all of whom are adults and of sound mind and that Wm. P. Cox, Rebecca M. Albritton, and Richard H. Cox are non-residents of said State.

It is ordered by the Court that publication be made in the *Vernon Pioneer* a newspaper published in the town of Vernon for at least three weeks prior to the first day of November next notifying the said Wm. P. Cox, Rebecca M. Albritton and Richard H Cox to appear at this court on the 1st day of November 1877 to show cause why said paper shall not be admitted to Probate, and that citation issued to John E. Cox and Medora E. Weir according to law. Alexander Cobb, Judge of Probate. Source: *The Vernon Pioneer,* October 31, 1877

Will Cox

The grand jury returned three bills against Will Cox, the young white man confined in jail two for burglary and one for grand larceny. Source: *The Vernon Courier,* September 28, 1888

(Mrs.) Levi Danner

Gattman Woman Kills Self With Both Knives and Axe.

Levi Danner (Mrs.) of Gattman (Mississippi) committed suicide at her home Saturday morning shortly after breakfast. She took razors and slashed both her wrist and then used an axe to crush her skull.

Mr. Danner had left the house only minutes before leaving his wife to do the housework. Upon returning to the house, he found her lying in the back yard in a pool of blood. Mr. and Mrs. Danner were considered good Christian people. The late Mrs. Danner had been an inmate of a sanitarium and her mind had been considered all right. Source: *The Sulligent News*, August 2, 1928

G. B. Darnel

Notice – Land Sale
Application to sell land.
State of Alabama, Sanford County

In the matter of the estate G. B. Darnel, late of said county, dec'd, this day came James P. Young, administrator of said estate, and filed his application in writing and under oath praying for an order to sell certain lands therein described –when. It is ordered by the Court that the 10th day of March next be a day set for hearing and passing upon the same, when all parties in interest can come forward and contest the same if they think proper.

Given under my hand this 20th day of January, A. D. 1877.

Alex. Cobb, Judge of Probate   Source: *The Vernon Pioneer*, February 23, 1877

Lillie Millican Evans Davidson

This Christmas memory was sent to my mother in a card this year from a dear friend, Mary Evans Kelley. Mary lives in Olive Branch, Mississippi and takes time to stay in touch with mother. Mother doesn't get out very much, so her visits to the mail box finding news from friends and relatives are special. Mary's mother was Lillie Millican Evans Davidson. Lillie was a sister to Roscoe Millican. The "Aunt Mamie" in the story below was Roscoe's wife Mamie Owens Millican.

"During World War II sugar was rationed and hard to come by, but mother had saved enough back to bake that wonderful lane cake that was a Christmas tradition with us. Mother and I walked across the woods and fields to aunt Mamie's to bake together. We shelled pecans and grated coconuts and baked those 4 layer rich gooey cakes. On our way home, we stopped to cut a Christmas tree. We set our precious cake on a stump and proceeded to hack down a tree. When we went back to the stump a stray dog had eaten our cake. What a disaster! But my dear mother, we used to call her the "Queen of make do" managed to combine molasses and the little sugar that was left and made the best sweet potato pies I ever tasted! The next year we watched our cake more closely."

Isaiah S. Draper

Died of pneumonia on the 23rd inst, near Fern Bank, Ala. Isaiah S. Draper. Mr. Draper was one of Lamar's most promising young men, having chosen the profession of teaching for which he had been earnestly preparing himself for years and with every promise of taking a high place in his chosen profession The many acquaintances and friends of Mr. Draper will lament his untimely taking away, and sympathize with the bereaved family, and hope that their sorrow may be turned into rejoicing with the hope that they will all meet in the bright forever. Perry McNeil   Source: *The Vernon Courier*, January 30, 1890

The many friends of Mr. ISAIAH DRAPER were shocked to hear of his death from pneumonia last week. He was one of Lamar's best young men. He was a student of the Institute during last year, and was held in high esteem by the people of Vernon and his fellow students. Source: *The Vernon Courier*, January 30, 1890

Mose Duke

Died From His Wound

Mr. Mose Duke died at his home a few miles east from town, on Tuesday morning. His death was due to wounds from a pistol ball, received in a difficulty which occurred just before Christmas between himself and Jim Flinn. In the difficulty Mr. Duke received a pistol shot in the groin. At the time it was not thought that he would prove fatal, although it was quite serious. The wound was treated, but Mr. Duke did not recover, as expected, the wound proving more serious than it was at first thought to be. Source: *The Vernon Courier* January 26, 1893

Carolyn Black Edgeworth

The road of life we travel often takes a turn we never imagined, such as my cousin Carolyn becoming sick and leaving us way to soon. When Carolyn was in end-of-life her special friends Sammy and Judy McSpadden, Wayne Myers, Sharon Williams, Shelia Rasbury, Sammy Jones, Ludy and Telita Randolph were all there, whether in person or in thoughts showing love during her last hours. I'll never forget sitting in the hospital room with her two days before death, witnessing the look on her face as she had a dream or vision......seeing her face glow is forever etched in my mind.

Carolyn Beatrice Edgeworth, age 70, of Detroit, Alabama passed away Thursday, January 7, 2016, born July 25, 1945 to the late Sumpter D. and Hazel Marie King Black in Jefferson County, Alabama.

She was a 1963 graduate of Sulligent High School, and a long time employee of First State Bank of the South in Sulligent, Alabama. She attended Detroit United Methodist Church. Blessed with a wonderful memory and a gift of telling funny stories, Carolyn had a genuine love for other people. Her motto for life could have been "If a person truly cares about you, they'll get more pleasure from the way they make you feel, rather than the way you make them feel." She was preceded in death by husband Harold Edgeworth and her parents.

Clovis and Ola Edgeworth

Married 70 Years
November 17, 2003

Clovis Edgeworth and Ola Robinson were married November 25, 1933. They will celebrate their 70th anniversary soon. I drove to their home near Detroit on Saturday. They live off Dry Creek Road in a house high on a hill overlooking the community where they have lived and worked for years.

It was a pleasure to be allowed to come into their home and interview them. I talked with their daughter Shirley before going so they were expecting me. I was greeted with warm smiles from both which made me glad to be there.

I asked Mr. and Mrs. Edgeworth to tell me about their courtship and marriage:

Mrs. Edgeworth said "It was different back then I wasn't allowed to go anywhere with him alone. My sister, Etta, who was like a mother to me, went with us sometimes. My mother, died when I was two years old. My daddy was Willie Thomas Robinson."

Mr. Edgeworth said "When we were dating we lived about 2 miles apart. Back then, young people would fill a wagon and go to church. There wasn't many cars, most of our dating was going to church."

I asked them, who mentioned getting married first, she said "He asked me." I learned Mrs. Edgeworth's father, Mr. Robinson, was not exactly fond of the idea of her having a boyfriend much less a husband. You have heard the saying "Where there is a will there is a way," well, Mrs. Edgeworth's brother Leon Robinson lived near Aberdeen, Mississippi, so Mrs. Ola went to spend a week with him. Mr. Edgeworth secured the marriage license, S. D. Ritter was Circuit Clerk of Monroe County, Mississippi at that time. With his father's blessing, Mr. Edgeworth borrowed his father's car and went to Aberdeen to see her. Leon told them about Mr. J. C. Thompson who had a store and was a justice of peace, so that is where they went to get married.

Mr. Edgeworth said, "After we married we went back to Leon's and spent the night. The next day we came back home to my daddy's and lived with them until we could build our house. We started right after we married cutting the trees for lumber to build us a house. George Stevenson and his sons built it for us and charged $10.00. It was a four room house, with a fireplace for heat and no lights except kerosene lamps. When we married I was working at a sawmill for 50 cents a day. and you could buy 24 pounds of flour for 25 cents. Back then all we had to buy was flour, sugar and coffee, living on the farm, we raised the rest of our food."

The Edgeworth's had four children, Kenneth, Shirley, Ann and Alan Junior. As they talked, it was evident they are proud of their family. They have had fourteen grandchildren and have eleven great grandchildren. Their son Alan and three grandchildren are deceased. Mr. Edgeworth remarked with pride, " A wife and children make a man, I think a lot of my family."

The Edgeworth's shared the story of daughter Ann's birth with me. She said, "I had all my children at home, but Ann came before the doctor got there." Mr. Edgeworth spoke up and said " I had gone to take Cleve Collier to Jasper to see about a tract of timber and when I got back that night she was sick. It was raining, but I left to go get Doctor Sizemore. He was out on another delivery and I had to wait for him. When I got back, Ann was already born, without Doctor Sizemore. Granny Collier and Ida Gray had been with her. Granny Collier was good, she knew what to do." Mrs. Edgeworth remarked while smiling, "We had Ann all wrapped up lying at the foot of the bed when he came in."

This couple has seen many changes during their years together. I asked them for words of wisdom for myself and others to keep our marriages strong for 70 years. Mrs. Edgeworth said " When you marry, stay together, you just put up with one another. There is no perfect marriage, trust is important, we still love each other, I love him more now than when we married." Mr. Edgeworth agreed that trust was important and he said "my family is important to me I don't know what I would do without them."

The Edgeworth farm is beautiful, they bought it in 1955 and built their home, which as I said before, is on a high hill, in 1961. I said my good byes and drove down their drive to Dry Creek Road, looking out over the area, I could see in the distance, the houses of their neighbors a beautiful view and at the end of the drive, across the road there was a large cotton field, where the cotton had recently been picked. I thought how blessed are they, at their age, living in their home, in a community that he has called home his entire life, and it has been home to her since she was 7 years old.

Mrs. Ola Edgeworth writes poetry and she is author of *Poems* . She wrote the following poem about their life together.

We Stayed Together
We had our ups, we had our downs.
We had our smiles, we had our frowns,
But we stayed together.

Storms came and the winds blew.
But we stayed faithful, we stayed true,
We stayed together.

Being happy was our thing,
You would whistle and I'd sing,
We stayed together.

We did not always agree,
But love was there and we could see,
And we stayed together.

We won't live together much longer here,
But one thing, we won't have to fear,
We stayed together.

You've been faithful, you've been true,
I'm glad I lived these years with you,
I'm glad we stayed together.

But let's give tribute to whom tribute is due,
For it wasn't me and it wasn't you,
Christ kept us together.

John Bankhead Edwards

M. W. Cribbs Store Sulligent abt 1916

In delivery wagon are John Bankhead Edwards, born November 10, 1886, died August 12, 1947, and Henry B. "Brown" Cribbs, born June 19, 1912, died April 22, 1990.

John Bankhead Edwards worked for Myrt Winston Cribbs in the grocery store and delivered groceries. M. W. Cribbs was a step brother to John Bankhead Edwards' wife Maudie Wing Cribbs Edwards. Little Brown Cribbs was the son of M. W. Cribbs. Source: Research of Henry Tracy Edwards, submitted by Lola R. Edward.

Edwards Infant

A baby born dead to M. D. Edwards, Thursday, July 26th, was buried at the Primitive Baptist Cemetery near Sulligent on Friday. Source: *The Sulligent News*, August 2, 1928

Henry Tracy Edwards

Tracy Speaks to Group During "Show & Tell"

My history buddy, Tracy Edwards died December 19, 2016. A heart attack took him. Tracy was a "good one" always ready to help in anyway, big or small. Tracy was a very active member of Lamar County Genealogical & Historical Society, volunteering in our History room since we opened in 2009. He has been there at least one day a week, and many weeks more days than one doing whatever was needed. He was our "maintenance man", among other jobs, helping to maintain our room. He eagerly assisted many persons in researching their family history never expecting anything in return. I might add that he also found new cousins while volunteering in the room. It seems Tracy or Lola were related to almost everyone who visited.

Tracy's last project was a few days before his death, he made reservations at a restaurant for our Society's annual Christmas dinner. He made sure I called to remind everyone to attend. He was unable to join us on that night due to illness, then a few days later he was gone.

I can speak for all the Wednesday volunteers in our History room when I say, "Not a Wednesday goes by that we don't think of Tracy!"
In Memory
1934-2016

Henry Tracy Edwards, age 82 of Vernon, AL, passed away Sunday, December 18, 2016, at Northwest Medical Center in Winfield.

Mr. Edwards was born March 27, 1934, in Lamar County., AL, to the late John and Maude Edwards. He was a veteran and a dispatcher with a trucking company. He was also a member of the Vernon Church of Christ. In addition to his parents, Mr. Edwards was also preceded in death by his brother, J.B. Edwards, and his sister, Virginia Stockman.

Funeral services were held Wednesday at the Vernon Church of Christ with Eddie Finch officiating. Graveside services followed at the Bethel Cemetery.

Survivors include his wife, Lola Mae Edwards of Vernon, AL; one son, Scott (Leah) Edwards of Vernon, AL; one sister-in-law, Annie Edwards; and a host of family and friends.

Billie Brooks Elliott

In Honor of Bill Elliott World War II Veteran
2/17/2014

Billie Brooks Elliott was born April 2, 1924 to John Henry and Virgie Pennington Elliott out from Vernon in Lamar County, Alabama. Seventy-one years ago this month, February of 1943, a single male and before his nineteenth birthday, Bill was drafted into the Army at Fort McClendon and received basic training at St. Petersburg, Florida. To offset the enemy, they were dressed in full northern clothes and put on a train to Hammer Field, California where they set up in pup tents in cotton patches. From their newly, dug trenches, they could see the Sierras snow tops from the Squaw Valley.

While at Payne Field, Everett, Washington, he received his sister Evelyn's telegram of her marriage on April 15, 1944 in Seattle, Washington to Eldon Oakes from the naval ship USS Washington. The ship was being repaired at Puget Sound from battle before returning to battle. Later one night while on guard patrol at Puget Sound, Washington, on a gravel road Bill encountered a large brown bear. Both howled and the bear ran off.

They were shipped to New York and boarded the Queen Mary along with 20,000 troops and a ship crew of 2000 for a three-day cruise to Colchester, England 3200 miles away. They encountered the German enemy about midway and were followed or chased to England. Every five minutes the ship changed course dodging torpedoes. With an ear pressed against the inside ship wall, he heard the torpedoes.

They were shipped to London, England to prepare for invading their assigned beach of Omaha, France. He was in the 70th fighter wing attachment to the 9th Air Force. Bill was assigned with communication and stayed near the crip van talking back and forth for the Army escort. They set up signals with different codes which they changed often. They broke German code numbers.

While there he saw his friend, soldier Chester Yerby from Crossville.

Also while in London at the USO the famous boxer Joe Lewis toured. Some soldiers stood in long lines for a signature, but Bill said he didn't have anywhere to keep a signature and didn't stand in line. Bill was hospitalized sick there for about a month. The beach of Omaha was located on the coast of Normandy facing the English Channel. General Dwight D. Eisenhower added Utah Beach. The objective of the D-Day Battle of June 6, 1944 was to secure the beachheads of some five miles. Despite all the preparation, very little went according to plan. Difficulties in navigation, strong currents, some small boats sank and unexpectedly strong defenses inflicted heavy casualties on the landing US troops. Bill survived and received a Bronze Star for the Omaha Battle.

While in Nurnberg, Germany at a show for the soldiers, the Germans attacked. Their train was bombed and his company was missing with those remaining scattered. For two months he and a few other men were without a company, wandering the countryside, with different military groups before he was accepted as a Corporal with General George Smith Patton's Third Armored Tank Battalion Division. General Patton was known as "Blood and Guts" and not liked by the soldiers. General Patton threatened to send soldiers to front lines and maybe killed for various things. The soldiers never admitted to anything. One time the soldiers found a wine cellar poisoned by the Germans. There were twelve Spanish American men in their outfit armed only with knives sent ahead for disposing the guards for the troops to follow. They pushed Saint Lo, France while the German's pushed back until the town was completely destroyed all but one chimney left standing. The US liberated there. From there they went into Switzerland for duties and training. At Dutchland which is below sea level with dams built around it, they received a three-day pass. They hired three of their large horses with wooden shoes and rode the streets to see the beautiful sights.

Next was the holocaust. Everywhere the Germans conquered, they exterminated the Jewish population. Railroad tracks were built and people were hauled into concentration camps in train cars. From Buchenwaid, a concentration camp in Germany, he saw 3,000 dead naked Jews piled to burn. He went on to Austria and saw the worst of holocaust. A Frenchman ran up to them and in broken English expressed gratitude for their coming. He told them twelve people were killed from the Concentration Camp for each escape or attempt escape. He explained a priest knew the (the Frenchman) had children and the priest upon request died in his place. The US liberated there too. He saw the Nazi leader Hitler's home at Eagle Nest bordering Russia. At this point Hitler knew he was losing the war and had papers drawn up for his main men to burn his body and bury him before enemy troops captured him. Hitler committed suicide by gunshot on April 30, 1945. This was to prevent being hung and his body displayed in victory in the streets of Russia. They pushed on. At the Battle of Bulge, Rommel, a German Field Marshall popularly known as the Desert Fox, also threw everything they had on the US soldiers. The snow froze some of their guns. They had wool overcoats, but their hands and feet got the coldest. After the shooting and running, only a few Germans remained. Bill received a Silver Star from this battle. They pushed on.

Later they pushed into Belgium against the V1 and V2 bombers. The buzz bombs would take out a block and fell every five to ten minutes for about 6 weeks. There were underground bunkers in every town where 1000 soldiers and citizens took shelter together when they heard the bombs. They were pinned down in Liege, Belgium without food. The people gave them what they ate. Once they were pinned down in a field of sugar beets, their only source of food. They had food, but sometimes their trucks were blown up and would take longer to replace.

One night Bill was on patrol and looked for the rumored newly arrived Army soldiers in Liege. He found his infantry soldier brother Perry "Pete" Jackson Elliott. They talked at length before Bill had to go back underground when not patrolling. They did not see each other again until back home. When the troops pushed on, little was left of Liege, Belgium.

Throughout his almost three-year length of service, he received no furloughs. Eighteen months of this time were in battle and he received three stripes, one for each six-months of battle. He received Marksman medals. While Acting Sergeant in 1945, he received an early discharge because of earned extra points. It took him a month to get home from the Rhine River near Russian border, 10,000 miles away. He boarded a battle ship to New York which took 6 or 7 days and then trains again.

Bill married Grace Oakes (now deceased) and their children are Terry (also deceased), Kathy Elliott Lucas and Jeanette Elliott Lucas. Bill continues to live in the Crossville community. Thank you for your service Uncle Bill Elliott! All of your family is very proud of you and your service to your country. Submitted and written by Dianne Oakes Woods.

Charles Evans

Charles Evans, born October 16, 1821 in Alabama, and died July 30, 1865 in Millville, Marion County AL, married Margaret McDonald, daughter of Allen McDonald and Esther Blackford. She was born abt. 1823 in Kentucky, died December 16, 1864 in Millville, Marion County AL.

Charles C. Evans and his son Jasper N. Evans were in the Civil War, Co. G 16 Regiment Alabama Infantry, Confederate. The story passed down through the family was that Charles heard that his wife was very ill, so he left his dying son in Tennessee, and came home to be with her, she died soon after he arrived home. But it appears from Civil War Records in Washington D.C. that Charles actually was in Franklin County, Tennessee with his son when Jasper N. died, cause of death was not listed. But Charles was also hurt in the battle of Murfreesboro by a falling limb which injured his spine, causing poor locomotion, making him unfit for any kind of military duty, so he was discharged. The 16th Alabama Infantry regiment was assembled at Courtland, Alabama, on 6 August, 1861, and it contained men from Russell, Lauderdale, Lawrence, Franklin, Cherokee, and Marion counties. The unit was ordered to Knoxville, Tennessee, then Kentucky where it fought at Fishing Creek (lost 64 men) under General Felix Zollicoffer. Later it was assigned to General Sterling Wood's (with the 33rd AL, 44th TN, and 32nd and 33rd MS regiments), Mark Lowrey's (same regiments, with the 45th AL was added), and Charles Shelley's brigades. After taking part in the battles of Shiloh (lost 162 men) and Perryville (held in reserve, not actively engaged), the 16th participated in the campaigns of the Army of Tennessee from Murfreesboro to Atlanta (losses were 200 in the campaign), moved with Hood to Tennessee, then saw action in North Carolina. In September, 1861, the regiment totaled 867 effectives. It sustained 168 casualties at Murfreesboro, and lost fifty-nine percent of the 414 engaged at Chickamauga. During December, 1863, there were 302 present for duty and 202 arms. It lost 150 killed and wounded at Jonesboro and half its remaining force were disabled at Franklin and Nashville, including all officers. On 26 April 1865, about 50 officers and men surrendered, their unit having been consolidated with the 1st and 45th Alabama regiments.

Taken from the journal of Alabama Evans, youngest daughter of Charles and Margaret McDonald Evans, written in 1917. "His life was spent on the farm (Charles C. Evans). He served in the Civil War beginning 1860 and ending in the year 1864. His father's name was Noah Evans; his mother's maiden name was Lucinda Loggins. He had 3 brothers named, John, Jeptha and Thomas. He also had 5 sisters, Sarah, Lucy, Mary, Rhoda and Louise. About 1 Dec 1864, he left his oldest son in Tennessee on his death bed and come home to be near his wife and she died the 16 December 1864.

Both parents were dead by 1870 and the children living with relatives. One daughter, Alabama Evans was born after 1860 census was taken and before the 1870. Margaret Jane Sizemore Ollar (born 1877, long after the Civil War) told yet another story, that one of the boys was hanged from a tree in the front yard and was witnessed by the family. There is no unaccounted for son in this family, so the story is probably one she heard about another family. Alabama Evans was an orphan, so she is relying on the words of her older brothers and sisters.

Charles Evans was a farmer and was 5'10" tall, he weighed 160 pounds. He had black eyes and black hair. Source: Research of Clara Rolen and the following website http://www.tarleton.edu/

Richard Green Evans Family

Richard Green and Nancy Ann Noe Evans Family
Lost Creek Community northwest of Sulligent, Alabama

Left to right, front row: Green Benjamin (married Ludie), Richard Green, Nancy Noe, and William Thomas Evans(married Malinda Mary Ann Blaylock, Martha S. Taylor, and Delia B. Enlow). Back row, left to right: Mary Jane (married James Coleman Mozley), Martha E.(married George Black), Rachel Catherine (married John Loggins Sandlin), Eliza Ann (married William Hasten Blaylock), Louella (married W. Thomas Wright), and Sarah Telitha (married Willie Washington King)

According to research by family members, Thomas Evans (born abt 1791) came to Marion County (now Lamar County) before 1830. Census lists North Carolina as his birthplace. Thomas died May 3, 1856 and is buried in the Evans Cemetery near Sulligent. He married Mary Webb. Their known children are: (1) Elizabeth (b1822) married William A. Young and Basil Weatherford, (2) Mary A. (b1825) married James Green Young, (3) William Thomas (b1826) married Narcissa Jane Winstead, (4) Jane Louisa (b1828) married James M. Ray, (5) John (b1831) married Mary Lee, (6) Richard Green (b1835) married Nancy Ann Noe.

After Mary's death, he married her niece, Lucinda Webb. Their known children are: (1) Lucinda Emeline (b1836) married Joseph Webb, (2) Hiram Noah (b1838) married Julia Tooten (Tuten), (3) David (b1838) married Rosa Tooten (Tuten), (4) Frances M. (b1844 d 1860), (5) Charity (b1845) married A. J. Thompson, (6) Benjamin Winstead (b1848) married Elizabeth Dorsey, (7) Pleasant Jeptha (b1854) married Martha Nichols, (8) Martha Ann (b 1856) married John Brown.

Burrell Lanier Falkner

Born July 27, 1827 - Died April 24, 1897

He served as probate judge of Jones, Sanford and Lamar County, 1867-1871 and 1873 – 1875.

His father Isiac Dickerson Falkner came to Alabama from Virginia. He had four sons; three went to Arkansas and one stayed in Alabama. The one that stayed was Burrell Lanier and he became the first probate judge of Lamar County, which was Jones County at the time.

On February 4, 1867 Jones County, Alabama was established and the following officials were appointed: B. L. Falkner , Probate Judge; George

E. Brown, Circuit Clerk; William Boyd, Sheriff; M. V. Brewer, Tax Collector; Peter McGee, Tax Assessor; David E. Woods, Treasurer; Commissioners: William Brown, Jason Guin, Newton F. Morton and W. C. York.

Judge Falkner lived to age 69. Burrell Lanier Falkner and Susan Ann Cannon were married October 13, 1850 they had 10 children.

W. J. Flinn

W. J. Flinn Deceased-Mrs. M. K. Flinn Widow

In 1867 Alabama began granting pensions to Confederate veterans who had lost arms or legs. In 1886 the State began granting pensions to veterans' widows. In 1891 the law was amended to grant pensions to indigent veterans or their widows. According to Alabama Civil War Database:

W. J. Flinn

Discharge Date: 1865/05/00

Regimental Unit: 10th Alabama Regiment

Company Unit: C

Pension Record: Yes

Engagements: Wounded at Cain Creek, Alabama

Remarks: Pensioner: Mrs. M. K. Flinn, widow. Witnesses: G. W. Woods, G. W. Nolen. Source: Alabama Civil War Database.

Erma Jaggers Flynn

December 08, 2003

Mrs. Erma Jaggers Flynn celebrated her 90th birthday last Wednesday night with family at Jay's Country Squire Steak & Fish Restaurant in Sulligent. Dewey and I were eating there, and we kept hearing this group in the back laughing and it sounded as if they were having such a good time. As she and her group were leaving, I discovered they had been celebrating Mrs. Erma's birthday. I didn't get a picture, because I left my camera at home. I didn't have to ask, I knew they had a good time, I had overheard. It was such a rainy bad night outside, but their spirits were not dampened. It was a fitting tribute to Mrs. Erma to see all the smiling faces of family members as they were leaving. Happy Birthday Mrs. Erma.

Farmer Gibbs

Farmer Gibbs attended the Lions Club luncheon last week. He drank water but each time he would put the glass to his mouth, the water would seem to seep through and drip on his new suit and tie. He looked at the glass and wondered what could be wrong. He had his glass filled three times and the same thing always happened. He had been given a trick glass. Source: *The Sulligent News* October 22, 1942

John Thompson Fraizer Gilmer

Thompson Gilmer (1832-1892) the son of Archibald and Peggy Stewart Gilmer married Eliza Ann Woods in 1858. She was the daughter of Thomas Wells Woods and Juda Terry Woods. Eliza Ann died in 1860 leaving a young baby, Mary Amanda. In 1861 Thompson went into the Confederate Army leaving his baby daughter in the care of her Woods grandparents. He served in Co. M Regiment 16 with rank of First Lieutenant.

In 1864 he married Frances Elvira Woods, sister to his first wife. They had three boys: Jimmie, George, and Archie. Frances died in 1870, leaving him with four children.

In 1872, Thompson married Judy Malinda Hankins, niece of his first two wives, and they had ten children. Thompson Gilmer had fourteen children in all. He moved to the Shiloh Community northeast of Vernon from the Blowhorn Community in the 1870's.

Judy Hankins was very young when she married Thompson Gilmer, some of her step children were almost her age, but they were all first cousins and grew up together making a happy family. Judy had a merry heart, always smiling, lively and cheerful. She kept these qualities into old age. Often she played an Irish harp, singing old ballads. One of her favorites was "Barbara Allen". Judy loved roses and one fragrant clear, red rose has been passed through the Gilmer family as "Grandma's Rose." Several Gilmer relatives have this old rose today.

Thompson Gilmer died at the age of 68. He and his wives are buried in the Shiloh Cemetery in the Shiloh Community. Source: research and family history of Mrs. Virginia Gilmer and Mrs. Mary Gilmer.

Virginia Woods Gilmer

May 7, 2013

I am writing this post with a sad but happy heart. My sweet friend Mrs. Virginia Woods Gilmer passed from this life last night......entering heaven as her reward. Mrs. Gilmer, a member of our Lamar County Genealogical & Society was a wonderful southern woman, with an unmatchable love for the history of Lamar County and its people. She was always willing to help those searching for their ancestors.

Choosing teaching in public schools as her profession, Mrs. Gilmer never tired of hearing updates of the lives of her many former students. At the age of 97 she could recall the names of most of them still.

Mrs. Gilmer supported Daughters of American Revolution (DAR) for many years. In 2009 she was honored with a reception at her historical home in the Shiloh community of Lamar County, Alabama by the Daring Dicey DAR Chapter of Lamar County. As DAR members and friends gathered in her home Mrs. Gilmer gave a short talk rich with wisdom that only years of service could speak.

Chapter Regent Kay Koonce and State Regent Rita Horton Presenting Service Award to Mrs. Gilmer

Mrs. Gilmer authored several books and research papers preserving Lamar County history.

S. P. Goodwin

Mr. S. P. GOODWIN lost a valuable cow this week, from poison.
Source: *The Vernon Pioneer,* February 23, 1877.

Faustina Hankins Gosa

August 4, 1924 - February 13, 2016

Mrs. Faustina was an amazing talented lady. I will forever cherish the memories I have of our times together. She was a valuable member of Lamar County Genealogical & Historical Society. She was always ready to help when asked.

She was the devoted wife of I. V. "Pete" Gosa and the proud mother of four children. With their young family they moved from Sulligent, Alabama, to Bowling Green, Kentucky. While her youngest son was in high school, she started attending Western Kentucky University and graduated with 40 hours above the Master's Degree. Upon graduation she taught for Bowling Green City Schools. After retiring she and Pete returned to the family homestead in Sulligent.

Faustina's positive attitude and tremendous spirit touched all who knew her. Whatever Faustina did, she gave 100%. One of her favorite pastimes was quilting. She won numerous local and state competitions.

She was preceded in death by her parents, Foster and Pearl Hankins; her spouse, I. V. "Pete" Gosa; a beloved daughter, Bonnie Register; and her three sisters, Willa Rea Dubose, Onyx Childs and Jane Egger.

A. L. Guin

On Saturday afternoon about one o'clock Sulligent was shocked by the news that one of her citizens had been fatally shot. For some time bad feelings have existed between A. L. Guin and A. Q. Smith, growing out of a partnership business. Smith had been absent from there some days and had returned to Sulligent, either that day or the day before, and was at that time waiting for his brother to come and take him to his home at Bedford.

Smith and a number of gentlemen were sitting in front of Ogden's store when Guin was seen coming from the back of the Pennington house. He had one hand behind him and walked on to where the gentlemen were sitting and seemed as though he was going to pass, but when opposite Smith, he raised his hand and struck Smith with an ax handle, Smith dodged but the lick fell on his arm and knocked him over. While on the floor he drew his pistol, and shot. Three shots were fired all taking effect, one in the wrist, one in the arm and one in the abdomen. In just what position the two men were when all the shots were fired will not be known until the preliminary trial is had. Some say the shooting was justifiable, others say it was not.

Guin lived until 2 o'clock that night and it is said that his suffering was intense. Smith is still in the county and so soon as arrangements are made for a hearing he will give himself up. Source: *The Vernon Courier* April 23, 1896

D. R. Guthrie

Mr. D. R. Guthrie of Pine Springs has a new plan of breaking mules from jumping. Simply tie a tree chain around the neck of contrary stock. They soon lose their vaulting proclivities. Source: *The Vernon Pioneer*, May 26, 1876

John Strawbridge Guyton

John Strawbridge Guyton born in 1842 in the Shiloh Community southwest of Sulligent served in the Civil War and was one of the early mayors of the town of Sulligent.

He was known as "Squire" Guyton. It is said that he owned land from Vernon Street in Sulligent to Gattman, Mississippi at one time. He was also justice of the peace and performed many weddings. He prepared most of the deeds of the area after the Civil War, when flour sold for $300 a barrel and coffee was $20 a pound.

The Lamar News October 1, 1882. " Miss Ellen Guyton, daughter of Mr. and Mrs. John S. Guyton of Sulligent, died of fever Sunday night. She was 18 years old and a bright and intelligent young lady."

The Lamar News October 22, 1885 . "We are pained to hear that an infant son of J. S. Guyton Esq. of Cansler was seriously burned by the over turning of a kettle of water on last Saturday." Cansler was a small community about two miles south of where Sulligent is located today.

The Eagle Eye November 30, 1895. " Mr. J. S. Guyton, foreman and business manager of the gravel pit informs us that this enterprise is in a prosperous condition. They load from 50 - 75 cars daily, furnish employment to about 50 hands which would otherwise be idle. This gravel pit is worth a great deal to the community."

The Guytons were among the first members of the Sulligent United Methodist Church. John S. "Squire" Guyton died in 1917 and is buried in the Guyton Cemetery in Sulligent.

Harrison Hale & Abraham Murdock

Harrision Hale and Abraham Murdock, manufacturers and merchants from Columbus, Mississippi, built Hale and Murdock Iron Furnaces in 1859, by the works also included the nearby Wilson's Creek Forge erected in 1857. Hale and Murdock also built and operated some of the first cotton mills in Mississippi.

A new furnace erected by Joseph Weston, replaced the older one in Vernon, in 1862 and employed 150 men. Much of the labor used in furnace construction and operation was slave labor, the Confederate government supplying the skilled workmen. Source: Hale & Murdock Furnaces Historic Marker Information

W. F. Hamilton

CAPT. W. F. HAMILTON is farming five miles above Detroit. Source: *The Vernon Pioneer*, May 26, 1876

Huse Hankins

Mr. Huse Hankins presented us with a fine specimen of the tomato on yesterday. Source: *The Vernon Pioneer* July 5, 1878

John Franklin Hankins

John Franklin Hankins (1831-1861) died in Richmond, Virginia from typhoid fever while serving in the Civil War. He was the son of Stephen Hankins and husband of Sarah Angeline Woods and father of Sarah (Franky) Hankins. Source: Mrs. Virginia Woods Gilmer

Stephen Hankins

Stephen Hankins (1805-1870) was a planter and landowner in the Union Chapel area of Lamar County, Alabama. He had seven sons, John Franklin, Isom Green, Joel Smith, David Crockett, Thomas Benton, Samuel Houston and William Burton Hankins and 4 sons-in-law, Leroy Hampton Smith, Davis Pitts, John Barnes and Madison Oaks, who served in the Confederate Army during the War Between the States. Samuel Houston and Thomas Benton Hankins were twins. Source: Mrs. Virginia Woods Gilmer

Thomas Hankins

1884 – 1981

Thomas Jefferson Hankins, born August 20, 1884, in Lamar County Alabama, was the 11th child of Samuel Houston Hankins and Vicie Langston Hankins. His mother died in 1891 and he was raised by his father and stepmother Alcie Walker Hankins.

Thomas Hankins married Cora Adline Black in 1902. He built a house in 1915 with local help at a cost of $32.00 for windows and doors with lumber from his farm. Hankins died at the age of 97 years.

Thomas Hankins, son of Samuel Houston "Hous" Hankins, and his second wife, Vicie Langston. Vicie Langston Hankins, died February 18, 1889. Samuel Houston and Vicie had married on July 26, 1883. They had one son, Thomas Hankins, born, August 20, 1884, died November 26, 1981.

On Tuesday, February 20, 1979, Mr. Thomas Hankins, who was 94 years 6 months years old arose early and related this incident from his childhood to his daughter, Mrs. Loree Hankins Butler Christian, "On this day, 90 years ago, I very well remember what happened. The date was

February 20, 1889. It was cold, windy and a very bad day to be outside, but my mother, Vicie Langston Hankins, had died two days before, and the body had to be buried. My half-sister, Annie Hankins Cunningham dressed me, and along with her husband, Frank Cunningham, prepared to start on the day's journey to the Spring Hill Cemetery in the Bluff Community in Fayette County Alabama. Frank's father, William Raymond (Bill) Cunningham had a fair wagon and two fine oxen, Buck and Ball, with long horns. Fodder was placed in the wagon bed and later served for feed that night for the oxen. The wooden homemade box was covered with a homemade quilt, that had been tied over it. A plank was placed in front of the wagon crosswise, and Frank, Annie and I, huddling close to her, rode all day. Nearing dark we reached the cemetery and the box was placed in the hand-dug grave and covered. My grandpa Langston, my mother's father, carried me home with them, and I spent a lot of my early years with grandpa, grandma, mother's sister Maddie Roland, Tannie Barton, Jane, Polly, Jess, Adline and Calline were twins, and both were deaf and dumb, and John William Langston, who was also deaf and dumb. In about a month, my daddy, Hous Hankins came, and Preacher Nick Dyer preached her funeral service. Everyone marched around the grave in tears, and placed a cedar twig on the mound. This was in 1889, and I was 4 ½ years old then and these memories are sweet to me. Later, my father married again and I came here to live and have been a resident of Lamar County all these years. I'm still able to walk over a mile a day, when the weather permits, and look forward for the postman to bring me a paper to read. I'm staying with my youngest daughter, Loree since January 1st, but I'm looking forward to springtime, and warmer weather. so I can return to my home."

Mr. Thomas Hankins lived three more years after relating this story to his daughter. Source: Written 2005 by Mrs. Laverne Cunningham Perkins (Mrs. Perkins is now deceased.)

Milas Harris

Murder Friday morning while Jas. And Geo. Sanders and Milas Harris were at work in a field on the Vick place, 12 miles south of town, pulling fodder, someone, unknown to the men, rode up to the fence and burst to caps. The men in the field were not sure who the man in ambush was, or what his purpose was, and did not leave the field until 12 o'clock. Harris told a neighbor that someone had made an attempt to take his life, and inquired of him if he had seen a certain man pass his house that morning. Why Harris thought an attempt had been made to take his life, or why he enquired about one man only, our informant did not know.

After dinner the three men returned to work, as if nothing had happened, little dreaming that one of their number would soon be launched into eternity. Sometime near the middle of the evening a gun shot was heard, the report coming from the fence, and Harris was seen fall. He called to his companions to see who had shot him. Two more shots were fired after Harris fell. The men at work with Harris left (as was stated at the Coroner's inquest) as soon as the first shot was fired, and ran off about 100 yards and halted. They saw a man climb the fence and go to where Harris fell. He had his hat drawn down over his face so that they not tell who he was. When he saw that Harris was dead he seemed satisfied, re-crossed the fence and disappeared to the woods. The deceased is said to have been an honest hard-working man, and at present his assassination is a mystery.
Source: *The Lamar News* (Fayette Journal), September 2, 1886

Maggie Lee Davis Hayes

Birth: May 14, 1892 - Died Jan. 2, 1981

Mrs. Hayes' parents were Charles Hurt Davis (1849-1924) and Victoria Hasseltine Wimberley Davis (1857-1944). She married Walter Blaine Hayes (1889-1976).

Memories of Maggie Lee

Coffins, in those days were made to fit the body. Miss Maggie Lee, who remembers trimming coffins, says, "some were trimmed in velvet but most were trimmed in domestic. And I remember when my grandfather died" she says, "it was so cold they had to keep a log pile fired all night to thaw the ground. Then when they'd shovel the dirt out it would freeze. We couldn't stay for the funeral, it was so cold."

Genealogy

Miss Maggie Lee, whose hobby has been genealogy as long as she can remember, says, "Oh somebody's always coming here wanting help. I got two letters yesterday." Now-a-days she refers people to the Records Room or to some other person but over the years Miss Maggie Lee has compiled literally hundreds of books of genealogical information.

She estimated she has traced between 300 and 400 family trees. "I've been as far East and West, North and South, as you can go." Miss Maggie says. She has records dating back as far as 1667 and says you have to "take off your high heels and go under fences and into the woods and bushes looking for original documents."

"Sometimes you look for a week and find the answer at your doorstep," she describes her search. She is presently involved in researching the Davis Genealogy. The Davis family originated in England, and Miss Maggie Lee has recorded the family back as far as 1430.

"I don't have any idea I'll live to see it published." She says of the 551-page genealogy. But it's about ready."

Recalling that her interest in family history goes back a long time. Miss Maggie Lee says "Papa was a Primitive Baptist preacher. I'd go with him to church and after it was over I'd ask, 'who was that Papa?' and 'are they kin to us?' and 'well who are they kin to?' " Source: Newspaper article in Mrs. Hayes' personal files, author and source unknown

Volunteers of Lamar County Genealogical & Historical Society (LCG&HS) have Maggie Lee Hayes' collection on the shelves for viewing in the History room of Mary Wallace Memorial Library in Vernon, Alabama. Mrs. Hayes' research notes and material are invaluable to researchers of the area.

Hilda Hays

Little Hilda Hays, 18-month-old daughter of Mr. and Mrs. Brown Hays of Star Community, died July 8th, after an illness of two weeks. She was buried at Springhill. Source: *The Lamar Democrat,* July 12, 1916

Paul Hays
08-18-2004

Paul Hays spoke with the Lamar County Genealogical and Historical Society in Vernon on Monday, August 9, 2004. Hays, an interesting speaker, is Reading Clerk of the U. S. House of Representatives in our Nation's capital. He told us, "I never speak my own words but words of someone else." Our Society was fortunate that Paul took time out of his busy schedule to spend time with us. Hays, born in Mississippi but has relatives in Lamar County, Alabama through his father, William Clarence Valentine Hays (son of John Freeman Hays and Sarah Jane Brown Hays) and mother Auggie McDougal (daughter of Cornelius Stephen and Martha Abigal Moore McDougal).

June 2005   Paul Hays Update

When he is not reading in the U. S. House of Representatives, Paul Hays is most likely home working on a cemetery database of Lamar County, Alabama Cemeteries. Paul has taken all available cemetery indexes and entered into one index database. When completed, he will make it available to the general public at no cost.

In addition, Paul has taken the listing of cemeteries on the Lamar County Cemetery map compiled by Gene Gravlee adding township and range for our convenience. Thank you Paul.

L. N. Henson

Mr. L. N. Henson has sold the Henson Springs place to Dr. Walden of Aberdeen. We learn that Dr. W. and family have moved over. Source: *The Vernon Pioneer*, May 26, 1876

Rose Marie Gardner Smith Hocutt

Words cannot begin to describe the aids researchers of Lamar County history acquire from Rose Marie Smith Hocutt's historical collection donated to the City of Vernon/Lamar County Genealogical & Historical Society. These documents are housed in the History Room archives of Mary Wallace Cobb Memorial Library and may be reviewed by the public.

We are frequently reminded and appreciative of her service in preserving the Lamar County High School building which is now the Vernon City

Complex as we walk the halls of the building volunteering in the History room.

C. C. Holladay

Western Wilds And the Men Who Redeem Them.

An authentic narrative, embracing an account of several years travel and adventure in the West, by J. H. Beadle. A most attractive feature of this work consist of the romantic tales of Western life and adventure which makes up about two thirds of the book. The author has fully succeeded in his aim to both interest and instruct, and competent critics declare this book the most finished work on the Far West. Our young friend Mr. C. C. Holladay, of Moscow is the agent for this work, and we bespeak for him a liberal patronage. Source: *The Vernon Pioneer* June 28, 1878

James Holladay

Memory Of Jas. Holladay

Mr. James Holladay, an old man and full of years, died on Saturday the 23rd day of April 1887. He was 72 years of age; had lived in this county from his infancy. He was a good and peaceable citizen; had been a member of the Baptist Church for many years, a good and charitable neighbor and a kind husband. He has left an aged companion and many relatives and friends to mourn his loss. But we trust that our loss is his eternal gain. Therefore we should be content, and may the good Lord bless and comfort his faithful and disconsolate companion until they shall meet where parting is no more, is the prayer of the writer. A Friend. Source: *The Lamar News* May 5, 1887

John Daniel Holladay Sr.

John Daniel Holladay Sr. Born March 10, 1798, in Kershaw District, S.C.; died Dec. 31, 1862; m. (April 16, 1822, in Kershaw District, S.C.) Catherine Beasley Higgins (daughter. of Benjamin Higgins and Katherine Pickens; b. Nov. 14, 1797; d. April 19, 1877). They moved to Moscow,

Marion (later Lamar) County, Alabama, in 1826.

After embracing Christianity in June, 1844, John Holladay sold his plantation, freed his slaves and moved his family to Utah. Six children accompanied him on the trek; John Daniel, Jr., 20; Karen H., 17; Keziah D., 15; David H., 13; Thomas m. w., 11; and Lenora, 8 years of age.

In 1847 they migrated to Santaquin, Utah (20 miles south of Provo). John Daniel is buried in Spring Creek (Spring Lake), two miles northwest of Santaquin. Source: *The Holladay Family* by Alvis M. Holladay, Sr. Brentwood, TN 37027

Mrs. Joe Holliday

Mrs. Holliday, widow of Joe Holliday deceased, was born in 1813. She has during this year spun and wove 120 yards of cloth and picked one bale of cotton. She resides at Holliday's Mill, in the neighborhood of Moscow. The above work is remarkable for a lady of her age. Source: *The Vernon Courier*, December 3, 1886

Hollis Family

Derrell Upright Hollis born in Winnsboro, South Carolina and lived in Kershaw District before moving to Marion County, Alabama, with his stepfather, Thomas Cusack.

Derrel Upright represented Marion County in the State legislature from 1831-1834, again in 1838 and in 1863. On May 1, 1836, he volunteered at Moscow, Alabama, for the war with the Creek Indians which was also known as the Florida War.

D. U. Hollis was captain of his company and led the following men to Montgomery for muster into the service of the United States: Leroy Kennedy, first Lt.; T. C. Moore, ensign; James Whitesides, Orderly Sgt.; David M. Hormback; John Johnson; T.K. Guyton; John Custar; John Cauble; John C. Stanford; Robert Patrick; Joseph Miller; W. R. Redus; Lewis Almon; Reexus Weaver; J. G. Bankhead; A. W. Moore; Wilson Kennedy; Kibble Terry; G. P. Sullivan; Bysha Taylor; William Carter, Sr.; H. B. Alberson and Hiram Tarwater. Derrel Upright Hollis served one month and twenty-five days and was honorably discharged at Montgomery on July 25, 1836.

On September 28, 1850, Derrel received forty acres of bounty land for service in the Florida War.

Derrell U. Hollis was first married to Mary Elizabeth Goodwin of Pickens, County, Alabama. They had two children: Daniel William and David H. He was married a second time to Margaret Rebecca "Peggy" Bankhead of South Carolina on January 17, 1844. Thomas Cusic and James Knox Polk were born to this marriage. One of D. U. Hollis' hobbies was riding horseback over the country side. Derrell died February 23, 1870. He is buried in the Hollis cemetery that is located across the road from the old Hollis family home. He was the first person buried in the family plot.

Daniel William Hollis, born near Moscow, Alabama, owned and operated a large plantation. He was mustered for the Civil War on August 15, 1861; he enlisted on August 19, 1861, at Courtland, Alabama, as an orderly sergeant in Co. K of the 16th Alabama Infantry Regiment. Daniel William first saw action at Shiloh.

Later, at Murfreesboro, he was captured after being severely wounded in the thigh and in both arms. These injuries were on January 6, 1863. He was then sent to the military prison at Louisville, Kentucky and then on to Baltimore, Maryland. On March 27, 1863, he was sent to City Point, Virginia, for prisoner exchange. During his next two battles, Franklin and Chickamauga, he was wounded again. Daniel William later fought at Missionary Ridge and Lookout Mountain.

After the war, Daniel William Hollis later represented Sanford County in the Alabama Legislature and was a member of the Methodist Episcopal Church South. He was past master of the Sulligent Lodge #532 F & M.

Daniel first married Margaret Miller of Winnsboro, South Carolina, and had three children: Mary "Mollie Elizabeth, Daniel Dix and Acklin Upright. His second marriage was to Sopronia Guyton of Pickens County, Alabama. They had seven children: Whitt, Enral, John Dorman, Forney Knox, Della, Cara, and Florence. Daniel was known by his nieces and nephews as Uncle Daniel William and to his grandchildren as Captain Daniel. He died from a stroke while working in his garden.

Mary Elizabeth "Mollie" Hollis married Dr. Robert Hames Redden on January 15, 1874, at the home of her grandfather Derrell Upright Hollis.

Daniel Dix Hollis was the second child of Daniel William Hollis. He learned to play the fiddle from a former slave, Ben Guyton. He could play all of his tunes by the age of ten. He played the fiddle with his neighbors, John Tucker, Dick Holmes, Dr. R. J. Redden, B. H. Holliday, and Marion and Levy Gibbs. While in Baltimore, Maryland, in 1884, and Italian violinist taught Dix some of the classics. He went to New York City in 1924 and recorded twelve records with the Paramount Recording Company. Dix showed this gift for music with other instruments also.

Dr. Dix Hollis studied at John Hopkins University, College of Physicians and Surgeons at Baltimore, Maryland, at the session of 1883-84.

He practiced medicine in Sulligent. He owned a store in Sulligent dealing in drugs and perfumery. Dr. Hollis was noted for his humor and his many practical jokes.

Dr. Hollis bought land in Lamar County including the land of Aaron Pennington with the extant deed signed by President Martin Van Buren in 1838.

In 1888, Dr. Hollis married Minnie Miller. She may have been his first cousin. Minnie died about a month later, when she fell out of a wagon coming back from a dance. One of the wheels hit a tree stump resulting in the accident. The fall broke her neck and badly battered her body. She was wearing her wedding dress and was buried in it.

On August 12, 1891, Dr. Dix Hollis married Annie Molloy. She was called Mama Ann by her loved ones. Their children were: Daniel Lester, Katie, Benjamin Ross, Annie Chloe, Mayme, and an infant. They adopted Jack Lloyd Hollis (Lloyd Hastings Hughes) from the Methodist Orphanage of Selma, Alabama. He was later returned to the orphanage. Source: Mrs. Peggy Adair (now deceased)

Darling Hollis Jr.

Visitors to the History room researching the Darling Hollis family from Lake Worth, Texas, were George Hollis and friends Chuck and Katy Ebert. Mrs. Edith Hankins, a local Hollis researcher and LCG&HS volunteer was there to help. They are looking for information on Darling Hollis, Jr , (born 1823 died 1884) who was accidently shot at Cansler near what is now Sulligent, Alabama in 1884. Darling Hollis Jr. was married to Sarah Ann Nolen (born 1833 died 1921).

We regret to learn of the sad death of Darling Hollis Jr. who was by accident shot at Cansler, on the 31st ult. by Green Hollis, (a colored man) while attempting to shoot John Miller missing him with the fatal effect as above stated. Cause of difficulty is altogether rumor, so we are not able to give the correct cause. Both, Hollis and Miller, we learn are absent. Source: *The Lamar News* June 5, 1884

D. U. Hollis

Below is the roll of the Company of Capt. D. U. Hollis, which was organized at Moscow for the Indian war of 1836. Truly may her citizens be proud of their record, which shows that the sons of Moscow have always responded to the call of their country whenever the drums beat for the bugle sounds.

D. U. Hollis, Capt. Leroy Kennedy, 1st Lieut., T. C. Moore, Ens. James Whitesides, Ord. Serg. David M. Hornback, Jesse Bean, Anthony Johnson, Joeseph Holliday, John Mayson, Daniel Holladay, John Johnson, T. K. Guyton, John Custar, John Cauble, John C. Stanford, Robert Patrick, Joseph Miller, W. R. Reddus, Lewis Almos, Rufus Weaver, J. G. Bankhed, A. W. Moore, Wilson Kennedy, Kibble Terry, John Matthews, Berry Hollis, J. W. Guyton, Isaac Rasberry, G. P. Sullivan, Byaha Taylor, Wm. Carter, Sen. H. B. Alverson, And Hiram Tarwater. Source: *The Vernon Courier* August 26, 1887

Homan Family

07-28-2004

Sunday I attended the Homan family in Kennedy, Alabama. The family gathered at the old school agriculture building which is now a beautiful community center. The building is a perfect place for reunions. My granny, daddy's mother, was Lucy Lula Homan, born April 15, 1887. She was the daughter of William Jesse Homan and Alie Harris Homan, who had 16 children. My granny was number ten in the line of children. I have not been to a Homan reunion in years and it was fun seeing cousins that I had not seen in such a long time plus I met new cousins too.

Granny's granddaddy, Andrew Ike Homan is an interesting person to research. He was born in Pendleton, South Carolina according to war records. Land records reveal that he was in Tuscaloosa County, Alabama in 1858. He fought with the Union Army in the War Between the States. He did not believe in slavery, he thought everyone should be free. His wife was Thriza Burchfield. Andrew Homan was killed at Stevenson, Alabama May 1, 1865. His widow went to Mississippi to live with a son and died there. Jack Homan of Millport and Thomas Homan of near Birmingham have both done extensive research on the Homan family.

Back to my grandmother, Lula Homan. She married Hobbie Woolbright 20th January 1904. He died in 1905 before my daddy, Hobbie "Jack" Woolbright was born on January 7, 1906. He had appendicitis which was fatal. According to oral history, granny then married a man by the name of Dewberry, who worked in the coal mines near Cordova. He was killed in a mining accident and granny was a widow again. Granny later married Ezra Ruffin, a widower. Mr. Ruffin had children and needed a wife and mother for his children. She helped raise those children and she and Mr. Ruffin had five children of their own. Granny was a small petite woman who witnessed and overcame many hardships in her time. Granny was buried Christmas 1973 at Tabernacle Cemetery in Pickens County.

Louise Bankhead Ingle

03-15-2005

Funeral services for Mrs. Louise Bankhead Ingle, owner of the James Greer Bankhead house in Sulligent, will be Tuesday, March 15, 2005 in Sulligent. Her grandfather, James Greer Bankhead was the son of George and Jane Greer Bankhead who were pioneer settlers of our area.

Mrs. Ingle's father Greer E. Bankhead known as Green was a brother to John Hollis Bankhead. John Hollis Bankhead and his two sons, William Brockman and John H. Bankhead Jr. served over 56 years in the United States Congress. It has been said that if one of the Bankheads was elected to Congress, he stayed there until he died. William Brockman known as Will was speaker of the house when he died. They were all born and lived for years in Lamar County, Alabama.

Mrs. Ingle loved the Bankhead house, sitting high on a hill and loved the history that goes with the house. She was most happy that Keith Bryson took an interest in the house and she rejoiced in the house being brought to life again.

At an Open House held there in 2003 and 2004, she was there greeting persons touring the house, renewing friendships and acquaintances. She shared her family history and area history as well on those days.

I have only known Mrs. Ingle for a short time; it was a privilege to be with her. When in her home I felt comfortable and at home. She was elated to be back in Sulligent. She could have chosen another place to spend her last years, but she came back to Sulligent and Lamar County. Her roots were deep her and she did not forget.

Irvin - Norton Families

Joseph Irvin and his wife Susan Ray were residents of Lamar County, Alabama for nearly fifty years. The son of Rigdon Irvin and Rosamond Mary Ann Lowry Irvin. Joseph Irvin was born on January 25, 1835 in nearby Monroe County, Mississippi in the Northwest ¼ of Section 30, Township 13 South, Range 16 West.

When Joseph Irvin and Susan Ray married, her parents John H Ray and Susan Berry Ray, gave them, land, a cabin, a team of mules, 1 cow, 1 pig, 12 chickens, a girl and a boy as slaves.

The children of Joseph and Susan Ray Irvin were (1) Robert Rigdon, (2) John Franklin, (3) Alice Lenore, (4) Joseph Hoyle (Bunk), (5) William Roy, (6) George Washington, (7) Minerva Ellis, (8) Waco C., (9) James Erby, (10) Ellie Green, Sr. Ellie Green, Irvin Sr. married Carrie Bessie Munn and their children were : Joseph Stanley, Mildred, Willie, Bertie May, and Ellie Green Jr.

Mildred Irvin married Richard Pearson Norton in Detroit, Alabama on July 21, 1928. Richard P. Norton was the son of Elmer Rudolphus Norton and Mollie Jane Markham Norton of Pine Springs, Alabama.

Elmer Norton was born in the Pine Springs Community in Lamar County, Alabama. Elmer bought farm land , built the first house that he and Mollie Jane lived in himself. He was a farmer in his early years, later he became a trader, buying and selling animal hides, mules, and cows. He would kill a cow, dress it out, put a white sheet in a wagon, put the cow on the sheet and go to Sulligent going from house to house, selling the beef.

Elmer Norton was killed in Sulligent, on October 17, 1942, hit by a train. It was said to be an accident, but there were persons who believed it was no accident that Elmer was murdered. His head was laid on the train rail as if he were sleeping. Some family members believed his death was over a card game in Sulligent. Another unsolved mystery.....

Richard and Mildred Irvin Norton had one son, William Alton, born in the Pine Springs Community near Sulligent, Alabama. Richard Norton farmed the first year of marriage and later worked for the Lamar County Road Department. In 1938, he moved his family to Miami, Florida (Dade County). William Alton lives in Florida today.

Three generations of Irvins are buried at Wesley Chapel Cemetery in Lamar County: Joseph, Ellie Green Sr., and Ellie Green Jr. Joseph Irvin was in the Second Mississippi State Cavalry, Company F, (private) and Ellie Green Jr. served in WWII. Source: William Alton Norton (deceased)

Clytee Turman Jaggers

March 25, 2006 was a special day on Lost Creek near Sulligent. It was Mrs. Clytee Jagger's 81st birthday. She has been my neighbor all my life, living across the creek from my house. As I grew up if I looked out our front windows, I could see her house. After a few months of married life, Dewey and I moved to Lost Creek, building a house on the same side of the creek as she and Mr. Moman. She is and has been a great neighbor for more than forty years. She bakes the best carrot cake that you ever put in your mouth. When Mr. Moman was living, we didn't see them unless we needed them. Somehow, they always knew just when we needed them.

Mrs. Clytee's family surprised her Saturday with a birthday celebration. They smoked chicken and ribs served with all the trimmings. She had chocolate cake with chocolate icing baked by Judy McSpadden that was delicious. Since we live close, Dewey and I were honored by sharing her special day with her family.

Clytee Turman Jaggers born March 25, 1925 to Troy and Columbia Strawbridge Turman. Her mother died when she was a young woman. Mrs. Clytee married Moman Jaggers and they had three sons, Lehman, Richard and Joe. She loves her sons and family. Richard lives next door to her; Lehman lives in Northport or near Northport, Alabama; Joe died a few years ago. She is blessed with wonderful grandchildren and looks forward to their visits

Mrs. Clytee is a quiet Christian woman, who enjoys working in her flower and vegetable gardens in the spring and summer growing many different kinds of flowers and vegetables. Her yard is always well groomed and beautiful. She makes the world a better place

Harold Jones 1917-2003

September 8, 2003. Mr. Harold Jones left us last week. He has been in Sulligent for as long as I can remember coming into town. When I think of him, I think of the smell of freshly popped popcorn and a cool breeze. I grew up in the Lost Creek community and didn't get into town much in my younger years. I went to school at Pine Springs until the 7th grade, I didn't come into Sulligent unless mother needed something from the grocery store or for the movies or "picture show" as we called it. I loved the "shows" even if most of the ones we went to see were westerns. My daddy loved westerns! I loved the smell of the popcorn and enjoyed eating it too. I can remember leaving the movies, walking up the aisle to leave, feeling the cool breeze from the night air in my face coming in from the open outside doors, as we went into the night going home discussing with the family about the movie we had just seen. That was about as good as it got back then.

Sometimes, I saw Mr. Jones there. I knew he owned the movie theater and thought he was a very important man. As I grew older, I got to know him. I have always admired Mr. and Mrs. Jones as a couple. I have never heard anyone speak ill of him or her. All I ever saw or heard from them were smiles and kind words.

Mrs. Jones was secretary at the school and made my transition from Pine Springs to Sulligent School much easier. I had lots of questions, and she always had time to answer them and always tried to help. She too, is a special person and I love her.

As I write this, my heart is heavy, Mr. Harold Jones touched many lives with his many kind deeds, words, encouragement and they will be remembered for years to come. I know that he is now seeing the ultimate "picture show" and has a place with the One who rules the world.

Jim Jones

Died: Jim Jones at the age of 58. He was a dementia from his birth. His sister Miss Kate Jones has cared for him all along though his life, she was kind and devoted to him. Source: *The Vernon Courier*, December 3, 1886

Hiram Jordan

Born November 24, 1889-Died May 26, 1890
First Person to be Buried in Furnace Hill Cemetery

Uncle Charley Jordan was babysitting Hiram, for George W. Jordan. Hiram was on his shoulder and accidentally slid off onto a chicken coop which was behind him, injuring the top of his head. Hiram died because of this injury. Mother, Martha Ann, did not want Hiram buried at Wofford Cemetery, or Old Nebo Cemetery because she would be too far away. She did not want him buried at the Furnace Church (now Springfield Free Will Baptist) because of the water level in the graves. Grandfather, Green Berry, told Martha Ann, "Stop worrying, I'll take care of the burial." He went to Jerry Pennington and G. B. and Pink Pennington started part no. 1, of the Furnace Hill Cemetery. Hiram was buried and Martha Ann cried day and night because little Hiram was all alone at the cemetery. She stopped crying when little lady Arkader Gifford was buried 15 days later. They were having the burial services under a huge oak tree at this time. Source: Furnace Hill Cemetery history.

J. E. Jordan

MR. J. E. JORDAN has gone into the soap business and has a legal right to sell receipts in Lamar County, Ala. and Monroe and Lowndes counties, Miss. Source: *The Vernon Pioneer* February 6, 1878

Cynthia Mary Jackson Kabell

Not long after arriving in Vernon, Alabama from Pakistan, Cindy came to our History room to visit. I felt a kinship or bond to her immediately. Though we are not related by family blood our Lamar County roots run deep. Her grandfather was Dr. John A. Jackson (1872-1950) who practiced medicine in Sulligent.

Cindy was a thoughtful, kind considerate, loving person, who cared about those around her. The few years she lived in Vernon she was always busy helping (volunteering) with the church, schools, history room, food pantry and anywhere else she found needing help. I am thankful God let our paths cross.

In Memory
1946-2016

Mrs. Cynthia Mary Kabell, age 70 of Vernon, AL, passed away Wednesday, June 1, 2016, at her residence.

Mrs. Kabell was born February 21, 1946, in Quantico, VA, to Mary Emma Jackson and the late Noel Alexander Jackson. She was a volunteer with many schools.

Funeral services were held the Vernon First United Methodist Church with Patrick Cooley officiating. Graveside services followed at Shiloh Cemetery in the Hightogy Community.

Survivors include her husband, Jerry Kabell of Vernon, AL; two sons, Ian Kabell of Weidman, MI and Kenneth (Amy) Kabell of Mount Pleasant, MI; her mother, Mary Emma Jackson of Sun City, CA; one brother, Noel (Bay) Jackson, Jr. of Murrieta, CA; one sister, Paula (Steven) Obermeyer of Santa Margarita, CA; three grandchildren, David Janetski, Erika Janetski, and Harley Baldwin; and four foster grandchildren in Pakistan.

Mary Lou Kinard King

My aunt, Mary Lou, age 93, Greenwood Springs, Mississippi died Sunday, January 30, 2000, at Beverly Care in Amory, Mississippi. Aunt Mary Lou lived most of her of her life in the Greenwood Springs, Mississippi area. She was the daughter of Calvin Burley and Bessie Crenshaw Kinard and the wife of Thomas Clyde King. The Crenshaws came to Monroe County, Mississippi from Virginia. Aunt Mary Lou was a strong-willed person and it seems it must have been a family personality trait passed down to her.

Her grandmother, Mary Emma Wood Crenshaw was the daughter of Robert B. and Mary E. Tyrone Wood. She married William Thomas Crenshaw, who was the son of Robert and Jane Ashford Broderick Crenshaw, on October 23, 1873.

Just a few weeks before aunt Mary Lou died, while in the nursing home in Amory, she was writing thoughts she could remember about her life and her family. She gave me a few sheets of her writing, to type for her, telling me to be sure and check my typing, she didn't want errors! Below is one of the stories I typed, written just a few weeks before her death at age 93.

Crenshaw Brothers move to Mississippi

"Mother enjoyed telling us stories about her ancestors. Many, many years ago, three Crenshaw brothers heard there was lots of crop land for sale in Monroe County Mississippi. They had been wanting for some time to move to a warmer climate, so they saddled up their horses and headed for Mississippi. After days of travel and hardships, they arrived at their destination. They bought up several hundred acres and headed home to tell their families the good news. All winter they made preparations to move to Monroe County. By the first sign of spring, they loaded up, driving the cattle and horses behind them. Day after day, they traveled up and down streams hunting a shallow place to cross. After crossing they had to stop for some time to dry out clothes and bedding.

After traveling for many days, they were tired and hungry. One spring day, unexpectedly, they came upon a large patch of greens. Grandmother yelled 'Halt, I am going to gather us a mess of those greens.' She jumped out of the wagon, gathering up her apron, began to gather fresh greens. Suddenly the cabin door opened, a woman in it yelled 'Get back in your wagon, those are my greens.' Grandmother replied, 'You have plenty of greens and we are hungry, shut your mouth and get back in the house.' The travelers ate scrumptiously that day."

Aunt Mary Lou was a graduate of Mississippi State College and retired principal and teacher from the Monroe County School System. She was my aunt by marriage. I certainly enjoyed spending time with her. Aunt Mary Lou was the mother of Charles King, who preceded her in death, and grandmother of Michael King.

Robert Kirk

It is always a source of pleasure to our citizens to know of the esteem in which Lamar boys are held, abroad. We learn from visitors to Louisville, that Mr. Robt. Kirk, the handsome son of Dr. Kirk, of Military Springs is progressing finely at the Medical College, and is taking a high place among his classmates in all branches of the science. All speak of him as both a talented and studious young gentleman, and evincing a proper pride in the noble profession he has chosen. An honorable career beckons BOB to future usefulness, and we are assured his friends and relatives will realize their brightest expectations in regard to him. Source: The Vernon Clipper December 26, 1879

Girthie Coker Knight

01-26-2004

Girthie Coker Knight celebrated her 99th birthday on Saturday, January 24, 2004. Mrs. Knight is the mother of Robbie Knight, Jewel Sandlin and Dennis Knight. Having served on the Lamar County Board of Education for a number of years and his love for sports, Dennis Knight is widely known throughout the area. Robbie Knight, who worked at the pants factory, lives with her mother. Jewel Sandlin lives out of state, but is visiting with her mother and family.

I had a nice visit with daughters, Robbie, Jewel and granddaughter-in-law Lucy Knight late Sunday afternoon. Mrs. Girthie was taking a nap, so I missed speaking with her. When, Robbie, Jewel and Lucy spoke about Mrs. Girthie's life, their faces filled with love and admiration.

Girthie Coker, born January 25, 1905, was the daughter of Murt and Susy Lindsey Coker. She and Curtis Jackson "Pat" Knight were married January 28, 1923, when she was eighteen. J. T. Maddox was probate judge of Lamar County at the time of their marriage. A humble beginning, married by Justice of the Peace Mays near where J. D. Knight lives today on the Alabama/Mississippi line, at the fork of a road. This couple surely saw many changes in their married life. She was living in the Bethlehem community in Monroe County, Mississippi and he was living near Detroit. They eloped, since her father, Mr. Coker was not too fond of his daughter getting married, a marriage that would last 67 years until death parted them. Mr. Pat died in 1990. Being a helpmate to her husband was something she did well. Always at home, taking care of the house and family, doing whatever needed doing.

Mrs. Girthie Knight has devoted her entire life to her husband, children and grandchildren. Pat was the son of James Madison "Jim" Knight and Elizabeth Brown Knight, who came to this area by wagon about 1901 from St. Clair County, Alabama. Mr. and Mrs. Knight had four children: Dennis, Jewel, Robbie whom I mentioned at the beginning of this article, and Carman Knight. Carman was killed in a truck accident on March 20, 1948 having served in the armed forces, he had been discharged about a year before his death. Jewel married John D. Sandlin March 16, 1946, and they have four children: Alan Sandlin, Mary Cook, Linda Searfini and Debbie Sandlin. Dennis married Louise Stanford, September 8, 1956, and they have five children: Wayne Knight, Dale Knight, Kathy Lepicier, Sandy Otts and Denise Knight. Robbie never married but she lays claim to all of Dennis' children as she and her mother have such fond memories of fun times spent with them.

It was remarkable to hear, Jewel, Robbie and Lucy tell memories that the family have of their mother and grandmother. Robbie remembers her mother making clothes, toys or whatever was needed, or wanted for the grandchildren. If she could do it or make it she did.

It seems that Mrs. Knight cooked meals until she was about 95 years old. It that not wonderful, to be active at 95? I discovered in this interview that Mrs. Knight has spoiled Robbie through the years. Robbie and her mother have a special relationship.

Besides the three children and nine grandchildren, Mrs. Knight has twenty-one great-grandchildren and six great-great-grandchildren. Mrs. Knight's half-sister Mrs. Jim Brock lives in Amory, Mississippi and they keep in touch.

Sunday afternoon as Mrs. Knight slept on the couch, we were on the other side of the room discussing her life. She was sleeping peaceful as we talked, I wondered to myself if she ever thought she would live to be ninety-nine years? I know she has many memories that she could share. Happy birthday Mrs. Knight, your family loves you.

James Knight

On Sunday April 12, 2009 James Knight local citizen celebrated birthday number ninety seven. I was privileged to interview James in his home located on Highway 278 west in Sulligent. During my visit Mildred Lowery and Lockie Noe stopped by to wish James a "Happy Birthday" loaded with cards and a treat of homemade brownies.

We sat around James' kitchen table and talked about all the changes that he has seen in his ninety-seven years. I said to James, "You have seen many changes in your time. What is the biggest change that you can remember?" After thinking a few minutes, James said "It would be when we got electricity. Before we got electric power, we used lamps for light and cooked and heated with wood." Speaking of cooking, James talked about his parents with admiration on his face. He loved his parents. His mother was a wonderful cook she filled the table at mealtime with homegrown vegetables and meat. A favorite desert of James was her peach cobbler. The family raised all their food in that day, except flour and sugar.

James was born to B. M. and Daisy Gilliland Knight in the Wesley Chapel Community on April 12, 1912 near Detroit, Alabama. Brothers and sister are: Flois, Raymond, Leamon, Elmer, J.D., E.D., and Kathleen. Memories of growing up on the farm are very clear to James. He began helping out on the farm and sawmill at an early age, using mules and later motorized vehicles for transportation. I grew up knowing the Knight family in the Wesley Chapel community. A family respected and loved by their neighbors. Always ready to help when there was a need. James' mother "Mama Daisy" as everyone called her was always at Wesley Chapel church when the door was open. We usually visited Wesley Chapel during revival. Mama Daisy and my grandmother Sarah King were friends. They both wore little black hats to church if I remember correctly. James attends services at Wesley Chapel Methodist Church carrying on the tradition with other relatives.

James told us of going to school when Miss Addie Ruth Lochridge was his teacher. Miss Lochridge told the pupils to not be wrestling. Well James and Theron Scott didn't take her rule serious, and one day while wrestling they looked up and there stood Miss Lockridge. Taking each boy by the arm, she guided them into the school room and said, "Haven't I told you boys to not be wrestling?" She punished James first with four or five licks and then Theron. Miss Lochridge then said "Don't let me catch you boys anymore."

James married Ruby Irvin and they have two daughters Betty and Annette. Mrs. Ruby is deceased and James lives alone. He has a nice house with lots of windows which I thought were very appropriate since he is a retired trucker. He can sit in his living room/kitchen and keep an eye on Highway 278.

James began driving a truck in 1954. He drove for different people until 1976 he bought a truck and drove for himself using a broker in Memphis. He began driving in the days before there was a Commercial Drivers License (CDL) requirement. In later years he went with his son-in-law Bill Ballard and took the test and obtained a CDL. I think James was about age 80 when he got a CDL license. James said he did pretty well with trucking. He tried to be a good manager. After retiring from trucking, James held different odd jobs such as police dispatcher in Sulligent, a paper route and lawn mowing.

I said to James, "I think God has blessed you, what do you think?" He was quick to reply. "Oh yes he has and I thank him."

Wrapping up the interview I asked James if there was anything he would like to do if age and health permitted. He looked out his window, for a minute his mind seemed to be someplace else, and with a look of longing for days gone by he said "You see that truck that just went by, well, I'd be on the road."

Lucius Quintius Curtius Lamar

We are informed that by an act of the last General Assembly, the name of this county has been changed from Sanford to Lamar, in honor, we presume of a Lucius Quintius Curtius Lamar, who lives somewhere in the State of Mississippi.

We have, as yet, failed to get hold of a copy of the Bill, making the change; but have sent to Montgomery for it, and will publish it for the information of our San—Lamarites, as soon as received. Source: *The Vernon Pioneer*, February 23, 1877

Lawrence

Boo" Lawrence wishes to become County Treasurer. Source: The Vernon Pioneer, February 23, 1877

E. W. Lawrence's new house nearly done. Source: The Vernon Pioneer , May 26, 1876

Anderson Lowery

Notice – Sheriff's Sale
State of Alabama, Sanford County
Anderson Lowery
vs.
NO. 27 – Tilman Irvin, J. S. Guyton, J.B. Gilmore, M. C. Clippard, D. I. Guthrie And D. J. Molloy and Anderson Lowery
vs.
No. 37 – Tilman Irvin

 Under and by virtue of two Fi. Fa's to me directed from the Clerk of the Circuit Court of Sanford County and State of Alabama, I will proceed to sell to the highest bidder for cash, in front of the Court House door of said county, within the hours prescribed by law, on Monday the 5th day of March 1877 the following described property, lying being situated in the county of Sanford and state aforesaid to with…(land description)…sec 22, T 13, R16 as the property of Tilman Irvin and the sec 7, T13, R15 as the property of D. I. Guthrie to satisfy said Fi Fa's.
 S. P. Kemp, Sheriff
 Jan'ry 26, 1877
Source: *The Vernon Pioneer*, February 23, 1877

Author note: A fieri facias, usually abbreviated fi. fa. (Latin for that you cause to be made) is a writ of execution after judgment obtained in a legal action for debt or damages for the sheriff to levy on goods of the judgment debtor.

Richard Livingston

 The many friends of our esteemed townsman, Mr. Van Livingston, deeply sympathize with him in the death of his venerable father, Richard Livingston, which occurred at the home of Mr. R. G. Livingston, near Vernon, last Monday.

 The deceased was 72 years of age on July the 25th. Two months ago he suffered a stroke of paralysis from which he never recovered. Twice during the present year has death broken the Livingston family circle and me thinks that in both instances it was the handiwork Omnipotence.

 Let us so live that we may meet our loved ones "Where the Tree of Life is Blooming", eternally. The interment took place at the Williams Grave Yard, four miles west of Vernon. Source: *The Lamar Democrat*, December 21, 1904

Lusk and Pennington Families

John Lusk, was in Lincoln County, Tennessee before 1820, moving there from, Warren County, Tennessee. He was the youngest son of Thomas Lusk and his first wife Susannah Davidson. Thomas and Susan's children were: (1) Andrew, who married Nancy Rhea, moved to Lawrence County, Missouri; (2) Isaac, who lived in Franklin County, Tn.; and John Lusk, born 8 February, 1794 on Thickety Creek, Union District, South Carolina.

Thomas Lusk's wife, Susannah died in 1810 and he married Barsheba Smith, widow of David. Thomas Lusk died 3 January, 1826 of "an overweight of cold."

Thomas Lusk's parents were Robert and Mary Vance Lusk. Robert Lusk was a ruling elder of Fishing Creek Presbyterian Church in Chester County, South Carolina in 1786. They possibly migrated to Illinois about 1799 and were in Carrsville, Livingston Co. (now Crittendon County) Kentucky in 1804 when Robert died. Mary Vance Lusk was born 1735 and died 1803. Their children were : Major James Vance, born 1754 died 1803; Agnes Nancy (Betsy) married William H. Steen and lived in Rankin County, Ms.; Thomas, born 1760 married (1) Susannah Davidson (2) Mrs. Beshaba Smith and died 3 January, 1826; John, born 1769 married Martha Davidson 8 January, 1789 and died 11 June, 1844 in Cherokee County, South Carolina.

John Lusk and Rachel Tenason were married 14 March, 1814 in Union District, South Carolina. Rachel, born 2 February, 1795, was the daughter of John Tennyson and his wife, Elizabeth.

John and Rachel Lusk moved to Warren County, Tennessee; Lincoln County, Tennessee; Fayette County, Alabama; Choctaw County, Mississippi and Lafayette County, Mississippi. Their eleven children: (1) John Davidson born 7 March, 1816 married Lucinda Boswell and Lucinda Davis. John in died 1890 in Louisiana; (2) Elizabeth Ann born 4 May, 1817 died 8 Sept. 1817 in Union District, South Carolina; (3) Thomas David Jefferson born 12 February, 1819, married Nancy Pennington on 16 December, 1841 and Druscilla Phelps 14 May, 1870. He died 8 January, 1895 at Webster County, Mississippi; (4) Sarah Louise born 22 November, 1821 married George Washington Pennington about 1838 and died 1870 in Calhoun County, Mississippi; (5) Martha Lucretia born 9 August, 1822; (6) Susan Jane, born 2 March, 1824 in Lincoln County, Tennessee married Henry Pennington; (7) Cynthia born May, 1826; (8) Nancy C. Samantha born 20 June, 1828 and married William W. Sharp on 10 September, 1851, died 17 Sept. 1899; (9) Frances Marion born 30 October, 1829 married Cassandra Cross 19 August, 1857, died 13 August 1889;(10) Robert Andrew Jackson born 8 December, 1832, died 18 September, 1859 in Lafayette County,

Mississippi; (11) George Vance born 7 November, 1835 died 17 November, 1921 in Lafayette County, Mississippi.

Rachel Lusk died 29 April, 1870. John Lusk died 24 June, 1870. They are both buried at Paris in Lafayette County, Mississippi.

Henry Pennington, married Susan Jane Lusk. He was born in 1813 or 1815 and died 1888 in Lamar County, Alabama, the son of William Pennington and Elizabeth Suratt. William Pennington was the son of Levi Pennington, Jr. Levi Pennington Jr. was the son of Levi Pennington Sr., born 1714 in Randolph County, North Carolina. Levi Sr. married Martha Mendenhall. He died in 1790 in Randolph, North Carolina.

Henry and Susan Jane Lusk Pennington's children were: (1) Amelia Clementine born about 1839; (2) Cornelia C. born 1841, married Jim Neal on 23 March, 1867; (3) Narcissa born about 1842 married a Mr. Overton;(4) Rachel born about 1843, married J. Mack Neal on 5 October, 1866; (5) Nancy Louise born 13 August, 1847 married John Thomas Thompson on 19 September, 1866, died 27 May, 1914 in Lamar County, Alabama; (6) Elizabeth (Betty) born 14 April, 1849, married W.H. (Will) Morris on 20 August, 1871 died 6 July, 1920; (7) Emily born about 1850 married William Peters; (8) Greenberry W. born 28 January, 1851 married Katherine Malloy died 22 November, 1940; (9) Martha L. born about 1853 married Sam Guyton; (10) Lydia Catherine born 13 November, 1855 or 1856, married DeWitt Thompson 14 November, 1878.

Susan Lusk Pennington, died sometime between 1860 and 1862 in Fayette County, Alabama. After her death, Henry Pennington married Susan Townsend and they were parents of three children: (1) William Giles, born 9 May, 1863 married Carrie Mae Beatrice Jackson in February, 1892. William Giles died 28 February, 1907; (2) Sarah J. was born 1865; (3) Aaron Edward was born 16 August, 1867 married Mary Loretta Jackson. Henry Pennington died 1 July, 1901. Henry Pennington and his two wives are buried in what is now Lamar County, Alabama, on east side of the highway between the town of Vernon and Emmaus Church. Submitted by Bo Morris.

Marchbanks

DIED: Also, in the neighborhood of Moscow, infant child of Mr. and Mrs. J. I. Marchbank. Source: *The Vernon Courier*, December 3, 1886

Adine Marler

A telegram was received by the relatives of Mrs. Adine Marler announcing her death on the 24th at her home in Florida.
Source: *The Vernon Courier,* September 28, 1888

Jim McClung

Jim McClung's Confession
December 18, 1889
Aberdeen, MS.

"My name is James McClung. I am twenty-two years of age. I have known Rube Smith for five or six years, but have not seen much of him until the past few weeks. I returned from the Indian Nation three weeks ago next Tuesday. I went to Henry Smith's in Itawamba County, Miss., thirteen miles from Tupelo, and there found Rube Smith and Rube Burrow.

Rube Smith was sitting on his horse at the gate when I arrived, about two hours after sun-up. About an hour after I arrived, Rube Smith told me that Rube Burrow was there. Smith invited me to go down to the woods where Rube Burrow was. I went down a hollow on the west side, and then went to the south side of the house, in an old field, where Rube Burrow was lying on his coat. Burrow asked Smith what he had decided upon, now that I had come. Burrow said he wanted to go into Alabama and to this we all agreed.

Rube Smith and I went to Tupelo that night. We ate two meals in Henry Smith's house. Rube Smith carried Rube Burrow his dinner and supper in the woods. Burrow promised to meet us at old man Jim Smith's in Alabama, about five miles from Crews Station. Rube Smith and I got off at Quincy, Miss. and walked over to Jim Smith's. We were afraid to get off at Crews.

Burrow did not join us until last Monday morning. Burrow made his appearance at the spring of Jim Smith's on Monday morning, the 7th of December. I went down to the spring. They were talking of robbing a train at Bigbee trestle, two miles north of Amory, Miss.

We all decided on robbing the train on the K. C. M. & B. Railroad on Friday night, the 16th of December. The plan was that Smith and I should board the train at Sulligent and come to Amory. Burrow was to walk and join us Thursday at Bigbee trestle. Smith and I got off at Amory at 3 A. M. Thursday. We went into the woods and slept, about one-fourth of a mile from Amory. We went to the trestle about 9 A. M. Thursday. We found Burrow on the south side of the trestle in the hollow. Smith told Burrow he had taken in the situation, and did not think it would do to board the engine at Amory, because there was a night watchman there, and it could not be done. Burrow said all right-he did not care for a night watchman, but was willing to leave it to Smith. It was then agreed to abandon the robbery of the train.

We agreed to go down to Winfield, Alabama and rob Jonathan Jones a merchant there. Smith proposed that he and I would go over to Hester's grocery, about three quarters of a mile from Amory, and get some beer. Burrow said he would remain until we got back. We were absent about one hour and when we came back, found Burrow there waiting for us. All three of us then went to Amory. We stopped at Tubb's Spring, one quarter of a mile out of Amory, and stayed there awhile. We went then to Mrs. McDaniel's getting there about one hour before sunset. Rube Burrow did not go in. We found no one in the house, but got some bread and meat. Smith brought some out to Burrow. It was nearly dark. Rube Burrow proposed that he would go into the woods on the north side of the track and sleep. Smith and I went to Mrs. McDaniel's and stayed all night. Next morning (Friday, July 13th) we met Rube Burrow in the woods. We waited until Mrs. McDaniel went into the field and then we went to the house and cooked some breakfast for Burrow, because he would not go into the house, nor would he allow us to bring anything out while Mrs. McDaniel was there. We remained there until ten o'clock A. M., then Smith and I went to John Marsh's and got dinner. We gave Burrow enough for dinner and breakfast.

We all got together at Amory Junction, about one mile out of Amory, late in the evening. Burrow said there was no danger of any one knowing him, and he was not afraid to come into Amory. So we all started in about one hour before sunset. We came up the track until we got near the depot. Burrow went over towards the round-house, among the side tracks, where we went over later, and joined him." Source: *Rube Burrow King Of Outlaws, And His Band Of Train Robbers* by G.W. Agee circa 1890

Albritian McDaniel

Mr. Albritian McDaniel, living in Strickland's Beat, this county has arrived at the ripe old age of 84, and is hale and hearty. Mr. McDaniel is now living with his second wife, Mrs. Nancy McDaniel, aged 64. Has resided near the same place for 45 years, has had 23 children, 19 of whom are living, 115 grandchildren and 45 great grandchildren. Source: *The Vernon Pioneer* February 6, 1878

Peter McGee

The funeral of Rev. Peter McGee, late deceased, will be preached by the Rev. T. W. Springfiled at Bethlehem church 8 miles south of Vernon on the 5th Sabbath in this month. Source: *The Lamar News*, May 5, 1887

Veneta McKinney

Thanks to Veneta McKinney who is doing a wonderful service for all of us to enjoy. She is transcribing historical Lamar County newspapers from microfilm and posting on the internet for us to enjoy.

Bobby McReynolds

Bobby McReynolds, age 70, died March 15, 2004 at the Fayette Medical Center.. Bobby put up a good fight. A retired Air Force person he knew what it was like to face a challenge. Bobby and wife Rachel have been faithful members of our Lamar County Genealogical & Historical Society and have done much work to preserve the history of Lamar County.

Metcalfe Family

Family of Wiley St. Clair and Virginia Ellen Bradley Metcalfe
1905 Sulligent, AL

Standing (back): John Edward Metcalfe, James William Metcalfe, H. Rudolphus Brown, Leander St. Clair Metcalfe, Henry Franklin Metcalfe and William Arthur Cobb.

Standing (front): Amanda May Metcalfe, Luella Brown Metcalfe, Jala Guin Metcalfe, Bessie Lee Stanford Metcalfe, Malinda C. Shaw Metcalfe and John M. Bannister.

Sitting: Sarah Anna Elizabeth Metcalfe Bannister, Harriet Estelle Metcalfe Brown, Virginia Ellen Bradley Metcalfe, Wiley St. Clair Metcalfe, George Tolliver Carrington Metcalfe, and Rosa Ellen Metcalfe Cobb

Wiley Saint Clair Metcalfe born in 1837, married Virginia Ellen Bradley in 1858. Wiley and Virginia were early settlers of what is now Lamar County and Sulligent. It is said that once Wiley Metcalf shipped 400 bales of cotton to Columbus, MS by way of the Buttahatchie river. It is hard today to imagine that the Buttahatchie was once navigable. He shipped harvested virgin timber by the Frisco railroad as did others in the area.

Mrs. Virginia Metcalfe was known in Sulligent as "grandma Metcalfe." The Metcalfes reared nine children and had 36 grandchildren. The Metcalfe's children were: Martha Elvira, who married Perry Evans; Leander Saint Clair "Lee", married Jala Guin. (Lee served as Lamar County Sheriff);

Henry Franklin married Melinda Shaw (Henry worked for the Frisco railroad.); Sarah Anna Elizabeth, married John Bannister (John was Sulligent Marshall.); James W. "Jim Buck" married Amanda May; Rosa Ellen, married first William Cobb second Cannon Richard Weaver, (after Mr. Cobb's death); John Edward "Ed" married Lou Ella Brown (Ed founded the Metcalf Grocery and Market that was in business in Sulligent for 70 years); Hattie Stella married Rudolphus Brown (A brother to Lou Ella Brown.); George Tollivar Carrington "Toll" married Bessie Lee Stanford (Toll worked as stock broker in Kentucky.).

Leander Saint Clair "Lee" and Jala Guin Metcalfe

Leander Saint Clair "Lee" Metcalfe, son of Wiley Saint and Virginia Ellen Bradley Metcalfe, married Jala Guin in 1889. Lee farmed near Crews, served as Lamar County Sheriff and Tax Assessor. While he was sheriff he pursued the Burrow gang. He helped capture Leonard Brock who was a member of the train robbing gang. Brock's alias was Joe Jackson.

Lee and wife Jala moved to Texas in 1911 with their three sons, Wiley, Jason and Rayburn. They had a son Dempsey Lee who died when he was 5 years old in 1901. Source: Metcalfe Family records

James Middleton

We enjoyed a rare treat of excellent peaches at MR. JAMES MIDDLETON on the Fourth. MR. MIDDLETON is first in the field with peaches this year, and as a grower of small fruits he has no superior. Source: *The Vernon Pioneer*, July 5, 1878

We should have stated in last week's News that the house purchased by JAS. MIDDLETON, Esq. cost him $762.50, instead of $662.50. Source: *The Lamar News*, September 23, 1886

MR. JAMES MIDDLETON is teaching a public school in the BICKERSTAFF neighborhood. Source: *The Vernon Pioneer*, July 5, 1878

J. W. Mixon

J.W. Mixon, captain and center on the Sulligent High football team has developed interests across the river and heads toward Detroit quite often. Quinon Duncan and J.C. Hollis can always be found in town on Brown Street. Source: *The Sulligent News* October 22, 1942

William Pierce Mixon

A friend of Lamar County Genealogical & Historical Society passed away in 2012. Bill, a wonderful man, is missed by researchers of Lamar and Marion County history.

William P. Bill Mixon, 65, of Sulligent, Alabama passed away Sunday, December 23, 2012 at Baptist Memorial Hospital-GT, Columbus, MS. Funeral services were Thursday, December 27, 2012 at 11 AM at Lowndes Funeral Home Chapel, Columbus, MS. Interment was in Cedar Tree Cemetery, Hackleburg, Alabama.

Bill was born June 27, 1947 in Russellville, Alabama to the late Lecil Clyde Mixon, Jr. and Caroline Fite Mixon. He lived in the Molloy Community of Lamar County, Alabama, graduated from Hamilton High School in 1965, attended Northwest Alabama Junior College, where he met his future bride, and graduated from Mississippi State University. Mr. Mixon served seven years in the Alabama National Guard, was a member of the Teamsters Union, and retired as a truck driver for Consolidated Freightway after 30 years of service. He was a member and Past Master of Columbus Lodge #5 F&AM. Mr. Mixon was also a member of Scottish Rite and York Rite Masonic Bodies, Order of Eastern Star, Vernon Masonic Lodge #389, Vernon, Alabama, Southern Cruisers Car Club, Columbus, Mississippi, and the Lamar County Historical Society. He also was a member of the Lamar County Sons of Liberty SAR, where he held various offices. Mr. Mixon was a member of Border Springs Baptist Church, Caledonia, Mississippi, where he served as a deacon and other various positions and he was a Gideon. He was a frequent customer at local coffee shops and was an avid Mississippi State fan. Mr. Mixon enjoyed throwing out Christmas candy in Christmas parades from his antique cars. He married Jackie Knight Mixon at Border Sprigs Baptist Church, Caledonia, MS on December 23, 1973, they have one daughter Jane.

Thomas Molloy

At Mr. Thomas Molloy's, a few miles south of town, an enthusiastic lot of people had gathered to make merry eating fish and tripping the light fantastic toe to the time of good music. They had a general good time, and many are the encomiums we have heard expressed regarding Mr. Molloy's hospitality. All in all, the Fourth of July, AD 1878, was a grand and glorious one, and many hearts made happy by its coming will revert back to it in kindly remembrance, wishing that the Fourth just past gone is only like unto the many that are to come.

The land sale in the matter of Thos Molloy vs Sarah A. and H. P. Hays, advertised for Monday last is again postponed to the first Monday in August. Source: *The Vernon Pioneer*, July 5, 1878

Mrs. George Moore

Mrs. George Moore dies in Sulligent suddenly. Mrs. Moore was daughter of the late Rev. Mose McGee. She leaves 4 small children and was laid to rest at Mt. Harmony Cemetery 5 miles south of Vernon. Source: *The Lamar Democrat*, July 12, 1916

James Field Moore

James Field Moore born March 21, 1789 in North Carolina moved to Tennessee. He was a surveyor of what was known as the military route from Mississippi to New Orleans. He held the rank of major under General Andrew Jackson. He was a special friend of Henry Clay. Major Moore moved to Alabama about 1821. They stayed in Franklin County for a short time. Pressing further south, they stopped on the Buttahatchie River in Marion County. The next year, they moved four miles south to Bogue Creek. They built a large home there which stands today just outside Sulligent, Alabama.

He served as a member of both houses of the state legislature of Alabama later moved to Monroe County, Mississippi near Aberdeen after remarrying. He was very wealthy at the outbreak of the Civil War.

Moore died in 1865 at Aberdeen, Mississippi. It is not known where he was buried but he was probably buried with his wife Abigail in Alabama. Source: Writings of Mrs. Virginia Woods Gilmer (deceased)

John T. Moore

Mr. John T. Moore, two miles south from Vernon, in addition to his excellent facilities for ginning cotton and grinding corn, is putting in a new bolting apparatus. With this acquisition and greatly needed improvement, he is enabled to make flour equal to any similar establishment in the country. Mr. Moore is on the order of progress and development and alive to the importance of any enterprise having a tendency to help individual man and improve the country at large. Mr. Joel F. Sanders is placing the machinery in position for this new feature in the mill, and when completed there will be no quibbling about the job not having the finishing touch of a master machinist. Raise wheat at home, grind wheat at home, and with this understanding the people who use home-made flour will live longer, die easier and enjoy the real comforts of a stomach not gorged with tale, half of the foreign flour now sold being composed of this deadly stuff. Source: *The Lamar Democrat*, July 2, 1898

Thomas B. Moore

Mr. Thomas B. Moore, who lived three miles west of Vernon, met with an accident last Friday, receiving injuries which resulted in his death on Monday night.

His remains were laid to rest in cemetery in town Tuesday evening in the presence of a large number of relatives and friends.

Last Friday morning, Mr. Moore was engaged in digging brick from the foundations of the old Iron Furnace one and a half miles west of Vernon. He was working in a trench about six feet deep and on one side the bank rose eight or ten feet higher and overhung the trench in which he was working. He had straightened up to rest a few moments, and while standing, the bank from above, slid in upon him, burying him to the top of his head. His little son and another small boy were nearby and ran to him and scratched the dirt away so that he could breathe. Some men who were nearby were quickly summoned and they proceeded to dig him out. Mr. Moore said that he would never get over it, that he was killed. Dr. W. A. Burns was summoned and did what could be done for the injured man. Mr. Moore received no external injuries, and gave evidence of improving for a couple of days, and his friends began to hope for his recovery.

Mr. Moore was an upright man, industrious farmer and a good citizen, and his death will be a great shock his many friends. Mr. Moore was middle aged man and leaves a wife and several children.

Floyd Morris Jr.

Bo Morris Sits and Talks at History Meeting

Floyd Morris Jr. aka Bo Morris a long time member of Lamar County Genealogical & Historical Society is recognized for his knowledge of our local history not only in Lamar but outside of West Alabama. Bo has quite a large network of historical followers from probably all states and maybe some outside the states. It is amazing at how many people actually know him and rely on his help to solve mysteries of their family tree. Bo grew up listening to his father tell stories of days gone by. He can't remember when he was not interested in history. If he has heard or read about it...he remembers it which is amazing. He has helped steer me in the right direction many times. I think Bo's idea of pleasure is traveling to some courthouse, cemetery or other place to unravel a mystery.

John Morris

During the Civil War the John Morris family who lived a mile away could hear the drum beat when the death lists were read at old Moscow. Source: *A History of the Boman, Chandler, Todd and Morris Families of Lamar County, Alabama*, written by Mrs. Edna Boman

Ruby Cash Morris

September 29, 2003

Mrs. Ruby Morris of Sulligent celebrated her 100th birthday at her home recently with family and friends. I talked with Mrs. Morris' son Bo about interviewing her, but with all my responsibilities or perhaps I just don't plan well, I have not found the time to visit.

Mrs. Morris and legendary County Music singer Roy Acuff shared the same birthday September 15th. Roy Acuff, born in Maynardsville, Tennessee, was known for "Wabash Cannonball." Mrs. Morris is known for the life she has lived in Sulligent.

In the Oak Hill Community, located between Sulligent and Vernon, Alabama, Ruby Cash was born to Robert Houston Cash and Tezzie Thompson Cash. Mrs. Morris married Floyd Mack Morris Sr. on February 27, 1927 and has lived in Sulligent since 1927. She loves her family and they love her.

In 1990 when First Baptist Church celebrated 100 years, I learned Mrs. Ruby Morris had been a member for over 60 years. She always had such a sweet smile and was such a gracious lady. She has made an impression in my life by seeing how she lived hers.

When I drive past her house, I always think of her, she has been there as long as I can remember. It has been some time since Dewey and I stopped to talk with her, but I know she is there and I say a prayer as I pass.

Happy Birthday Mrs. Morris, you are loved more than you know!

Dr. M. Morton

An incident occurred to Dr. M. Morton the other day which taxes that gentleman's vim and energy far more than the game of croquet which he is wont to play so well. The Dr. was going to see a patient at the house of Mrs. Munroe, and upon entering the yard, was attacked by the noble mastiff Frank, who was proceeding to make mincemeat out of the son of Lisuiapius. But the Dr. knew what he had to deal with when he went there, and was prepared, and soon put Frank hors du combal with a ponderous can he carries with him. Dr. Morton suffered no injuries from the attack of the ferocious canine other than being somewhat scared, and he now cries "Brave" wherever the name dog is mentioned in his presence. Source: *The Vernon Pioneer* June 28, 1878

James M. Morton

Death of J. M. Morton

Mr. James M. Morton, Register in Chancery, died Friday Night at 9 o'clock. He had been confined to his room for more than a month from paralysis, during which time he sustained two other slight strokes, the last of which proved fatal. Mr. Morton was in his 70th year and was reared in this county. He became active in public affairs in the early sixties and served as postmaster at Morton's Mill during the civil war or until the town of Vernon was established, when the post office was moved here, where he continued to serve as postmaster for several years.

When Lamar County was formed, he was appointed Register in Chancery, which position he held continuously until the day of his death. His predominating characteristic was his fidelity to trust his State, his friend and his people were his all, and he never refused to give generously to every public and charitable cause, but saying nothing to others about his good deeds, and declining to accept thanks from those he favored. He more truly kept his left hand from knowing what his right hand did than anyone in

Vernon. In private as well has public life, he was modest, genial, tender and timid to offend. He possessed not a single quality that gives him artificial or predunctory friends, and there is a great wave of sorrow in this community for the loss of this excellent citizen. The final exercise took place from the residence Saturday evening and the body was deposited in the vault in the Odd Fellows cemetery at 4 p.m. to await the sounding of the last trumpet which shall call all nations to the judgment bar of God. Source: *The Lamar Democrat*, December 20, 1899

Mose

MOSE, the Negro confined in the county jail says he would rather be at work in the cotton field than be confined in a gloomy cell and that he's so tired of restin'. Source: *The Vernon Pioneer* June 28, 1878

John Coleman & Mary Jane Evans Mozley

Mary Jane Evans, born December 21, 1858, the daughter of Richard Green and Nancy Noe Evans, married James Coleman Mozley on February 1, 1880. James Coleman, born June 5, 1861, was the son of Caleb and Mahala Mozley.

The Evans family lived in northwest Lamar County, Alabama. Mary Jane's grandfather, Thomas Evans was a pioneer settler of Lamar County who owned land in what is now the Pine Springs & Shiloh North Communities N and NW of Sulligent.

The Mozleys arrived in Maysville, OK, October 2, 1902 on the Santa Fe Railroad, the day the Santa Fe Depot was dedicated. In 1904, they lived near the Love Ranch at Story, Oklahoma, then moved to Lindsay, Oklahoma, in 1906. It seems that they began spelling their name as "Mosley" after moving to Oklahoma.

The Mozleys had 9 children, James Luther, Viola Jane, Mary Eliza, Nancy Clementine, Millie Louvenia, Sarah Mildred, Baby Boy, Richard Cleveland and Gladus Alvin. Nancy Clemetine lived to be 102.

Maysville is a town located in Garvin County, Oklahoma. As of the 2000 census, the town had a total population of 1,313.

T. B. Nesmith

COL. T. B. NESMITH fully domesticated at his new home. We trust he will become a fixture. Source: *The Vernon Pioneer*, May 26, 1876

Dr. W. L. Nixon

Dr. W. L. Nixon graduated from Baylor School of Pharmacy and the Chicago School of Chiropody before entering St. Louis University in St. Louis, Missouri. He transferred to the University of Alabama in July 1944 as a junior. Graduating May 1946, he taught embryology in the existing medical school and helped move the school of medicine to Birmingham. He finished his medical school classes to graduate with the class of 1950. He did a two-year residency at City Hospital in Mobile where he was head of the surgery department. After completing his residency, the family moved to Sulligent July 1, 1952, where Dr. Nixon went into practice with Dr. Haig Wright. They had been classmates at the University of Alabama.

Dr. Nixon practiced in Sulligent and Vernon until July 1963 at which time he moved to Clearwater, Florida. Dr. Nixon born 1910, died 1981 in Cullman, Alabama. Source: Mrs. W. L. Nixon (deceased)

According to *History of Lamar County* by Joe Acee, the Sulligent Clinic was built by funds contributed by the citizens in 1947. Dr. J. M. Burnett and Dr. W. B. McDonald were the doctors. Both doctors were called to active duty. The clinic reopened July 11, 1951 with a new doctor, Dr. Haig Wright.

Noe Family

5-26-2003. This past Sunday was "Decoration Day" at Pine Springs Cemetery. I went to the cemetery this year, in spite of the shower it was a beautiful day. A newly discovered cousin of mine, MarEllen Benson and her husband Theo "Doc" came from Oklahoma City last week for the "Decoration" on Sunday. MarEllen is related to me through the Noe family. She wanted to meet Noes and that she did.

My grandmother, Sarah Evans King's mother was Nancy Ann Noe, whose father was Samuel C. Noe. Samuel C. Noe was a brother to Thomas R. Noe, murdered in 1867. Samuel C. Noe had a son, Thomas R. Noe, who left Lamar County in the late 1800's and settled in the hill country in Oklahoma. MarEllen Benson is the great granddaughter of this Thomas R. Noe. There were several Thomas R. Noe's in Lamar County.

MarEllen and I had a wonderful week-end visiting in the Pine Springs and Lost Creek Communities. It meant much to MarEllen to travel to the area where her ancestors lived, to walk where they walked.

Lockie Reese Noe

09-01-2004

Things around at Sulligent City Hall will be different beginning Monday as well as things at the Glenn Noe home. Lockie Noe has retired from her job with the city. I went by on Friday to wish her well like lots of other folks. Lockie has been kind, considerate and helpful to me through the years. This didn't start with her work with the city. Lockie has been nice to me for a long time back when they had the grocery store on Front Street. She has a special family and I know she looks forward to spending more time with them especially the grandchildren. Happy Retirement Lockie!

Noe Murders

On December 1, 1867 Thomas R. Noe, Sr., his wife Mary Fitzgerald Noe and Dr. Metcalfe "Mack" DeGraffenried were murdered in the Pine Springs Community located between present day Detroit (then Millville) and Sulligent (not a town until abt 1887).

Horrible Tragedy by a Lunatic

A man name Briggs was confined in the jail at this place on Sunday last for the killing of two men and a woman with an axe, in Jones County, Ala. --- For years Briggs has been deranged, but this, we understand, is the first act of violence he has committed and or attempted to commit. At one time he belonged to the Alabama Methodist Conference, and was regarded as an able and efficient minister until he lost his mind. Source: *The West Alabamian*, 18 December 1867, Pickens County, Alabama.

Wholesale Murder by a Preacher

Near Melville, Ala., on the night of the 30th ult., a Methodist preacher named Samuel Briggs murdered Dr. DeGraffinreed and Mr. John R. Noah. According to the Tupelo Mississippian's account. Briggs and DeGraffinreed were in conversation when Briggs arose from his chair, seized a piece of wood, and struck DeGraffinreed, knocking him into the fire and killing him; whereupon Mr. John R. Noah, an old gentleman, at whose residence Briggs and DeGraffinreed were, jumped out of bed apparently to rescue DeGraffinreed, when Briggs fell upon him with his stick of wood and beat him to death. The wife of Mr. Noah attempted to escape by the door but was overtaken by the murderer and killed with the same instrument. Briggs escaped and at last accounts had not been arrested. Source: *Memphis Dailey*, Memphis, Tennessee, December 21, 1867

Triple Murder with Axe Handle

A Methodist minister named Briggs killed two men and a woman at Milleville, Ala. He was a lunatic who had been released as cured. He committed the triple murder with an axe handle. The victims were all aged persons in the house where he was staying. Source: *Boston Herald*, Boston Massachusetts, December 27, 1867.

Ellie Ester Birmingham Nolen

On August 3, 2001, Mrs. Ellie Ester Birmingham Nolen celebrated her 100th birthday. There was a celebration honoring her on August 4th, at the American Legion Building, in Sulligent. Mrs. Nolen lives in Norton Estates in Sulligent.

The family of Mrs. Ellie Nolen has truly been blessed. It was an honor to interview her and learn so much from what she had to tell me.

Mrs. Nolen's parents were W. Thomas Birmingham (born 1878 -died 1942) and Mary Lou "Mollie" Otts Birmingham (born 1882-died 1974), they lived in Lamar County, Alabama. Mrs. Nolen has lived here for most of her 100 years except for living a short time in Mississippi.

Thomas and Mollie Birmingham had eleven children with Ellie Ester being the oldest. Their other children were Myrtle (married Rufus Weeks), Clifton (married Madge Otts), Grace (married Earlie Evans), Gertrude (married Howard Crew), Hazel (married Roy Otts), Clarence (married Robbie Weeks), Ralph (married Gladys Burks), Ray (married Ruth Murrow and Jean Sorrells), Delbert (married Helen McDonald and Gail Harris), Evelyn (born 1922 - died 1925), Daisy (married Roland Egger).

It is a different day than when Mrs. Nolen was born that is for sure. According to the *The Vernon Courier*, August 1, 1901: lady's umbrellas were selling from 50 cents to $1.50 at J. E. Morton's store and he also had the latest thing in lady's straight front corsets. You could buy 9 pounds of coffee for $ 1.00 in money at N. Edgeworth & Son. At W. B. Clearman's store, 16 pounds of sugar sold for $1.00 and domestic and calico cloth was 5 cents per yard.

Mrs. Ellie Nolen grandparents were John Otts, Americus Catherine Newell Otts, John Birmingham and Mary Jane Birmingham. John Birmingham's first wife was Mary Ester). Both of Mrs. Nolen's grandfathers were farmers and served the South in the Civil War.

Growing up in rural Lamar County meant doing chores on the farm. She remembers picking cotton in cold weather, with her hands freezing from the early morning dew or frost.

At night, in front of the fire, a sheet was lain on the floor and the family would all shuck and hand shell corn onto the sheet. The corn was then bagged to carry to the mill to be made into corn meal.

The houses back then had cracks in the floors, she can remember living in a house with a dirt floor at one time. In the summertime it would be hot and they would often bed down at night on the porch to be cooler.

Her mother must have been a wonderful cook, because the baked sweet potatoes, she described baking in an oven in the fireplace, and the food cooked on the wood stove sounds very tasty. Mrs. Nolen said, "Some of us liked brown biscuits and some liked light brown biscuits, mother would cook some of each kind. One day my mother cooked an apple stack cake, I took the top layer off and ate down through the center of the cake. I can't remember what mother did to me." Mother had two cows that she milked. She would mix a tub full of hulls and cottonseed meal to feed the cows" said Mrs. Nolen.

She told me another story, "I had a sister Evelyn that was sick, the night she died we were all on the porch, there was a loud noise like a wagon and team of mules running loose, we all heard it rattling but there was nothing there. Everyone was scared so we went in the house. Later that night Evelyn died." said Mrs. Nolen.

Mrs. Nolen married E. B. "Birt" Nolen whom she had grown up with, at age 14. They married at Gattman, Mississippi. They had eight children: J. K. (married Ruby Northam), Annie Mae (died age 15 months), Marie (married Frank Gilmore), Mary (married Ray Stephens), Jewel (married Clarence Quick), Lois (married Benny Collins), Carl (married Mary Crossley), and Billy (married Ruth Hankins). At the time of this interview, J.K., Annie Mae, Jewel and Billy were deceased. Her husband E.B. "Birt" Nolen was the son of John and Catherine Flynn Nolen.

Mrs. Nolen has been affectionately known for years as "Nonie." She was given this name by her first granddaughter, Gwen Nolen Buckley, daughter of J.K. and Ruby Northam Nolen.

Mrs. Nolen talked of hardships in her life. She had a daughter, Annie Mae who died as a child. She remembers they cut stove wood to pay the doctors that treated her. When times were hard, they shelled 3 bushels of white corn and sold for $1.00 to buy necessities.

Before electricity or iceboxes, the family kept milk cool by lowering it down into the well or placing in a spring of cool water. Later they had an icebox and would buy block ice to keep things cool. She washed clothes by hand and the dirty ones, she beat them clean with a "battling stick" and hung on a barbed wire fence to dry.

When I asked her about Christmas past, she shared a memory, "When I was a child, we usually got an apple, an orange and a stick of candy for Christmas. One Christmas when we lived near Tol Anderson's place daddy bought me a doll. I remember running over to granddaddy's to show him. On the way I fell and broke the doll and cut my arm." To this day, she still has the scar from that cut on her left arm.

I asked if she remembered picnics. She said, "There was a place at Beaverton where they would have picnics. One time Myrtle (her sister) and I went over there, we each had a dime. They had tubs of lemonade, which they sold. At the end of the day, they would sell the lemonade, two glasses for the price of one. Myrtle and I waited and bought at the end of the day. We got more for our money."

When asked if she could remember anything unusual about the weather Mrs. Nolen said, "One time there was thunder and lightning when it was snowing. Another time there was a tornado below our house; we got under the house under the rock chimney."

I asked what she could remember about the Fourth of July. Mrs. Nolen said, "After I married some friends came over and we made ice cream. One freezer wasn't enough so we poured it out and made another freezer full. The first ice cream almost melted before the second was finished. The friends were my cousin Dudley and Ruth Otts."

Mrs. Nolen has been a loving wife, mother, grandmother and great-grandmother (I am not sure how many greats). She has quilted many quilts which family members have enjoyed and are enjoying them. She loved working in her garden when she had one. She enjoyed going to gospel singings with her husband, Earlie and Grace (her sister) Evans.

I spent ninety minutes talking with this great lady and the time went by fast. She is remarkable. I asked her for words of wisdom for living a long life, she had none. I think that she has taken whatever fate dealt her and made the best of it. To a precious lady, Happy 100th Birthday.

August 4, 2001

Two hundred and fifteen persons registered Saturday at the birthday party honoring Mrs. Ellie Ester Birmingham Nolen, at the American Legion Building in Sulligent. Mrs. Nolen was 100 on Friday, August 3, 2001. Believe me Mrs. Nolen doesn't look one hundred. This lady has had a special week. I often hear someone say "if I live to be a hundred." Mrs. Nolen has done that with such grace and dignity. I visited with her a few minutes before the party. She was dressed in a red outfit and looked great. Her family beautifully decorated the building and there was lots of good food. I commented to Mrs. Nolen that it looked like they had a good "spread" on the table. She said " I know, I have been hearing them talk about it."

Distance didn't matter, folks came from Florida, Illinois, Texas, Kentucky, Georgia and it seems from all over Alabama to honor this precious lady. Mrs. Nolen received many gifts, cards and of course she had flowers. She enjoyed her son Carl's guitar playing and singing. His daughter and granddaughter joined him in singing. Her daughters, Marie Gilmore, Mary Stephens and Lois Collins were there. Honorable Roger Bedford stopped by to offer his birthday wishes.

In my interview with Mrs. Nolen last week, I asked her about her school days. She said, "I went to school at Prospect. I remember playing baseball when I was 10 or 11 years old. I was catching, a boy was batting and he hit me in the head." She walked to school, but not too far, about half a mile.

She has witnessed things that most of us can only read about.

Mrs. Nolen remembers taking short trips on the train. When she was growing up they would catch the train at Crews and ride to Beaverton. Later when she lived at Greenwood Springs, she would ride the train to Sulligent and back.

Mrs. Nolen told me that her daddy pulled one of her teeth with the pliers. She said, "Daddy carried me to Dr. Collins because I had been keeping them up nights with the toothache. Doctor Collins was going to pull my tooth, but I wouldn't open my mouth. Daddy carried me back home, later I woke up in the night crying with the toothache, so Daddy pulled the tooth himself."

Birthday 101-August 5, 2002

Mrs. Ellie (Nonie) Nolen celebrated the big 101, August 3, 2002, quietly, with a luncheon, at the home of her granddaughter Mrs. Gwen Nolen Buckley, in Sulligent. Among those helping her celebrate were Mrs. Lois Collins, Mrs. Mary Stephens, and Mrs. Daisy Egger. Mrs. Nolen commented about her birthday, "they just keep coming." Happy Birthday to a precious lady!

Nonie Nolen Celebrates 102nd Birthday on August 3, 2003

On her birthday she attended church services at Mt. Hebron United Methodist Church near Crews with family members.

Nonie Nolen Celebrates 103rd Birthday on August 3, 2004

Ellie Ester Birmingham Nolen celebrated birthday 103 on August 3, 2004. She is known as "Nonie" to all that love her. Knowing Mrs. Nolen is special as I've heard many remark, "To know her is to love her." Mrs. "Nonie" spent a quiet day with family on this birthday.

Ellie Ester Birmingham Nolen on the Right

During these 103 years she has seen many changes. When I interviewed her before her 100th birthday, she told me about her life. There have been sorrows along her journey. Yes, times were hard, but they were good too. Mrs. Nolen has memories of good times too, like picnics on the Fourth of July, riding a train from Crews to Beaverton, good lemonade mixed in a tub.

Mrs. Nolen lives with her daughter Lois Collins in Norton Estates in Sulligent. Talking about Lois, Mrs. Nolen said, "She takes good care of me." Her daughter Mary helps Lois takes good care of her too. I know because I have seen them together. Mrs. Nolen is fortunate to have Lois and Mary and they have been so blessed to have her all their lives. There are many who do not know the love of a mother such as Mrs. Nonie. She is a genuinely good person, kind, and considerate. She was a loving wife and is a loving mother and grandmother. She has been a smart shopper, a seamstress, a gardener, a good housekeeper, and she trained her children with wisdom. She has loved gospel singing and hearing the word of God as her attendance in church on her last year's birthday proved. She has been an inspiration to all who were blessed to know her. Happy Birthday Mrs. Nolen.

Passed Away - December 28, 2004

Mrs. Ellie Ester Nolen was 103 on August 3, 2004. I believe she passed away on Christmas Eve. I'm reminded of the Christmas Cantata "Home for Christmas." How fitting for her to leave this life on Christmas, a time when we celebrate the hope that God brought to the world through His son, Jesus.

Mrs. Nolen lived longer than most. There is no one living that remembers life without her. She has always been here. She touched many lives in her 103 years and her memory will continue to influence those lives.

George Washington Nolen

Full Name: George Washington Nolen - Present Post Office address: Crews Depot, Ala ; Was born on Aug 19, 1838 in the county of Lamar then Marion in the state of Ala; first entered the service as Private on July 1, 1861 at Courtland, Ala in Co K 16th Ala Inf and continued until after serving through the war was paroled at Decatur, Ala in the Spring of 1865. Source: No. 114, *1907 Census of Confederate Soldiers* transcribed and submitted by Veneta McKinney

Elmer Norton

The body of Elmer Norton, Pine Springs farmer was found on the Frisco railroad tracks in Sulligent early Saturday morning. Apparently he had been dead about three hours. Source: *The Sulligent News* October 22, 1942.

Evelyn Elliott Oakes

Evelyn and Eldon Oakes

Around 1938, Eldon Oakes left for DeKalb, Mississippi for the CCC camp, a Roosevelt program for six months. Evelyn Elliott was in high school. Then in 1940 he left for the navy while Evelyn was still in high school where she graduated in December. Her school friend Mary Woods Barnes (named after her mother Betty Woods, sister to Belton Woods) came by her home. Mary Woods had a new job in Birmingham and was moving out from the home where she cared for landlord's children. She wanted to know if Evelyn was interested in her old job. She had recommended Evelyn. John Elliott had planted a crop. Pete and Bill were gone in the army with Johnnie V. only at home. John and Virgie along with Johnnie V. harvested the crop.

Evelyn rode the bus with her clothes. She received room and board for babysitting in the home of a family at Edgewood over the mountain. With Mary Woods leaving, the family needed someone to watch the children for room and board. One of the children was named Dianne. During this time, Evelyn rode the street car to Massy Business College a few months but did not graduate. Because it was war time, there were many jobs available. Evelyn got a new job at Western Union and moved to the YWCA in Birmingham. She took the Civil Service test and went to Mobile as a clerk typist at the base there. Edith and D.B. Leigh went to Marietta, Georgia to work with Bell Aircraft, where B-29's like the Enola Gay were built. He was turned down for overseas duty. Later they worked around Washington D.C. until his service time was up.

The ship USS Washington went to Seattle for repairs. Eldon sent for her to get married. She quit her job and wrote a letter to her parents of their plans to get married. The repairs were made ahead of time. Eldon told her to watch for his ship with two stacks each evening coming back, because any day the ship would return to war and not return to Seattle. When he didn't return home, she left and went to Birmingham and got a job with a lawyer on First Avenue until the war was over. Eldon's sisters Onnie and Jewel came to get jobs and they all lived at the YWCA near their jobs. Onnie and Jewel worked at a soda fountain in a drug store. The drug store was located near the Grey Hound Bus station. Jewel met Jesse there, although she was engaged to a man Selman in Columbus, Mississippi Jesse was discharged to Ft. Benning, Georgia going to Monroe, Louisiana. There was a layover when he went to the drug store. He decided to stay in Birmingham where he got a job and married one month later. Onnie met Lamar on a bus. Because Eldon still had service time remaining of his six-year enlistment after the war, he was stationed in California. Jewel married Jesse first. Onnie and Lamar lived with Jewel until they could get an apartment across the hall. They helped Jewel with Judy who had nine months of colic.

Evelyn left Birmingham and rode buses and trains to meet him in California. Eldon and Evelyn lived on base in Indacyrn, Mojave Desert. She worked as a civil service clerk typist at a motor pool with the navy ordinance testing station. Eldon's service was up in January and they left California in February for Lamar County, Alabama. They lived with Bill and Grace in the other half of the dog-trot house until they built a house. Dianne was born in April and Wade 3 years later. Source: Written and submitted by Dianne Oakes Woods.

Mrs. Evelyn Elliott Oakes recently celebrated her 96th birthday on October 9, 2017. We owe Mrs. Oakes a debt of gratitude, she is one of the charter members of Lamar County Genealogical & Historical Society. She was very involved in the formation of the organization in 1993-1994 and has been active since its beginning. She doesn't make the meetings now, but continues helping others with their research and promoting historical research from the retirement/long term care facility in Fayette, Alabama.

Renzo Franklin Odom

(1875-1963)

Left to right Charles P. Odom and Renzo Franklin Odom

Renzo Franklin Odom married Alma Propst daughter of H. G. Propst. He entered into business with his father-in-law. After Propst's death in 1911, R. F. Odom and his wife Alma ran the business until son Charles Propst Odom was old enough to enter the business. The firm was named

R. F. Odom and Son and was in the general merchandise, cotton buying, lumber and real estate business. Charlie P. Odom was in the New Orleans Cotton Exchange and the Chicago Board of Trade. They were the only business in the area to have a ticker tape. Photo courtesy of L. Peyton Bobo

Green Pearson

Green Pearson who has been running a "blind tiger" near Buttahatchie on the Kansas City, was arrested by Sheriff Pennington and possee, latter part of last week and lodged in jail. He was also found to have a concealed pistol for which he will have to account. Source *The Lamar News*, March 31, 1887

Pennington Family of Lamar County

The first Penningtons to immigrate from England arrived in the 1600s settling in the New Haven Colony. They eventually made their way down the East Coast where their presence is documented through land and probate records in North and South Carolina in the 1700s. Levi Pennington Sr. (1714-1790) and at least one of his sons, Levi Jr. (1758-1808) were members of the Quaker Religion while living in North Carolina, before relocating to South Carolina. In 1780, Levi Jr. was expelled from the Quakers for marrying out of unity. As a Quaker, Levi Jr. would have been a conscientious objector and therefore would not fight or aid and abet the Patriots during the Revolutionary War. Levi Jr. had thirteen (13) children, nine (9) boys and four (4) girls.

The Pennington Family first appeared in Northwest Alabama in the mid 19th century when five (5) of Levi Jr.'s sons left South Carolina and settled in the Fayette (now Lamar) County area.

The original five Pennington brothers migrating to Alabama from South Carolina were; Ben Sr. (1783-1868), William M. (1788-1868?), Jesse (1797-1884), Solomon (1804-1870?), and Noah (1807-?). According to census records, Ben and Jesse were slaveholders in Alabama.

Ben Sr. donated land on which the town of Vernon was founded. His original homestead is located on Highway 18 abutting the Vernon Cemetery, where many Penningtons are buried. The five brothers fathered more than 50+ children with their wives while residing in Alabama-- so their children will not be identified in this article. There is also evidence that one or two of the brothers fathered children with a slave named Martha (Patsy). Pennington family oral history is that Serena (Rena) Pennington was fathered either by Ben Sr. or Jesse Pennington. Rena's death certificate only contains her mother's name (Martha) so we may never know which, if either, brother was her father. Many of the African-American Penningtons from Lamar County can trace their ancestry to Rena's children; Richard and Robert Pennington. Serena's sister, Jane Pennington (Woods') death certificate names Martha as her mother and Ben Pennington as her father.

After arriving in Alabama, the Penningtons purchased original land patents from the Federal Land Office ranging in size from 40 acres to 700 acres primarily in Townships 13, 14, 15 and Ranges 15 and 16. The Penningtons owned mills and farmed various crops including cotton and raised cattle. The Penningtons appeared to have been a large close-knit family, often marrying cousins. However, when the Civil War broke out, the Penningtons, like other families, were deeply divided on the issue of secession. The Civil War disrupted their lives and resulted in the loss of financial stability, property and status in the community.

Pennington brothers, fathers, uncles, nephews, and cousins joined the Confederate Army, the Union Cavalry, Union Navy or served as the Home Guard. Several Penningtons remained at home working at the Hale Murdock Blast Furnaces during the war making iron cannon balls and bullets for the Confederate army from pig iron. At least one Pennington, William (Big Bill), was hung by the Home Guard in front of his family for refusing to join the Confederate Army and other family members were involuntarily conscripted in the Confederate army.

Penningtons fought on both sides, survived the siege of Vicksburg, were taken prisoner and were killed, maimed, or wounded in battle. Some Penningtons who served in the Confederate Army were sent to Rock Island Prison in Illinois where they were given the option of joining the Union Navy or suffer the inhumane prison conditions until the end of the war. At least two family members elected to join the Navy.

Ben Sr. died in 1868. His will was probated in the court house in 1869 and it provides a snapshot in time of his wealth following the Civil War. It must be assumed that his wealth was significantly diminished as a result of the war. However, this document describes significant real and personal property that he owned at the time of his death shortly after the end of the war. In addition to property, the will identifies his heirs and where they were residing at the time of his death and the distribution of his assets, several years later. Not contained in his will is the location of the gold that he allegedly buried on his property for safekeeping. Pennington descendants still visit Ben's old homestead with metal detectors searching for the missing buried gold.

Many of the Pennington family members lost their land during the war and moved to Mississippi, Arkansas, and Oklahoma where they became sharecroppers.

However, a significant number of Pennington descendants of the original five brothers remained in Lamar County after the war and remain there today.

If you are an Alabama Pennington descendant and wish to research your roots, the Pennington Research Association has an extensive data base beginning with Levi Pennington (1714-1790). http://online.dralex.com/Senora1890/index.html Search by looking up your oldest known Pennington ancestor in the data base. Additional sources of information can be found using census, land grant records, Quaker records, cemetery and probate records. Additionally, US Pension and state Confederate pension records can be helpful in researching relationships because they contain affidavits of marriages and family relationships. Unfortunately, many of the probate court records before 1865 were destroyed during the civil war. Source: Written and submitted by Nancy Pennington Markey

Hugh Pennington

Mr. Hugh Pennington is building additions to the blacksmith ship, now occupied by Mr. J. W. Morton, with the view of using it for a livery. Source: *The Lamar News* September 23, 1886

Mollie Pennington

The Wonderful Girl

If there is anything that the average Vernonite wants it is a first class sensation and this he has had during past week. Little Mollie Pennington, daughter of Mr. Geo. Pennington who lives a short distance out of town, was taken seriously sick on the 15th, medical aid was summoned and her sickness more nearly resembled hydrophobia than anything else.

On the 17th a party of physicians consisting of Drs. Reed, Brown, M. W. Morton, E. L. Morton were called on with Dr. Burns and decided measures were taken to prevent the frequent paroxysms during which the patient would attempt to bite everyone in reach and even herself.

On the evening of the 18th, she told her friends and physician that she would die for one hour exactly and at the expiration of that time to charge her hands and feet and that she would come back. At the time predicted she died away and the physician present says that every known evidence of death appeared and that life appeared at the expiration of an hour, exactly. She told those present that she had been to Heaven and that God had cured her and that she was now well and could get up - and was assured by her physician that she was too feeble to get up - she asked his permission which was given, he thinking it impossible and no sooner than permission was given she jumped nimbly from the bed and walked to the door. And then began an exhortion to say the least was simply marvelous.

At appointed times of evening she has continued her exhortations telling before hand at what hour God would be with her. Almost everybody in town and surrounding country have been in attendance. Ministers of all denominations have followed her discourses with sermons and the audiences were moved to shouts and tears.

Men of strong minds and acknowledge intelligence say that there is something supernatural about the girl. She is but thirteen years of age and heard but one sermon in her life and can't read, and the good language used by her in her discourses and Bible teachings strike her hearers with wonder. Source: *The Lamar News* June 24, 1886, Transcribed by Veneta McKinney

More About The Wonderful Girl
Vernon, Ala, July 20, 1886
Editor of Lamar News:

Because of the great number of letters that I receive addressed to me as post master and minister of the Gospel, growing out of an article published by you concerning Miss Mollie Pennington. This article has been copied by so many papers and the inquiries are so numerous, I beg space to answer them all through your columns. The following is statements I know to be true. She was taken violently ill on the 15th of June; convulsions being of Hydrophobia type, and was so pronounced by the distinguishing physicians: Dr. Mortons, Brown, Reed, And Burns. These convulsions continued up to Friday in the evening. At that time she told those present that Dr. Burns was coming, but they informed her that he was not to be back until morning, when she said that was true that he did not expect to when he went away to come back but that he would be there soon. Dr. Burns about this time called, being as he says impelled by strange convictions that he ought to go back. When she remarked "Did I not tell you he was coming?" She then told the Dr. and friends that she would only have one more of those dreadful spells and that the Lord would cure her and that she would be as well as ever in life. She told them that she would die and go to the Spirit land for one hour and then come back. And then asked the Dr. to remain with her till she returned. She did die - had no pulse, no heart beating and that Dr. pronounced her dead. Her friends and relatives stood agonizing and weeping around and thought she had parted with life. At the expiration of one hour by the watch, she revived and breathed again, and told them that she was well and that the Lord had cured her and she desired to get up. The Dr. told her that she was too weak to get up. She jumped up and began to shout and praise God and to warn the people. She said that she had been to Heaven and had seen the Lord and many who are dead, some who died long before she was born. She said that she saw Mrs. Bickerstaff who had died about five miles from her home that day and it is a certain truth Mollie had not heard of the death. I had officiated as minister at the burial that morning. She told her friends that I went with her to Heaven and that the Lord had sent a message by her to me.

When asked what it was she told them she was to tell no one until she told me. This conversation I did not hear but I vouch for its truthfulness - every word of which can be established beyond any doubt should any doubts arise.

Up to this time I had not had opportunity to go out and see her nor had I seen her in four or five years.

I was in bed asleep on Friday night, spoken of before when two young men called at my home and related the circumstances and told me of her request that I come to see her. I rode out with them and found her I think one of the happiest mortals I ever saw and I have been a revivalist for thirty years and have witnessed many happy persons but nothing like this. She told me she had been to heaven and saw the Lord, and that she saw my son Jimmy who has been dead three years there, and that the Lord told her if I kept on that I would get there when I died and meet my children. She said she could not read a word and had never been to school a day, but that the Lord could put words in a child's mouth and that all must become as little children before they could be saved, and exhorted all to repent and believe, or they would be lost. Told me that the Drs. had given her medicine to kill or cure and that she would have died and not the Lord saved her and that he had cured her and that if she lived until she was twenty one years old she would never have another spell. She got up right away and has eaten of everything she wished and has had no illness since. She has said so many things in keeping with the Bible and her lamentations are great. She is not able to read the Bible, but rejoices that the Lord had put words of exhortation in her mouth. When I remarked that was better, she replied not, for the Bible was God's Word, and continued to exhibit the strongest faith I have ever witnessed among mortals, repeatedly that she did not dread the stings of death.

And that she loved the Lord and his ministers and all Christians and manifested great zeal for the salvation of sinners. A great many other things said and done by her are equally convincing that is it s a great supernatural work. Lamenting her limited opportunities of attending church and school and not being able to read the Bible. She by her own appointment talked to the people or three successive evenings; large concourses of persons attending and the fear of God was most fearfully demonstrated many shouting and praising God On the first Sunday in this month she joined the church and was baptized by the writer. Since that time she has at appointed times been talking to the people at stated intervals and the power of God over the hearts of her hearers has been wonderfully magnified.

I will continue my letters in your next and until the many wonderful things said and done by her are all told the people.

Yours truly,

T. W. Springfield   Source: *The Lamar News*, July 22, 1886, Transcribed by Veneta McKinney

Messrs Evans & Sims, representatives of the New Orleans Picayune, were in our town yesterday writing on "the Wonderful Girl" for the leading dailies of this country and Europe.

Pennington
To the Lamar News:

In this my second letter in regard to Miss Mollie Pennington, I will first correct three slight deviations you made from the manuscript of my first letter. First, she told them that Dr. Burns was coming, they told her he would not come until morning. She said he did not think he would come but he would be there soon. Dr. Burns did not expect to go but being called to see a patient neat by did call on her. When he arrived, she said there, I told you he was coming. Second, she named Mrs. Bickerstaff who had been buried that morning, not whose burying I had officiated as minister. Third, that I had not saw her in four or five years that I know of. This is not very material, but as I vouch for what I write, I prefer it just as it is.

After the baptism nothing special occurred until Sabbath evening following at preaching, she went off into a state similar to three following. The first when she revived was very happy, talked to those present and said she must suffer more and would talk the following evening at four o'clock, and sent out for the people to come and hear. A large concourse of people assembled. At the time, when she revived from the aforesaid similar state, she called the ladies and particularly the young girls to her one by one and lectured them on the sin of pride. Told them it was a sin to bang their hair, to wear bustles, hoops, or hats. That these fashions were an abomination in the sight of God and was ruining the world; that it was her duty to tell them so. It seemed to be great pain and a heavy cross for her to tell them so. She labored hard to extort a promise from all to quit it. Some agreed, others like some of Christ's disciples, turned back and said, who is sufficient for that? The Devil being present took in the situation - made a grand charge and gained a great victory for many, who said, just as I expected all a farce. Glory to the Devil! She's going deranged. (Selah) She talked on until about midnight. With great joy and happiness she has talked several times, shouted and sang from six to eight hours at a time without the slighter injury. She talked Tuesday and Wednesday nights following, saying many strange things, convincing many that God was in the child working wonders. Again on Sabbath evening following while in a similar state and while the preacher was preaching, she told someone to tell the preacher to stop and listen, pointing up and saying she heard a voice. At that moment her jaws were locked and she was carried to a neighbor's house, and late in the night when her jaws became unlocked, she talked with telling effect to all present, saying she would talk next morning, which she did, with power, convincing and telling effect. Giving out she would talk at home at three in the evening, telling me she could hardly get home, that it seemed that every bone in her would burst. Said if the preacher had stopped son enough he could have heard the voice, but could not have known what it said. Some of this last I did not hear but vouch for all I write. She said to me if I had been there I could have heard the voice but could not have known its meaning. I was a little after three arriving in the evening, but when I arrived her jaws were locked and could only make motions, in which condition she remained about one hour, during this time I will not try to describe my thoughts and feelings, for I could not. When she commenced to talk, how glad would I have been had all of those been present who had gone back in unbelief, yea and all the world. I am certain all doubts would have been removed from everyone who had one spark of humanity remaining in them. Her grief seemed almost unendurable, praying God in trust and anguish of heart to bring something upon the people that would make them believe, saying she had suffered miseries no tongue could tell for the people, that her pillow had been hard but thanked God it would in death be soft and her rest would be sweet in Heaven, exhorted sinners to repent or in death their pillows would be hard and their miseries eternal.

She tells the fashionable ladies who wear bustles, that if they had been made that way they would seek some great Doctor to take them off. Many visit her and ministers and all ask many hard questions, and she has always gained the victory and gives satisfaction. She is a great puzzle to skeptics and unbelievers, but the power of God to believers.

I am writing facts such as I am ready to prove. I have not written all by a great deal, and may write again.

Yours truly,

T. W. Springfield   Source: *The Lamar News*, July 29, 1886, Transcribed by Veneta McKinney

Vernon, Ala., Aug 11, 1886
Editor Lamar News:

    I will not trouble you with a long letter this week, in regard to Miss Mollie, the "wonderful girl," but am proud to be able to say to all skeptics, doubters that she is neither dead, sick, or insane: but is stout, hearty and healthy and able to preach, pray, exhort, sing and shout two and three hours at a time without the least hurt. She is sound and strong in the faith, perfect in love and practice too much for any skeptic, and greatly beloved. Yes, almost worshiped by all good people who have kept up with the wave and wonderful works of God's love displayed in and through her. The whole current is heavenly, evenly and upward. She is possessed of that charity that "suffereth long and is kind, that envieth not, that vaunteth not itself, that is not puffed up, that seeketh not her own, that is not easily provoked, that thinketh no evil."

    I may write again.

    Yours truly,

    T. W. Springfield   *The Lamar News*, August 12, 1886, Transcribed by Veneta McKinney

    Messrs. Davis and Upchurch of Shannon, Miss were in town yesterday, being here to see Miss Mollie Pennington. Little Mollie Pennington, of Vernon is attracting more attention now more than any person in the United States, Sam Jones not excepted. - [Journal] Source: *The Lamar News*, August 19, 1886, Transcribed by Veneta McKinney

An Unprovoked Attack
Editor Lamar News:

    In the Vernon Courier of Aug. 20, I notice an unprovoked attack on Miss Mollie Pennington and those who have seen and heard and know it to be the wonderful works of God. Stating "those who believe it are on a sandy foundation or superstition and ignorance, for any man indorsing her knows no more about the teaching of Holy Writ than a parrot knows about the science of language. Stating that Vernon has medical men that could diagnose the and is signed J. P. Collins M. D. Now we don't know Dr. Collins, but we do know by his unprovoked attack, that he knows as little about the grace of God as he does about little Mollie. He is one of those hearsays red-hot from his father's kingdom and his lust he will do and spits forth his persecutions in style. Now, Dr., we have Doctors here the pears (sic) of any in the State, and gentlemen at that. Dr. M. W. Morton, whose judgement we will put against any Doctors in the State of Alabama, says he could not diagnose the case, at all, and Dr. G. C. Burns was with her off and on from beginning to the end and was there when she apparently died. She told them before, all about how it would turn out, and it was true prophecy. Dr. Burn's testimony corroborated by every person there which were about 15 or 20, and no one ever denying except some of those hearsay skeptics. Now, Rev. M.D. D.D. what do you know of Mollie, the innocent little girl and her prophecies? You seem to assume an angel of light, as Paul says Satan will do, and endeavor to diagnose a case of which I am sure from your position you know nothing of. No, M.D. D.D., if you are as ignorant of physics as you are of revelation I pity your patients. Rev. Sire, please don't shoot until you see the game, and don't condemn your betters before you know who they are. She has never pretended to have any new revelations and she has never said, or done anything the Bible does not justify. He who says she has is "a liar" and the truth is not in him. If you think her doings and sayings cannot be substantiated, come to the scratch and see; I know what I say and I am not as green as you or your blindness may think. I stand pledged before God to defend her against all the fiery darts of hell - so far and if you think there is no good in it come and see. Come to the light and don't bushwhack men you know nothing about on hear says your tirade of hear says amount to the basest persecution. I have written two articles, what I did not see I can prove and what I saw I will swear and am ready to go to judgement on it. I will stand by it and if necessary I will seal it with my life. Now, sire, if you think, disease and medicine give persons the love of God and make them happy as she is all the time, please sire take some for God knows you need it badly. What harm has she done you or anyone else to merit such an attack of malignant persecution? She has done and is still doing much good, all in the name of the Lord. Many hard hearts have been melted, many made to rejoice, many reclaimed from back-slidden state, many good persons visit her room a far and go away rejoicing. I have to meet the first Christian yet who has seen and heard her that is not truly satisfied that the work is from God and supernatural. You say the Bible is complete, so says Mollie and never has said anything to add, or take away but prizes it highly enough to obey this teaching by pure love to all.

Now, as far as God's wrath hovering over us, we are ready any time. Are you sure? And again be sure you many not haply be found fighting against God. For you are as sure as there is a God, and now where does infidelity come in from Satan's ranks, always opposing everything Christ-like opposing the works of the spirit, denying the power thereof.

Now dear sir in conclusion will you please come and see for yourself the little innocent girl whom you have attacked so savagely and unmercifully. She will forgive you as freely as Christ forgave his enemies and so far as I am concerned I forgive you for your harsh sayings, for you know not what you do, and I hope God will, and before you die you many see and know the truth as it is. I subscribe myself a lover of truth.

    T. W. Springfield.   Source: *The Lamar News*, August 26, 1886, Transcribed by Veneta McKinney

> *The pamphlets on the "Wonderful Girl" are at last completed. Call in and get one. Price 50 c.*

A Letter

Below we give a specimen of the letters received by many in our town since the remarkable circumstances occurred in regard to Miss Mollie Pennington. This letter was written by an intelligent and accomplished Christian lady and it's well worth reading.

Kingstree, S. C., Sept. 9, 1886

Rev. T. W. Springfield:

Dear Brother,

Your letter of Aug 14th reached me in due time. As I did not think it right to trouble you with a regular correspondence I hesitated. Though I felt it my duty to thank you for the trouble you took to give me so much interesting news. Your letter was a great satisfaction to me and many others. One minister read it and said it was another prophesy fulfilled. One of the wonders that was to take place, I suppose what seemed to be spasms from disease, must have been the evil spirit striving not to be cast out. We read of similar cases in the Bible. You no doubt heard of the terrible earthquake we had the last night in August. Charleston and Somerville are ruined. The people will never be able to rebuild even if they knew they would be safe in doing so. A small shower of pebbles from the size of a grape to an egg came down in two streets last Sunday. They must have been sent from some volcanic eruption but they have not been able to find it yet. Some think Charleston is liable to go down any moment. Well, I know God does all things for the best. There has been a general revival going on all over this country ever since. A great many sinners have been saved and the good work is still going on. It was the best sermon that was ever preached in S. C. It seemed to shake open the eyes of the people to see where they stood. As for myself, I stood firmly on the everlasting Rock. I find no other foundation safe and no other friend true. My Father died a soldier of the Confederate army and a soldier of the Cross. He was a class leader in the Methodist Church for many years and his five sons are exhorters, class leaders and Sunday School teachers.

We are the old time Methodist and believe in the old time religion. We praise God when we feel like it and are not ashamed for people to know we are Christians. When any one has a little bit of religion he is ashamed for people to know it, but when he gets full he can't hide it, he wants to tell the whole world. I want you and that dear little girl Mollie Pennington to pray for me that I may be more useful in the Church of God and that I may meet you both in Heaven.

Your stranger, but true friend

Mollie Epps   Source: *The Lamar News,* September 23, 1886 Transcribed by Veneta McKinney

Rena Pennington

Rena Pennington born 1831, died before 1943. Her mother was Patsie (Martha). Rena's children that we know of at this time are: Richard, born May 8, 1862; Martha, born October 15, 1862; Rody, born 1869; and Robert, born December 2, 1872. According to Riley L. Pennington, Rena is buried next to Robert Pennington (her son) in the Furnace Hill Cemetery near Vernon, Alabama. She does not have a grave marker.

Richard Pennington

02-16-2004

Richard Pennington born son of Rena on May 8, 1862. Not much is known about Richard's parents, Rena was a slave and it is said that his father was a white man.

Listed in the 1880 Lamar County, Alabama U. S. Census as children of Rena Pennington are Richard, Robert, Rody and Martha. Rena Pennington, born 1831, is buried in Furnace Hill Cemetery near Vernon in a grave without a grave marker. Her son Robert is buried next to her.

Whatever his beginnings, Richard Pennington proved that you can do something with your life if you desire. It is said that when Richard was a young man he went to Lowndes County, Mississippi to be under the instruction of a Mr. Williams to learn financial business. Mr. Williams usually charged $4.00 for a trainee to work under him, but Richard was such a smart pupil and asset to his business that he paid Richard $4.00. I could not find information on Mr. Williams, but I have been told his son was Metro Williams and he graduated from West Point. It is said Mr. Williams lived in the Border Springs area near Columbus, Mississippi.

In *The Heritage of Lamar County, Alabama*, it is written Rich Pennington was a farmer, who at one time owned five hundred acres. He was reputed to be the wealthiest Black person in Lamar County, Alabama. He sold the property about 1920.

According to an interview with Bo Morris, who owns and lives in the house Rich Pennington bought when he moved to Sulligent, Mr. Morris thought that he sold the land near Vernon and bought land in Sulligent around 1910, or that is what I understood. I have not checked the courthouse records. Mr. Morris said that Van Hayes bought the land from Richard Pennington. Additional research is needed.

Rich Pennington died September 4, 1938 and is buried in the Sulligent City Cemetery. After his death, wife Malinda put a card of thanks in the local newspaper thanking their white friends for their concern during the time of his death.

One of Rich's daughters, Minnie married Daniel Allman near Detroit, AL. When Daniel and Minnie married, he gave up teaching for full-time farming and began immediately to purchase additional acreage next to the Allman homestead. He steadily invested in additional acreage until he had 1,000 acres of farm and woodland at his peak acquisition. Daniel Allman left approximately 700 acres to his heirs.

Rich's son Eddie Pennington, who served in World War I, is buried in the Sulligent City Cemetery near him. Eddie died December 1, 1963. Eddie and Ramah Pennington had a son, Richard F., who died February 17, 1888 and is buried in the family plot in the Sulligent City Cemetery. Richard F. like his father Eddie, was a veteran, serving in World War II.

Richard F. Pennington's son Richard Pennington is currently the 22nd chief of police in Atlanta, Georgia. He is responsible for the overall operation of the largest municipal law enforcement agency in the State of Georgia which consist of 2,300 sworn and non-sworn employees, five divisions and an annual budget of more than $120 million. He has been active in law enforcement for over thirty years. He began his law enforcement career in the Metropolitan Washington, D.C. Police Department rising to the rank of Assistant Chief.

Hired in 1994, after a national search, to become the chief of police in New Orleans, LA, during his tenure in New Orleans, he dramatically reduced homicides by fifty percent, created a Public Integrity Division to root out internal corruption, implemented community policing programs and created effective partnerships between the police and community. He established new hiring standards for recruits and totally reorganized the department by decentralizing all enforcement and investigative functions, holding Commanders accountable, and implementing the Computer Statistics (COMSTAT) program. This resulted in a fifty-five percent decrease in violent crimes.

As chief of the Atlanta Police Department, Chief Pennington has established the Atlanta Police Foundation; established a weekly Command Operation Briefing to Revitalize Atlanta (COBRA) to discuss crime patterns and develop strategies to eliminate problems throughout the city; and reorganized the Department by decentralizing all enforcement and investigative functions. He has also proposed a new beat redesign to more evenly distribute officers' workload; formed the Cyber Crime Task Force with the FBI to develop skills and resources for investigating computer-related crimes; and established a new Homeland Security Unit within the Department.

Sources: personal research of the Pennington Family, Bo Morris Interview; Riley Pennington Interview, *The Heritage of Lamar County, Alabama* various articles, and the City of Atlanta Police Chief website.

Note: Richard Pennington died May 4, 2017 in Atlanta Georgia.

Silas Filmore Pennington

Silas Filmore Pennington (1852-1895.) S. F. Pennington was elected sheriff of Lamar County in 1884. In May before the election was to be held in August, he ran this ad in The Lamar News: "To the voters of Lamar County: Fellow citizens I announce myself as candidate for the office of sheriff of said county, election in August next, and if elected I pledge myself to discharge the duties of the office honestly and faithfully to the best of my ability, and would be very much obliged for your support."

Election results were reported in *The Lamar News*, August 14, 1884 : S. F. Pennington 911, W. R. Bradley 221, James Blackwell 423, Watson Brown 109 and J. F. Ferguson 52.

Taken from *The Lamar News*, August 21, 1884 issue, appearing in the local news column, E. J. McNatt, editor and publisher "We learned that some of the lawless citizens of our county are regretting that they voted for our fearless and energetic sheriff, S. F. Pennington, at the recent election".

During his term, which was only two years, S. F. Pennington was involved in the searching for Lamar County's notorious train robber, Rube Burrow. The story has been repeated by older family members that Rube Burrow stopped by Sheriff Pennington's house one night with the intention of killing him, but when he looked through the window and saw him holding his baby daughter, he would not shoot for fear of hurting the baby.

S. F. Pennington and his wife, Nancy E. Mahan Pennington were charter member of First Baptist Church in Sulligent. Taken from *The Vernon Courier*, October 8, 1892 "An oyster supper will be held at the Pennington store house on Saturday night October 20th for the benefit of the church. Let's all attend and thus aid a worthy cause."

He was serving as mayor of Sulligent when he died in 1895. Taken from *The Eagle Eye*, November 21, 1895. "The saddest occurrence in the history of Sulligent, was the deplorable death of Mayor S. F. Pennington who was struck by a train about two miles below here last Friday at about twelve o'clock killing him instantly. He had started down the railroad to meet the pay train at Gattman, and as he had to see some parties on the section between here and Gattman, he was walking. He met the gravel train at the curve about two miles west of here which was coming in with a lot of empty cars and through carelessness we suppose as some of the train hands had left a heavy plank on one of the cars which projected out, it is not known how far, which striking the deceased on the forehead did the rash deed."

S. F. Pennington's father was James Matttison Pennington, whose father Jesse Pennington (born 1798 one of five brothers) came by wagon train from Spartanburg County, South Carolina and settled in Fayette County, which later became Lamar County. Source: Research of Felix and Peggy Hollis Adair.

Laverne Cunningham Perkins

11-1-04

Hello Jean,

I've been thinking of you all week-end. Are you doing OK? We just have to go through lots of grief and tough times, when we lose our loved ones. Try to stay as calm as possible. I wanted to tell you how much I enjoyed the Lamar County LINKS edition last week. I couldn't put it down until I read the entire booklet.

I also wanted to tell you that on page 24 where the pastors are named, who served at Mt. Zion, that B. E. Cunningham was my grandfather. Also, the W. J. Cunningham, who served as pastor was a first cousin of my grandfather. I can remember visiting with the W. J. Cunningham family there in Vernon, with my parents and grandparents when I was a little girl. I grew up in the Fellowship Community of Lamar County, and that's where we attended church, as I grew up. At one time, about the 1920's and thirties, there were two churches there. As people grew up and left the area, and the older people passed on, one church ceased to be used and was torn down. My parents, and Cunningham grandparents, and numerous other Cunningham/Hankins relatives are buried in the Fellowship Cemetery. Lots of Perkins buried there too. My dad had a sister who married a Perkins, and my mother had an aunt, who married a Perkins. They are connected to my husband's Perkins family, but he and I were no relation. Different sets!

Laverne Cunningham Perkins

Both my parents were related to Minerva Hankins Lollar, who has paintings in the artist department at the Vernon Civic Building (the old Lamar County High School, where I graduated in 1941). Rebecca Holt from Birmingham has some art work there. She passed away 2 or 3 years ago at age 100. She wrote a book about her growing up years in Lamar County, and she gave one to me. She gave one to the Library at Vernon, too. It has a family group picture in it of my great grandmother's birthday dinner, Mrs. Mary Elizabeth (Betty) Collins Hankins in the book. I am a little girl on the front row about 4 years old I guess; she died in 1928, and I was born in 1923. I'm now 81 years old so that was some time back, but I remember that day.

My dad and Rebecca were 1st cousins. Just wanted to let you know I'm thinking of you. and wanting you to be ok; I know, like me. you have health problems, too.

Love, Laverne Perkins

P.S. Be sure to tell Mrs. Carruth what a good job they did with the Links (newsletter).

R. J. Perry

We publish by request the following obituary notice of Rev. R. J. Perry, who will be remembered by our people as the founder of Perry's Camp Ground, in this county, which stands a fitting monument to this good man.

Dr. Rigden J. Perry died at his residence in Gatesville, Texas, Jan. 5th, 1888 at 12:45 o'clock a.m. Dr. Perry was born in South Carolina, Jan. 13th, 1815, and was married to Miss Mary Kirk, of Pickens County, Ala. June 28th 1838. He professed religion and joined the M. E. Church, South in 1859, and was licensed to preach Jan. 11th, 1853 and joined the Alabama Conference, Nov. 3rd 1865; transferred to the Northwest Texas Conference 1858.

Dr. Perry commenced the practice of medicine soon after his marriage, and continued up to the time of his connection with the Alabama Conference, then he gave his entire time to the work of the ministry. Source: *The Vernon Courier*, March 9, 1888

Austin Pinkerton

Austin Pinkerton Found In An Abandoned Well Shot Twice In The Head; Twice In The Breast. Had Been Missing Since Sunday. Two Negroes In Jail Here.

Preliminary Trail Next Month

One of the most gruesome murder ever to occur in Lamar County, was perpetrated Sunday, July 15, about 5 miles southeast of Sulligent. The murdered man was Austin Pinkerton, 42 years of age, who lived near Kennedy school.

Mr. Austin Pinkerton left his home, Sunday morning and went over to a neighbor's house and stayed a while and then left stating that he was going home. That was the last that any person saw him except the murderer or murderers. Pinkerton according to his wife had about $125.00 in money on his person, when he left his home.

Monday morning, (July 16th) the people in the community began an intensive search for him and finally on Wednesday afternoon, his body was found in an abandoned well on the Old George Brock, house place.

County Solicitor, Guy Redden, who with Sheriff Smith, Deputy Sheriff, Dan Crossley, and Chief of Police, Lake Nolen of Sulligent made the investigation states that the dead man, had two pistol wounds in the back of his head and a shotgun wound in his shoulder, neck and breast. Mr. Redden states that the investigation discloses that Pinkerton was murdered near the house of one Gilbert Summers, a Negro, and that his body was placed in a pool of water, near the place and was probably left there until Monday or Tuesday night and then carried to the old abandoned well, where it was found.

Mr. Redden informs us that the preliminary trial of Gilbert Summers will probably be heard around the first Monday of August as the State is waiting for an analysis to determine if the substance found near the house of Summers is human blood.

Another suspect has been placed in jail, concerning this matter, he having been arrested yesterday morning. Source: *The Lamar Democrat* July 25, 1945

$400 Reward Offered For Conviction Of The Murderer Of Pinkerton
State Offers A $200.00 Reward Community $200

We have just been informed by County Solicitor Guy Redden that at his request the Governor of Alabama has offered a reward of Two Hundred Dollars for the arrest and conviction of the murderer of Austin Pinkerton, whose body was found on Wednesday, July 18th in an abandoned well, about 5 miles east of Sulligent, Alabama.

The citizens of that community together with the citizens of Sulligent, have supplements that reward with an additional sum of $200.00, making a total of Four Hundred Dollars as a reward. Source: *The Lamar Democrat* August 1, 1945

Murder Preliminary Trial

County Solicitor Guy Redden has just informed us that the preliminary trial of Gilbert Summers for the murder of Austin Pinkerton who was found in an abandoned old well near Sulligent two weeks ago, with two bullet holes in the back of his head, will be held at the Court House in Vernon on next Monday morning, August 13, 1945. The murder was one of the most brutal in the history of Lamar County and a great deal of interest has been manifested in the matter. Source: *The Lamar Democrat* August 11, 1945

Preliminary Trial Held For Summers

Gilbert Summers, negro, charged with the murder of Austin Pinkerton, whose body was discovered in an old abandoned well several weeks ago, was remanded to jail without bond, to await the action of the Grand Jury, following his preliminary trial that was held in Vernon on Monday, August 13th. Source: *The Lamar Democrat* August 22, 1945

Mr. Pollard

A Mr. Pollard was shot and instantly killed by a Mr. Darr, last week. The killing occurred near the Lamar and Pickens county line. We have not learned the particulars. *The Vernon Pioneer*, February 23, 1877

Elizabeth Rasbury

Mrs. Elizabeth Rasberry wife of Isaac Rasberry and daughter of Jesse Taylor, died April 22nd. 1887, after a long and painful suffering which she bore with Christian resignation. She had been twice married but had no children, and was about forty years of age; had lived a consistent member of the church since her youth, and died a triumphant death and gone to join her mother who died when she was very young. Peace be unto her ashes.

Sister, thou art gone to rest,
Thy toils and cares are o'er,
And sorrow pain and suffering now
Shall never distress thee more.

A Friend   Source: *The Lamar News*, May 5, 1887

Isaac Rasbury

PFC Isaac Rasbury, a member of the 357th Engineers oat Camp Swift Texas has recently been promoted ot the rank of corporal. He is the son of Henry Rasbury and Mrs. Nora Rasbury. Source: *The Sulligent News* October 22, 1942.

Charlie Franklin & Annie Rector

Charlie Rector

Remembering Charlie Franklin & Annie Rector
Charlie Franklin Rector was born March 8, 1888 near Vernon, Lamar County, Alabama. He was the 2nd child of James Edward (Jim) and Rhoda Alice (Duke) Rector. Charlie's mother died when he was 12 years of age. Martha Jane (Collins) Rector was his step-mother. Reared on a farm, Charlie was a small frame man being 5'7" tall with brown eyes and black hair. During World War I, at the age of 31, he enlisted in the U. S. Army on July 8, 1918. He departed the States on September 15, 1918. He served in the 47th Infantry in France. On one of their marches, he took pneumonia and almost died. He arrived back in the States March 26, 1919 and received an honorable discharge.

Bought Car in 1920 $400.00
In April 1920, Charlie bought a new little Overland Ford car for $400.00

with W. L. (Loyd) Turner and Arlie Turner as co-signers. This was the only car he ever owned. He was a member of Woodmen of the World.

Jaretta Ann (Annie) Lucas Rector was the 1st child of James Thomas and Emma Josephine May Lucas. She was born June 30, 1901 in Fayette, Alabama on Temple Avenue. In 2000, the white two-story house is still occupied.

In 1904, Annie's parents bought and moved to a farm near Winfield, Alabama. Her four brothers and two sisters were born there. The family farmed and her father was a school teacher and Fayette County Superintendent of Education.

Married February 28, 1922

Charlie and Annie married February 28, 1922 in the court house in Fayette, AL. She was 21 and he was 34 years of age. Their first home was about two miles east of Vernon, Alabama on the "Ice Hankins" farm, located near Morton Chapel Cemetery. Their first two children, Hoyt and Helen were born in this home.

In September 1924, they bought a house and an 89 acre farm for $1500.00. George and Etta (Wheeler) Jordan owned the home when they bought it. This farm is located about three miles east of Vernon, AL near Bethel Church of Christ, where the family attended worship.

At that time, the house had two bedrooms, a "side-room", a large kitchen with a dog-trot hallway through the house. Later two bedrooms were added. Charlie B. the 3rd child, was born in this home followed by Howard, Lavice, Lola Mae and Clyde. Charlie and Annie lived in this home the remainder of their lives.

Rearing seven children in the 1920's and 30's, especially during the "Great Depression" was a challenge to any parent. No electricity, nor indoor plumbing, made it more difficult, but with all the hard work and trying times, there was love and good memories and much adventure among the children.

In addition to raising corn and cotton there were cane, peanuts, watermelon, pea and sweet potato patches. There was also a large garden for all kind of vegetables to be canned on a wood-burning stove, then, kept in the cellar underneath the house to keep it from freezing in the winter.

We cannot forget the orchard located a short distance from the "Ole Cow Lot". There was always plenty of fresh Marshall apples, June apples, peaches and plums. Some of the fruit was dried on the tin roof on the barn to be used in fried pies and cakes. In the fall, we had pecans and black walnuts from the trees in the front yard.

Cow For Milk & Butter

There were cows for milk and butter. The milk had to be carried down the hill and put in the spring to be kept cool also in the fall, there were several hogs butchered. The hams and sausage were smoked and placed in salt for preservation and left in the "smoke house" located at the back of the house. Of course, the mules, Pete and Jack can well be remembered.

Annie Always Had Enough Good Food On The Table

We always had an abundance of food. Mama never knew how many would eat dinner with us on any Sunday, because it seemed some family would always come home with us from church, but it was stated, "Annie always had enough good food on the table."

Charlie Rector Man of His Word

Charlie was an honest, hardworking man; "a man of his word", leaving an example for his children. After working in the fields in his later years, he can be remembered as he sat leaning against the wall in his chair on the end of the porch underneath the shade of the Chinaberry tree, watching the younger ones playing in the yard. Charlie died in the Veterans Hospital in Tuscaloosa, Alabama, January 14, 1947 at the age of 59.

Annie Rector Kind And Devoted

Annie's hobbies were working in her yard, where she had many pretty flowers and doing all kind of crafts and needlework, especially crocheting dollies and tablecloths, which we still have and treasure. She was kind and devoted to her family. She was a good neighbor and a friend to all.

Annie Lucas Rector died September 2, 1961 in the Vernon hospital at the age of 60. They are both buried in Bethel Cemetery, Vernon, Lamar County, Alabama. Submitted and written by Lola Rector Edwards.

Digging Up Rector Kin

In mid-October 2004, we were in Gatlinburg, Tennessee and we decided to return home by way of Greer, Greenville County, South Carolina to do some Rector research. Greer is just across the mountains from Gatlinburg. We had never been to Greer. Before we left Vernon, Alabama, where we live, I got on the internet, and found names and telephone numbers, of some Rectors living in the Greer area. I picked a name from this list and gave this person a call. Can you believe this person (Joe Rector) was one of my cousins? Before this phone call, I did not know or had never heard of this person. Joe Rector and his sister, Helen Elizabeth Rector live together; neither have married. Lewis Rector (the Baptist preacher) was Joe and Helen's great-great-grandfather.

We left Gatlinburg Friday a.m. (10-22-2004) arriving in Greer mid-afternoon; checked into a motel and then we gave Joe and Helen Rector a call. They invited us out to their home, at 4028 Highway101 North, Greer, South Carolina. I met, two new found cousins, that afternoon and we had a good visit. Joe is 89 and Helen is 85. We stayed with them until almost dark.

Joe told us, his great-grandfather (Joel Rector) had bought some land in 1861, and it had been in the family until about ten years ago, a brother wanted his part, so they sold the old Joel Rector place

The *Bethel Association Minutes* reveal that Joe and Helen's great-great-grandfather, Lewis Rector represented Bushy Creek Baptist Church as minister and delegate at the 1796 Association Meeting. The Bushy Creek Church started many church branches during the thirty plus years that Rev. Lewis Rector was pastor of this church. One church that was started, 9-2-1802, was Clear Spring Baptist Church. This church is still going strong today. Lewis Rector was the first pastor of this church. During this time, churches only had preaching once a month, and preachers could pastor three or four churches at the same time. In 2002, Clear Spring Baptist Church had their two hundred year anniversary reunion. Joe Rector and Helen Rector were invited and they did attend. Joe and Helen attending a *Two Hundred Year Anniversary Reunion* at a church that their great-great-grandfather started two hundred years ago, I think this is pretty neat. It is written on Lewis Rector's tombstone, that he was a charter member of Bushy Creek Baptist Church until his death (04-14-1827) thirty plus years.

Joe told us where one of Lewis Rector's sons is buried. This son's name was Nathaniel, and he and his wife are lying at rest in the Glassy Mountain Baptist Church Cemetery, located on Highway 11 in Upper Greenville County. After we left Joe and Helen's house, we visited this cemetery. It got dark on us as we were checking the markers; before we left we had to use a flashlight to check the markers, we then headed back to our motel room.

Saturday a.m. early to rise we headed out to Greenville, South Carolina to do some Rector research in the main (Hughes) library. This is a new huge library. On Saturday a.m., we had no trouble with parking, and also the library was not crowded. This library has three floors and a total of 119,000 square feet of floor space. One huge room (the South Carolina Room) is where we did our research. We did not count the rolls of microfilm, I guess the count would be in the thousands. It took a while to learn our way around, and how their system worked; again we were in a hurry and only got to spend about 4-5 hours in the library. We found on the microfilm where my 3rd great-grandfather (Jesse Russell Rector) had bought one hundred and forty acres of land from a George Salman. This land was on the south Tyger River. This land purchase was made in 1808 (more on this land purchase later).

We found records listing the executors (two sons) of Jesse Russell Rector's Estate. Jesse died in 1853, we also found six names of Rector children, who R. M. Hughes had taken guardianship of, in 1923, after their father had died (more about this later). We also found an index of a Rector Family Cemetery. Joe and Helen had told us about this cemetery the p.m. before. Lewis Rector and his wife, other Rectors and a few no Rector names are lying at rest in this cemetery. This cemetery is located on Blacks Drive, off of Roper Mountain Road, in Greenville City limits.

We also found records on another Rector Family Cemetery. This cemetery is located at 2700 Highway 14 North, Greer, South Carolina. Fred and Kate Rector live at this address, the Rector Family Cemetery is a few hundred yards from Fred's house. We leave the library in search of more Rector cousins.

We found Fred Rector's house; Fred arrived just before we did; as we were pulling into his drive, he was getting out of his truck. My husband Henry Tracy Edwards got out of our car and walked up to Fred asking, "Are you Fred Rector?" He said, "yes" and Tracy introduced himself, and told him "We are from Vernon, Alabama." Tracy said "I think I have some of your kin folks in the car," then Tracy motioned for me to get out. As I get near Fred I say "We are kin folks." Here we find another Rector cousin. Fred gets in our car and we drive over to the Rector Family Cemetery. Fred keeps it cleaned off, keeping the bushes and tall grass cut. We were in a hurry but we did look at the markers in the cemetery, some real good markers, some not so good and rocks marked some graves. The last burial in this cemetery was March 30, 1927. We are most sure my 3rd great-grandfather, Jesse Russell Rector and his wife, Sarah Jane Cleveland Rector are lying at rest in this cemetery. This cemetery is on the 140 acres of land Jesse Rector bought in 1808 also this cemetery is near Jesse's old house place.

We found Nathaniel Green Rector and his wife's tombstone. Nathaniel

Green was Jesse's son, also Fred Rector's grandfather. We also found Jesse Russell Rector's tombstone, (this Jesse was Nathaniel Green Rector's son). There were other markers in the cemetery that we could not make out the names. As we stood in the cemetery talking, Tracy was going over his notes from the library. He was studying the Rector children's names, that R. M. Hughes had taken guardianship of in 1923. I thought Fred might shed some light on these names, so Tracy reads these names out loud, and when Tracy read the last name "Fred"; then Fred sticks his hand in the air and said "That's me," Fred then puts his glasses on and looks over the list of names. He said one of his sister's name was left off the list, her name was Agness. Fred also told us the "M" in Mr. Hughes' name stood for Murry. Murry was a banker. Fred said, "Mr. Hughes was real tight with the money he handed out to us children." Fred was five years old when his father died and Mr. Hughes took guardianship of the children. Tracy looks over his notes, and tells Fred that we had found records in the library, showing Jesse Russell Rector bought one hundred and forty acres of land from George Salman in 1808 on the south Tyger River. Then all of a sudden, Fred said, "We are standing on this land.". I could not believe what Fred was saying that we were standing on my 3rd great-grandfather's homeplace. This was surely the high point of our trip.

As we left the Rector Family Cemetery, (walking back to our car), Fred points out the old Jesse Russell Rector house place. Fred remembers this house very good and tells us the house fell in, and they cleared the lot. There is today, a big black walnut tree (still living) that stood in the yard. Fred also told us it was a fine house; he had heard that it was the first and only board house in this area when first built. All the other houses were log houses. Jesse Russell Rector was Fred's great-grandfather. Fred is 86 years of age and seems to be in good health. We went back to Fred's house, and he wanted us to go in and meet his wife Kathryn "Kate" and we did.

Fred and Kate told us about another cousin Norman Rector Thompson, who lives in Louisville, Colorado. Norman has put a book together on the Rectors and Ballengers, (they married into each other). We have talked to Norman and we ordered and have already received a copy of his book. It has copies of many of the letters, (between family and friends) that was written from 1812 to 1878. We have a copy of a letter from Jesse Russell Rector to William Elliott Rector (Jesse's son), dated October 14 1851. We also have many letters from Sarah Jane (Cleveland) Rector, (Jesse's wife) to her children.

Fred and Kate also told us of another Rector cousin, Jim Rector, who lives in Baton Rouge, Louisiana. Jim heads up a family reunion committee, and they have a family reunion every two years. We hope to attend the next reunion in 2006.

Fred Rector was lead pilot on a bombing mission over Germany in

World War II. German fighter planes did major damage to his B-17 flying fortress. The fighter planes shot off one half of his tail wing, (Fred calls this the stabilizer), and Fred and his crew had to bail out over enemy territory. Snow was on the ground, as he was gliding down, he could see his plane making two barrel rolls before it crashed into the ground. Fred said, "this is not the recommended method of travel, when you are alone in enemy territory with snow on the ground." This was on a Tuesday. Fred managed to stay hid from the enemy for a few days. He was taken prisoner the following Saturday, (it could have been Fred's cousins that shot him down). Fred's 3rd great-grandfather, (John Jacob Rector) was from Germany. Fred was a POW for fifteen months. One of his fellow prisoners was an artist. Fred ask him to paint a picture of his plane showing the damage,(the best that Fred could describe it). This painting is hanging on the wall in Fred's home today. Fred showed us pictures of he and his crew. Earlier in the War, Fred said he was grounded for two weeks with an inner ear infection. During this time his crew went on a bombing mission with another pilot. They crashed on takeoff and all his crew were killed except the tail gunner.

We left Fred and Kate's house assuring them we would return soon. We had an enjoyable visit with my new found cousins.

On this one trip, I met four new cousins and got information on four others. Maybe this article will find its way to other Rector kin, and bring us together. Submitted by Lola Rector Edwards, written by Henry Tracy and Lola Mae Rector Edwards.

Redden Family

On January 15, 1874, Robert James Redden and Mary Elizabeth "Mollie" Hollis of Moscow in Lamar County were married. Mollie was the daughter of Daniel William Hollis and Margaret Miller Hollis. She grew up in Moscow and Robert Redden in surrounding areas and settled in Moscow. The first house they owned was a log cabin on forty acres of land which they homesteaded. They later built a large house at Cansler, which was near Moscow, and lived there until 1888. The railroad came through and they moved to what was later called Sulligent. Robert Redden named the town of Sulligent in honor of two prominent railroad men, Mr. Sullivan and Mr. Sargent.

In this new town, Robert Redden was the first doctor, the first postmaster, and owner of the first drugstore. He had the first house in Sulligent and later, he owned one of the first automobiles. There were two other houses under construction when they moved to Sulligent, the Ogden house and the Bankhead hotel, but the Redden house was the first house to be occupied in Sulligent.

Redden House in Sulligent Owned by George Family

The Reddens had five children, Blanche Kathleen, Stella, Raymond Hollis and Robert Guy ,born at Moscow or Cansler and Margaret Inez, who was the first baby born in the town of Sulligent on August 10, 1888. These children all grew up, married, had families and lived in Sulligent for some years.

Mollie Hollis Redden died of a heart attack on September 10, 1928. Dr. Redden's daughter, Stella and husband Albert Gray moved in with him. They had been living on a farm between Sulligent and Vernon.

The information for this article was taken from the Redden Family History written by Clara Redden daughter of Guy Redden as told by Stella Redden Gray.

Mollie Hollis Redden, wife of Dr. Robert J. Redden, died of a heart attack on September 10, 1928. Dr. Redden's daughter, Stella and husband Albert Gray moved in with him. They had been living on a farm between Sulligent and Vernon.

Doctor Robert James Redden died, at age 83, on March 13, 1931. A few weeks before his death, he called his two sons, Guy, an attorney, and Raymond, a doctor, into his office for a talk. He told them that he wanted to help get all his affairs in order. He told them that he was having a vault built for himself at the cemetery. They protested, but he said "This will not hasten my death by one day, I want it done."

On the day, the vault was completed, the workmen came to his office and he paid them. As was customary, Dr. Redden walked home about 10:00 a.m., sat down in front of the fire and read the paper. As he got out of his chair, he had a stroke and fell. He died on March 13, 1931 only a few days after suffering the stroke. He was buried in Sulligent Cemetery with a Masonic Burial, attended by the Officers of the Alabama Grand Lodge. He had been Grand Master of the Grand Lodge of Alabama and Worshipful Master of the Masonic Lodge in Sulligent. He later served the office of

Grand Lecturer which was created for him. Source: *Redden Family History* by Clara Redden.

Reese

On last Monday night, a young man by the name of Reese, while on his way home from Fayette C. H. rode into an old well, near Musgrove's Store. His horse fell clear to the bottom, about fifteen feet, while fortunately for him, the foot hung in a root and jerked him from his saddle – suspending him about four feet from the top. He received no injuries but the horse was killed. Source: *The Vernon Pioneer*, February 6, 1878

Jimmy Paul Reeves

Jimmy Paul was born September 4, 1932 in Lamar County, Alabama to the Paul J. and Alice Belle Jackson Reeves. He grew up on a farm with five siblings: Polly, Carl, Jerry, Brock and Barbara. During their brother's memorial service Polly and Carl shared memories of their growing up days. Their parents were both Christians and taught their love of God to their children. Jimmy Paul passed this teaching on to his children and grandchildren.

Jimmy Paul made the statement that his life really began when he accepted Jesus as his Savior on April 1, 1969. He continued to live in Christ until he died in Christ on January 28, 2012.

Having worked for Ogden Management Company for years and then working with Liberty National Insurance Company, it seems like he knew everyone in Sulligent and everywhere else. I seldom saw him alone unless he was in the grocery store picking up items for Barbara. Usually he was with family, or drinking coffee with friends, talking and enjoying their fellowship.

If you talked with Jim for a few minutes, you heard how much he loved his wife, Barbara and their family. The legacy that he has left Bill, Jim, Bonnie, Cathy, Aaron, Holley and Ryan is worth more than any monetary or property inheritance. Dr. Charles Stanley's book *Leaving A Godly Legacy* explains walking with purpose and leaving a distinct imprint on the lives of the children God has given you to love and nurture. Printed in 1999 this book has been distributed around the world, but Jim's living book is printed in the hearts of his family. He began writing it on that April Fool's day in

1969. He fought cancer with faith and determination. His family and friends prayed for healing that we might keep him here longer, but those prayers were answered according to God's will and His plan. Jimmy Paul loved singing and listening to gospel music. Taking a few lines from the song, "If You Could See Me Now", written by Kim Noblitt, *"My prayers have all been answered, I've finally arrived, the healing that has been delayed, has now been realized. If you could see me now, I'm walking streets of gold. If you could see me now, I'm standing tall and whole. If you could see me now, you'd know I've seen Him face to face; if you could only see me now. You would not want me to leave this perfect place, if you could only see me now."*

Revolutionary Patriot Dedication Held

On October 3, 2015, a cool, rainy, windy, Saturday, the long forgotten village of Moscow in Lamar County, Alabama became alive with the Sons of the American Revolution (SAR) Honoring Ceremony held in Moore-Hill Cemetery aka Moscow Cemetery. SAR members, friends and patriot descendants traveled from Mississippi, Tennessee, Florida, Kentucky, Louisiana, and within Alabama to remember and to honor Five (5) patriots of the American Revolutionary War: (1) Sgt. Daniel Holiday, (2) Pvt. John Roebuck Sr., (3) Pvt. Thomas Stanford, (4) Pvt. James Lindsey, (5) Sgt. Richard Priddy buried in Marion county now Lamar county. Before the honoring ceremony, the color guard marched down Main Street in Sulligent during Old Fashion Day festivities, then traveled to the Moore-Hill Cemetery.

Rev. Robert Stamps (retired Navy), pastor and members of Mulberry Springs Baptist Church graciously allowed their fellowship hall to serve as a welcome center with Lamar County Genealogical & Historical Society members providing refreshments to travelers participating in the ceremony.

Barb Carruth, Lamar County Genealogical & Historical Society Vice President, welcomed the group to the Sulligent area. SAR Color Guard, Bob Anderson Commander presented the colors. Invocation was given by Rev. Robert Stamps, Mulberry Springs Baptist Church. Wayne Baines, President Lamar County Genealogical & Historical Society led the pledge of allegiance. Greetings were given by Joel Mize, President, Shoals Chapter ALSSAR.

A most distinguished roster of speakers was presented to those in attendance. Michael Wells, Vice President General, Southern District, stirred our hearts with "Remember Me" tribute to our departed patriots. Bill Stone, President ALSSAR, talked of "SAR Patriotic Outreach Within

Our Communities". Rick Hollis, Past Vice President General, Southern District; Board of the SAR Foundation, held our attention with "Our Obligation to Our Forefathers".

Kay Koonce presented each patriot's biography:

1. Sgt. Daniel Holladay (aka Holiday/ Holliday) S10867:SC Troops, under Lt. Fuller, for 3 years, served in 2nd Regiment of regular Troops (South Carolina Continental Line) under Lt. Hall, Capt. James McDaniel & General William Moultrie. From High Hills of Santee, Sumpter District, marched to Ft. Moultrie, Sullivan's Island, Charleston SC; after 2.5 years, hired a substitute, George Powell (paid 200 # currency). Stated he is known (in 1832) by Colonel John Hollis; Colonel James Moore & D. Hollis, Esquire.

2. Pvt. John Roebuck, Sr.: Spartan Regiment of Spartanburg South Carolina; aka Roebuck's Regmt. Mudlick Creek, March 1781; Under Col. Benjamin Roebuck & Lt. Col Henry White; at William's Fort, Newberry District SC. Roebuck & White led 150 men against a heavily fortified location, much outnumbered. Shown on roster in a "snapshot" of muster roll printed in Spartanburg newspaper.

3. Pvt. James Lindsey, S10992: Enlisted Orange County, North Carolina, Feb 1781, under Capt. Thompson & Col. Thomas Taylor. Battle of Guilford Courthouse; from Troublesome Iron Works chased British to Ramsey's Mill on Deep River, thence to Raleigh. Guarded British & Tory prisoners at Hillsboro.

4. Pvt. Thomas Stanford, S11463: Enlisted Chester District SC, Feb 1776; under Capt. George Wade & Col. Thomas Sumter. Joined army at Eutaw Springs and marched to Charleston SC > Sullivan's Island > Haddrell Point. Battle of Rocky Comfort Creek GA, Friday's Fort/Ferry (Ft. Granby) battle. Thompson's Fort/Siege of Belleville at Thompson's Plantation; skirmish. Marched to Wright's Bluff near Eutaw Springs, skirmish at Ft. Watson. Marched to near Camden SC; skirmish at possibly Ratcliff's Bridge (Lee County South Carolina).

5. Sgt. Richard Priddy, W5593: Enlisted for 3 years in Virginia by August, 1776 in 1st Virginia Line, Northern Continentals under Capt. John Fleming; Col. Isaac Read/Col. Richard Parker & Col. William Davies. Battle of Monmouth; taking of Stony Point Fort; served until Aug 1779, discharged from service at Rampaugh, New York. Thomas Hubbard, S17227 appeared on behalf of applicant and testified that he served as Quartermaster of same 1st VA Continental Line, was acquainted with Priddy and statements correct.

Descendants participating in the event, honoring their patriot were: (1) Sgt. Daniel Holiday: Kay Koonce and Paula Lampkins; (2) Pvt. John Roebuck, Sr.: Deana Newell-Vernon; (3) Pvt. Thomas Stanford: James Pruett and Bobby Stanford;(4) Sgt. Richard Priddy: Geoff Baggett. (5) Kay

Koonce honored Pvt. James Lindsey in the absence of a descendant.

Before closing a SAR Southern District Wreath, ALSSAR Wreath, and other SAR State/Chapter Wreaths were placed on-site along with an individual grave marking placed at Daniel Holladay's grave and Sgt. Richard Priddy's grave. Bob Baccus played TAPS then Colors were retrieved by the Color Guard. Rev. Robert Stamps offered the benediction and dismissal for the group.

As we were all walking away from the cemetery, I felt gratitude for these five (5) patriots, who served, and those men and women, who are serving today so that we might have the freedom to remember, and participate in a ceremony such as we had today.

After the ceremony, a convoy led by Shoals Chapter President Joel Mize traveled to gravesites of patriots not buried in Moore-Hill Cemetery, stopping first at James Lindsey's gravesite, nearby in Moscow- Armstrong Cemetery, then on to Old Nebo Cemetery near Vernon to visit the gravesite of Thomas Stanford, traveling next Northeast of Sulligent to John Roebuck's grave in Henson Springs Cemetery.

Sons of Liberty chapter president Carl Thornton and Shoals chapter president Joel Mize are to be commended for their service in putting together this grave dedication and marking event.

Roberts

Mr. Roberts, of Pine Springs Beat, an octogenarian, and one of Jackson's men, died a few days ago. He was drawing a pension at the time of his death. Source: *The Vernon Pioneer*, May 26, 1876

Dr. John Monroe Roberts

05-05-2004

Dr. John Monroe Roberts, born in Fayette County, Alabama in the year of 1881 died at the age of 91 in 1979. He practiced medicine in Lamar County for many years. Dr. Roberts, the son of William I. Roberts, lived in the Bluff Community before moving to Vernon in 1919. Dr. Roberts was the father of Mrs. Lavelle Redden who celebrated her 91st birthday September 9, 2003. Mrs. Redden lives in Vernon. Source: Lavelle Roberts Redden (now deceased)

Fay Robertson's Memories

These are a few of 94-years-old Mrs. Fay Robertson's memories on 7/20/06: When she was 4 years old, her mother Margaret (Maggie) Rebecca Thomas Franks died in 1916. A year later Mr. Franks moved with his children to a farm in the woods on the right past the Old Iron Bridge east of Vernon. Mr. Allen Mathis and wife Donnie were the owners. There was a path through the woods to the Allen Mathis Mill where Mr. Franks worked. Mrs. Fay called him papa. Papa would not let his children go to the mill because it was not safe for them. The water-powered mill was located upstream to the right of the bridge approximately 500 yards. During the dry weather in July of 2006, some boards or planks of a platform have been seen by Johnny Wayne McAdams. The workers backed up a pond with water-gates. The cotton-filled wagons where pulled by mules across the platform/bridge under the suction created for the cotton gin. Some corn was also ground here. Mr. Mathis drove the first car Mrs. Fay saw, before Fords.

There was a 1918 flu. Of the seven kids at home, Mrs. Fay and her papa were the only two not to take it. Walter and Ellie Elliott were nearby neighbors and brought food to their porch. One day they didn't come and papa went to see about them. Both of them were in bed with the flu. Mrs. Fay said her papa baked big biscuits in a wood burning stove.

Young Turner built a corn grist mill with a big wooden wheel just east of Vernon on Yellow Creek. Papa moved his family near the mill in 1918. His daughter Bertie Mae Franks had finished all grades offered at Morton Chapel School. Now she walked to Vernon school and graduated high school. She attended Florence College for 6 weeks to 3 months and qualified to teach. Miss Bertie Mae returned and taught school 42 years.

Mrs. Fay's brother Arthur Franks joined the Navy like his friend Onnie Turner, Young Turner's son. After World War I, Onnie bought his dad's mill to work there.

Mr. Franks moved about once a year as a 3rd and 4th share-tenant farmer. He received one-third of the cotton and one-fourth of the corn produced. The landowner kept the rest. Once they lived on Levi Maddox farm, currently located past the Vernon Trade School. Later Mr. Maddox sold the farm jointly to the Vernon banker Mr. Jones who had moved into the area and to Van Livingston.

Tommy and Mervin Jones put in the Crossville Cotton Gin in the late 1920's or early 1930's. This site is currently where Duckworth Motors is located. Mervin Jones built a store and ran it before selling to Willis and Loree Hankins Butler. They lived in the back of the store. In 1930's Willis Butler had a pickup truck fixed as weekly rolling store. Mrs. Loree continues to live there.

In 1920's Cullen Webster had a truck with a bed built up and around it. This was known as a rolling store. The peddler made weekly rounds. He would also buy chickens and eggs from folks. His truck was stocked, including kerosene and stick candy.

In 1940's Mrs. Fay remembered their ice man Finis Crawford, father of Edna Earl Crawford Lawrence and Maureen Crawford Turner. There was an ice house in Fayette which cut the 100 pound blocks for delivery. If the blocks were cut smaller, they would melt. She thought maybe the 100 pound blocks sold for 50 cents. The blocks would last a week in their iceboxes.

Mrs. Fay fondly talked of the old fashion telephones. Their house ring was 2 longs and 3 shorts. All telephones on the party line rang with incoming calls. Often everyone listened in on the calls. Jesse Corbett had a call bell that could connect lines from Crossville to Vernon. In the Fellowship Community, Joel Hankins had a call bell to connect to Fairview area. Mr. Hankins' daughter was Lettie married to Bert Cunningham. Bert Cunningham's father was Benjamin who owned and operated a store located in the area near where Bert Cunningham's daughter Marjorie Cash currently lives. The main staples bought were kerosene, sugar, flour and coffee. Sometimes folks traded eggs for bread, crackers and cheese. Written and submitted by Dianne Oakes Woods.

Tom Robertson

We learn, through Mr. Landford, that Mr. Tom. Robertson, in the southern portion of the county, had his house and household furniture, bedding and wearing apparel burned about 10 a. m. on Tuesday last. Mr. Robertson saved nothing, except his corn and meat. There was no one at the house at the time, as his wife, who has two small children, was in the field helping her husband, and had, as was not her custom, carried the children with her. The Vernon merchants and sympathizing friends have generously contributed to their immediate necessities. It would be far better for men to go to the field, and leave their wives in the house to care for the place. Source: *The Vernon Pioneer*, May 18, 1877.

Rush

Mr. George W. Rush commenced his school at the old Academy building on Monday last. Source: *The Vernon Pioneer*, July 5, 1878.

Mr. Philip Rush, who resides about a mile south of town, on the Columbus road, was very seriously hurt while in town Tuesday forenoon. He was in the act of backing his mule, and had just gained his position in the saddle, when the mule shied, thereby throwing Mr. Rush to the ground. His foot becoming fastened in the stirrup, the mule started on a run, dragging Mr. Rush for a distance of about fifty or sixty yards, bruising him fearfully. He was carried to Taylor's store, and Dr. M. Morton called. His injuries were ascertained to be quite severe and painful, and Mr. Rush hovered between life and death for some time. He was finally taken to his home, and at last accounts is resting easy and in a fair way to recover. Source: *The Vernon Pioneer*, July 19, 1878.

Sanders

Mr. Sanders the artist will only remain in Vernon one week from next Saturday. He goes from here to Kennedy. Those desiring pictures would do well to call at once. Source *The Lamar News*, March 31, 1887.

Bill Sanders

Millport, Ala. Dec. 6. It may be true that some people live in this world too long but seldom is it admitted. A man was found in Millport Tuesday who said "I've been living too long" His name is Uncle Bill Sanders, aged negro. Uncle Bill celebrated his one hundred fifth birthday Tuesday and informed the Commercial Dispatch correspondent he was born at Blue Creek, Va. Dec. 4, 1823 and was stolen from his parents when 12 years old and brought to Tuscaloosa where he was sold as a slave to Ennis Sanders and carried to Pickens County.

Bill says that during the War Between the States that he stayed at home and looked after things while his ol' Mos' fought the fight.

He has lived within a few miles of Millport 93 years and is as active as the average man of 65. Uncle Bill raised three bales of cotton and 100 bushels of corn this year, which is positive proof that he has learned something about farming during all the years he has been in this section". Source: *The Commercial Dispatch*, December 6, 1928

Thurman and Margaret McDill Shackelford

Thurman and Margaret were members of Lamar County Genealogical & Historical Society for years, during this time they were very active in helping preserve Lamar County history. They will forever be missed.

Margaret McDill Shackelford 1936-2015

Margaret McDill Shackelford of Columbus, Mississippi age 79 died Wednesday, July 22, 2015 at North Mississippi Medical Center, Tupelo, Mississippi. Services were held Saturday July 25, 2015 at Calvary Baptist Church. Burial followed at Pleasant Hill Cemetery.

Mrs. Shackelford was born on Thursday, January 30, 1936 in Liberty, AL to the late Joseph Dee and Z.O. Woolbright McDill. She was a member of Calvary Baptist Church and a retired employee of United Technologies after 48 years. She was a volunteer at the Vernon, Alabama Mary Wallace Cobb Memorial Library History room. In addition to her parents she was preceded in death by her brothers, Joe Reed McDill and Willie Dee McDill.

Survivors include: Her husband: Thurman "Bud" Shackelford, Columbus MS, daughters: Wanda Channell (Ronnie), Birmingham, AL, Donna Jenkins (George "Allen"), Columbus, MS. Son: Richard "Lee" Shackelford (Becky), Columbus, MS. Sister: Mavis Brown (Eugene), Ethelsville, Alabama. Seven grandchildren.

Thurman Lee Shackelford 1931-2015

Thurman Lee "Bud" Shackelford, age 84, of Columbus, Mississippi, passed away October 30, 2015, at Baptist Memorial Hospital. Funeral services were Sunday, November 1, 2015 at Calvary Baptist Church. The private interment followed at Pleasant Hill Baptist Church Cemetery.

Mr. Shackelford was born July 2, 1931, in Lamar County, AL, to the late Joseph Lee and Ruby Strawn Shackelford. He was a veteran of Korea serving in the United States Army. Mr. Shackelford retired from United Technologies after 40 years and was a member of Calvary Baptist Church. In addition to his parents, he was preceded in death by his wife, Margaret McDill Shackelford, and sister, Mildred Hannah.

Survivors include his son, Richard "Lee" Shackelford and his wife Becky of Columbus, MS, daughters, Wanda Channell and her husband Ronnie of Birmingham, AL, and Donna Jenkins and her husband George "Allen" of Columbus, MS, seven grandchildren, and nine great grandchildren.

Peter M. Shaw

The colored people in the vicinity of Esqr. J. T. Collins, have organized a Debating Society, at the school house called Temple Star. We learn from Peter M. Shaw, a member, that peace and harmony prevails, and all seem to have a feeling of civilizing interest in the organization. Source: The Vernon Clipper November 7 1879

Dr. L. F. Shelton

Dr. L. F. Shelton, Dentist. Will remain in Vernon but two weeks longer. Parties needing work in his line should call at once. Source: *The Vernon Pioneer*, October 31, 1877

Captain Shields

Captain Shields has returned from his visit to Aberdeen. Source: *The Vernon Pioneer* July 19, 1878.

Capt. S. J. Shields has been invited by the Memorial Association of Aberdeen, Miss., to deliver an address on the occasion of the decoration of the soldier's graves May 7th. The Capt. is somewhat an orator, and we are sure he will acquit himself with much credit on this solemn event. Source: *The Vernon Clipper* April 23. 1880

A. Q. Smith

A. Q. Smith, who shot A. L. Guin at Sulligent on the 11th surrendered to the sheriff last Saturday. He was brought before Judge Young and a new warrant was sworn out charging him with murder in the second degree. The first warrant having been issued before the death of the wounded party was only for assault with intent to murder. Mr. J. C. Milner is prosecuting the case. Messrs. McCluskey, Shields, and Nesmith appear for the defense. Bail at $1,000 was agreed on and the trial set for next Friday, 24th. Thirty-nine witnesses have been summoned. The defense will set up self defense, while the prosecution will contend that the force used exceeded that required and proper under that plea. Source: *The Vernon Courier* August 23, 1896

A. Q. Smith Trial
Preliminary
A Synopsis of the Evidence in the Trial of A. Q. Smith.
Testimony Will be Heard Today.

The case of State vs. A. Q. Smith, for the killing of A. L. Guin, was on trial last Friday and Saturday, and on account of absent witnesses the court adjourned until today. Some previous engagements of parties interested and the sickness of Capt. J. D. McCluskey, one of the attorneys for the defense, caused the continuance to be made longer than otherwise. There was considerable interest manifested during the whole trial. There has been a most solemn air pervading the court room. The mother of the deceased, with some other lady friends, have been in constant attendance upon the trial. The serious of the affray seems to have impressed itself on many of the witnesses in a way that they do not easily shake it off. In that awful struggle not a word was spoken. It appears from all the eye witnesses that though no word was spoken they knew at once it was a struggle to the death. The trial has gone on smoothly. There is but little clashing between the lawyers, when an objection is interposed, it is promptly settled. The examination of the witnesses has been thorough and covers the ground fully. The Courier gleaned the following from the testimony, being substantially what the witness said:

H. S. Henson

The first witness for the prosecution was Mr. H. S. Henson who testifies as follows: "I know defendant and knew A. L. Guin, who is now dead; was about sixty feet from front door heard noise, saw Guin at the door he had an axe handle drawn. Smith was leaning over, witness saw no lick – Smith shot, and Guin followed Smith about ten feet down the aisle in Ogden's store in the town of Sulligent, in Lamar County, Alabama. Smith fired second time, then Guin followed Smith two or three steps and stopped, and Smith turned walked back and fired upon Guin – think the ball struck deceased about the jacket pocket in front. Afliant was about twenty feet from defendant when the last shot was fired. Had talked with Smith in regard to decedent; defendant said Guin was making grave charges reflecting on defendant's character- that defendants character was worth as much to him as deceased's character — that there was a law to protect a man's character. There was a back entrance to the store house which was open at the time.

On cross-examination — "I was sixty feet from the door and heard a noise; saw Smith drawing a pistol. He was in a leaning position at the door as if he had been struck and had fallen back. Didn't tell Ed Molloy, in the post office, that Smith turned and cocked his pistol. Did not get under the counter part of the time; was not in the grocery department during the fight. Didn't say the presence of J. T. Thompson, at the post office in Sulligent, that Smith ran forward and cocked his pistol and run back and fired, did say that it looked like he went through the motion of cocking his pistol. At the firing of the third shot, deceased was standing with an axe-handle resting on the floor — deceased had followed defendant about three steps down the aisle and stopped and defendant walked six or seven steps down the aisle and returned to within about six feet of deceased and shot; defendant was rather to the South or East side of the aisle when he fired the last shot and Guin on the West side; defendant was about six feet further from front door than the deceased".

Van Livingston

The second witness for the state was Mr. Van Livingston, who testified as follows:

"I know both defendant and deceased. Guin is dead. On Saturday, about the 11th of April,1896 in Ogden's store my attention was attracted by a noise in front of the store. I am a salesman in the said Ogden's store and was about thirty feet from front door behind the counter in the dry goods department. I saw Guin in the door with an axe-handle. Smith had been sitting inside or outside the door. I saw that there was trouble and drooped behind the counter. There was two shots fired after which I looked up and Guin was about opposite me across the aisle. Smith was in a leaning position, leaning from deceased and was straightening up; when up he stepped forward and fired a pistol at the deceased. The pistol was pointed at the body of deceased; think it would range about the stomach. The parties were about six or eight feet apart. The defendant walked to the front door and out and the deceased followed and I took hold of his arm there at the front door; deceased walked slowly to the door, soon he remarked to me, 'He has killed me." The shots were in quick succession. I think the second and third were the closer together.

Dr. R. J. Redden.

Dr. R. J. Redden, the next witness says: "I am a practicing physician and was called to A. L. Guin on the 11th day of April, 1896, when I found the deceased suffering from three gun or pistol shot wounds. One in his left wrist ranging up breaking the bone in the forearm; another had passed through the fleshy part of the arm and the third entered the body just below edge of the ribs, about two inches to the right side and passed through the body and lodged under the skin in the back. This wound was mortal, producing profound shock and internal hemorage from which death ensused." On cross-examination "The deceased when intoxicated had reputation as quarlesome and dangerous man. Others spoke of him as rather a bluff than dangerous.

Capt. F. Ogden

Capt. F. Ogden, the next witness for the state testified as follows: "I was sitting leaning against the front of the store house of F. Ogden & Son in the town of Sulligent on the evening of the 11th of April 1896, when Mr. A. L. Guin came across the street from the office of Dr. R. J. Redden,. Mr. Guin had an axe-handle in his hand. He came by and went to the door. Mr. A. Q. Smith the defendant was sitting in the door. I heard the disturbance to my right and looked around and saw a blow with the axe-handle falling upon the arm of Smith. The blow was struck by Mr. A. L. Guin. I immediately rose up and my eyes were turned from the combatant. Two pistol shots followed in quick succession. I stepped back behind the wall. I again looked in either at the door or window. I think it was the door, and saw defendant and Mr. Guin standing facing each other. Mr. Smith had his pistol pointed at Guin and fired instantly. I think the pointed or ranged to the stomach of the deceased. The defendant walked back and out at the front door. The deceased followed and the defendant turned in the street and started back. Someone shouted 'go away' and he crossed the street. I stepped in the store and picked up the defendant's bat and laid it on the counter. There was not a word said that I heard by the combatants. The deceased was naturally slightly stooped in the shoulders; my best judgement is that he looked a little more stooped than he is at the moment of the last pistol shot.

J. A. Poe

Mr. J. A. Poe, witness for the state testified as follows:

"I was sitting in front of Ogden & Son's store on the evening of the 11th of April 1896. I saw Mr. A. L. Guin coming from across the street from what is known as the Pennington corner. His little son was with him - he stopped and sent his son back. He had an axe-handle in his hand he came on and when near the door he made a quick step and stuck defendant Smith with the axe-handle. They both went into the house. Two shots were fired in very quick succession. I then went to the door of the dry goods department and just before I looked in I heard another report. I then turned back and defendant came out of the front door and Mr. Guin followed after him to the door. The defendant stopped and turned, Dr.

Hollis shouted "go on and have no more fussing her." He crossed the street. There were only three shots fired. The first two were fired so close together as to be hard to distinguish from one report. The third report was after a longer interval. The third shot was a very short time from the second shot. The shots were fired almost as fast as could be counted. I was sitting about midway between the door and window I got up and went to the door - just before I looked in I heard third report. I was sitting about six feet from the door. I commenced to rise from my seat when the difficulty commenced

Perry Gilmore

Perry Gimore, another witness for the state testified as follows:

"I heard the defendant telling Mr. W. W. Ogden about one month ago that if Mr. A. L. Guin did not let him alone or if he run on him he would shoot him. That he had run on him the evening before with a knife."

A. U. Hollis

A. U. Hollis, the last witness for the state testifies., that on the morning before the killing that the defendant was in his office and said to him that he had heard that Guin was cursing out him and his friends and that Guin had better let him alone, he was not interfering with Guin.

Dr. D. D. Hollis

Dr. D. D. Hollis, the first witness for the defense said:

"I was sitting on the pavement in front of Ogden's store and the defendant was sitting in the door, his face was out of the door and his feet were on the door sill. Mr. Guin came up and made about three rapid strides and struck the defendant with an axe-handle. The handle was homemade and not exactly finished. Smith threw up one hand and possibly both and from the effort to evade blow or the blow itself and defendant fell back into the house on his ack. While e in a recumbent position defendant fired a pistol at deceased that the deceased pursued defendant with the axe-handle drawn and struck him again. As to whether both blows were stuck before the first shot, I am not able to say. When Smith had gained an upright position he fired again. The range of the pistol appeared to be at the breast of the deceased. The deceased continued to advance after the second shot. Affiant saw defendant presenting his pistol in position to shooting the third time the deceased was advancing with axe-handle drawn. Affiant jumped behind the wall to get out of range of the bullet. The defendant walked out of the front door and rather up the street. He then turned down the street in front of the door and affiant told him to go away - defendant made no effort to reenter the house, nor did the come toward it. The deceased came to near the front door where Mr. Livingston took hold of him. As to the difference in the time of firing affiant thinks and it is his best judgment that from the distance moved and the positions occupied that there was a longer interval between the first and the second shot then the second and third. Affiant examined the wounds of decedent. The wound in the arm and the stomach very nearly on the same elevation. The ball entering the body ranged downward about two or three inches. Affiant knows the reputation of the deceased for violence and peaceableness and the deceased was not regarded as a peaceable man when in liquor and the deceased had appearances of having been drinking. The whole time consumed was not more than seven or eight seconds, possibly less, and not positive as to the time between second and third shots. The bullet striking the forearm was evidently weakened in force or its penetration would have been greater. Some years back there was unpleasant feelings between affiant and deceased, the day before the killing the deceased while in liquor seemed to be angry with affiant and spoke unkindly. Affiant refused to bandy words or say anything unpleasant to the deceased. The deceased came next morning and apologized for his speech the day previous.

Thomas Harris

Thomas Harris, also for the defense says: "I was not present at the difficulty. Deceased made threats at different times. On Friday night before the killing he said to me, "Gus Smith has robbed me and we both can't stay in this town three days." He said, "you are a friend to me ain't you?" I said yes, he said, "you come down tomorrow and bring your big pistol, and stand by me." He said "tomorrow is you democrats election day - I will have an election." I have heard him at other times say that he and defendant could not live in the same town. About one month ago when he was drinking he wanted me to go down town and back him up that Gus Smith was trying to run over him. Communicated the threats Friday night. When drinking he was regarded as dangerous. At one time he said one or the other would have to leave the country or die. This was said on Friday night before the killing. Communicated these threats on Friday night before the killing. I told Guin that he had better watch Smith. I knew of the ill feelings existing, and thought that they would both fight. Smith told me that, "Guin had better let me alone," he said. "He would let him (Guin) alone if he let me alone." Did not tell J. R Guin in Sulligent on Sunday morning after the killing that both had made threats. I told him that I guess they both have made threats.

Pleas May

Pleas May testified for the defense as follows:

"I was sitting on the dry goods counter in the store of F. Ogden & Son at the time of the difficulty. The first thing at attracted my attention was the first pistol shot. Guin was striking the defendant with an axe-handle. Three or four blows were struck at the firing of the second shot Smith was down, not exactly flat one the floor. At the firing of the third shot Smith had gotten about straight. I think that Smith was nearer the front door. The entire difficulty was quick and there was no stopping of the fight until Guin stopped at the front door. Smith had gone out. The combatants were close together, rather too close for effective use of the stick in my judgment. No words were spoken. When the difficulty was over I went out at the back door which was open. judgment is that the second and third shots were closer together than the first and second. The distance covered by the combatant between the first and second report being about twenty feet, while the distance covered between the second and third shot was less. My best judgment is that the deceased struck defendant with the axe handle after the third shot was fired. The deceased was rather beside the defendant as they went back into the room. Defendant had his head tucked down. The blows appeared to fall on defendants head and shoulders.

Joe Noe

Joe Noe, another witness for the defense says

"I was standing in Ogden's store in Sulligent, and looked around after the first report of the pistol and saw deceased strike the defendant on the side of the head with an axe-handle; they came back toward where I was standing. Smith was stooped over. After the second shot was fired the deceased knocked defendant down, and defendant got up about straight and fired. There was no cessation in the fight from start to finish. After the third shot I got behind the counter. I had been standing in front of the counter up to that time. The combatants came to within fifteen feet of where I was standing; I dropped under the counter after the firing ceased, was very much excited, but remember distinctly what I saw. I am nearly 21 years of age."

J. A. Smith

J. A. Smith, testified for the defense as follows:

"I examined the person of defendant on the morning after the difficulty and found a bruise on this muscle of his arm; one on the back of his hand and two bruises on the back, well up on the shoulders. I knew the general character of the deceased. He was a dangerous violent man when in whiskey; when sober, otherwise. The relation between deceased and myself have always been pleasant. I and defendant are warm friends.

C. G. Swan

C. G. Swan testifies that he, on the day after the difficulty saw the person of defendant and he had a bruise on his arm and hand and there were three or four bruises on this leg below his knee and thinks it was his right arm and leg that had the bruises. The bruise on the arm gave indications of a severe blow.

Ed Molloy

Ed Molloy also for the defense says: "Heard shooting in Sulligent Guin had in my presence said that he and defendant could not be in the same town many days longer. I heard H. S. Henson say that defendant cocked his pistol and shot. I told him that the pistol was a hammerless pistol,. Henson said he acted as though he was cocking his pistol quite a crowd heard the conversation. I did not communicate the threats to the defendant.

Source: *The Vernon Courier,* April 30, 1896

In the case of the State vs A. Q. Smith in preliminary trail last week the result was the defendant held in $500 bond to answer the charge of manslaughter. The witnesses examined last Thursday gave testimony favorable to the defendant. The argument by the counsel consumed the entire afternoon session. The prosecution was opened by Mr. J. C. Milner for one hour and was then followed by Messrs Shields and Mccluskey for the defense for one hour each. The speeches showed preparation and would have done credit to any bar in the state. It is said by spectators that no more painstaking and dignified examination has ever been witnessed. Numbers of the friends of both the deceased and the defendant attended the trial The contention of the prosecution was that at the time the last shot was fired, which the state contends was the fatal one, that the defendant could have retreated without endangering his life or limb, or increasing his peril, or suffer great bodily harm. Even the proof supporting this contention was not sufficient to make the offense in the opinion of the Judge more than manslaughter in the first degree, while the defense offered contradictory evidence tending to show that he was at all times trying to get away and that he was being assaulted when the last shot was fired, and that the affray only lasted about eight seconds and was continuous from start to finish. Source: *The Vernon Courier* May 7, 1896.

The grand jury failed to indict A. Q. Smith for the killing of Guin. Source: *The Vernon Courier* - September 3, 1896

L. R. Smith

L. R. Smith well known and highly esteemed citizen of Military Springs died of consumption at his home near Bedford on the 5th inst. He was laid to rest at Friendship Church . Source: *The Vernon Courier* dated January 12, 1893

Rube Smith

Rube Smith Goes Up for Life

Birmingham News. Rube Smith, the last surviving member of the famous Rube Burrows gang of train robbers, was convicted at Jackson, Miss. On the charge of robbing the United States mails at Buckatanna, Miss. in September, 1889. The lowest sentence is imprisonment for life, and Judge Hill will pronounce it in a few days. The jury were out less than half an hour, as the evidence of Smith's guilt was conclusive.

Smith is already serving a ten year's term in the State Penitentiary of Mississippi, so that now he will never again be a free man unless he escapes. He is about 27 years old and bears every evidence of being a hardened criminal. As far as is known he participated in but one of Burrows' train robberies, and that was the Buckatanna robbery on the Mobile & Ohio road. Source: *The Kennedy News* November 21, 1890

Claud Smithson

Claud Smithson thinks baths are too expensive and maybe shouldn't be taken too often. While taking one several days ago and returned to put his clothes on, he found all of his money had been taken. Source: *The Sulligent News* October 22, 1942

E. M. Springfield

Mr. Myrt Springfield, a lifelong resident of Vernon died at his home here, Monday of this week. Mr. Springfield was 64 years of age. Residents of Vernon knew him as an influential citizen whose entire 64 years had been spent in this town.

He was a Christian gentleman, a member of Vernon I. O. O. F Number 45, active up until a short time before his death in the gin business here, and was loved and respected for what he has accomplished and for his desire to be of service to his fellow man.

Flower girls were Lema Perkins, Mary Joyce Stokes, Bess Springfield, Sarah Cartwright, Bobbie Springfield, Pauline Guin, Geraldine Duke, Jane Presson.

Out of town visitors included: W. O. Presson and family, Noa Robertson and family of Columbus, Mrs. Springfield's sister, Mrs. Sapp of Birmingham, Mrs. Springfield's father, Mr. Coleman of Millport, Mr. J. D. Springfield and family and Mrs. Theede of Birmingham.

Rev. M. W. McCain and Rev. Miles Wright conducted the funeral service, with burial at Pin Hook. Source: *The Lamar Democrat* Oct. 19, 1938

Harriet Springfield

Miss Harriet Springfield, daughter of Rev. and Mrs. T. W. Springfield died on the evening of the 24th after a long illness. In life, Miss Harriet was one of the sweetest Christian characters we have ever known. For years, she has been a meek and patient sufferer, stricken down in the very bloom of life she gradually faded away to the city of God. Source: *The Vernon Courier*, September 28, 1888.

Martha Brown Stanford Heirs

In the basement of Chester County Court House, in Record Book J, March 1822-1826, p.66, is this legal paper: "Thomas Stanford Vs Mrs. Ann Brown. Whereas George Brown, deceased, of Chester District, State of South Carolina, at the time of his death was possessed of a tract of land containing two hundred and eleven (211) acres, being part of a tract originally granted to John Bond. George Brown died intestate, leaving at the time of his death: Ann Brown, his widow and the following next of kin: John Brown, James Brown, William Brown, Thomas Brown, brothers of the said George Brown dec'd; James Hamilton surviving husband of Jane Hamilton, formerly Jane Brown, sister of the said George Brown dec'd, Thomas Hamilton, Robert Hamilton, Eby. Hamilton, Jane Hamilton,

William Hamilton, Moses Hamilton, Matty McDaniel, formerly Matty Hamilton, and John McDaniel her husband, the children, the children of the said James and Jane Hamilton; and Thomas Stanford, Senr., surviving husband of Martha Stanford, formerly Martha Brown, sister of the said George Brown dec'd, Thomas Stanford, Junr., William Stanford, George Stanford, James Stanford, John Stanford, Mary Morton, formerly Mary Stanford, and Willie Morton her husband, and Jennet Lamb formerly Jennet Stanford and Isaac Lamb her husband, Martha Mobley, formerly Martha Stanford and Daniel Mobley her husband, Peggy Bennett, formerly Peggy Stanford and John Bennett her husband, Jane Perry, formerly Jane Stanford and William Perry her husband, and Rebecca Almon, formerly Rebecca Stanford and Jacob Almon her husband, the children of the said Thomas Stanford, senr., and Martha Stanford dec'd., heirs of the said George Brown, deceased. Whereupon the said Ann Brown widow of the said George Brown dec'd became entitled to one half of the said tract of land and the aforesaid Heirs to a distributive share of the remaining half. Source: Page 116, *The Revolutionary Soldiers of Catholic Presbyterian Church Chester County, South Carolina* by Mary Wylie Strange (Mrs. R. M. Strange) Historian of the Catholic Memorial Association 1946.

In the clerks's office, Chester County Court House, Book W, p. 438, No. 479, appears the following: " The State of Alabama Marion County (8/30/1821) We William Stanford, George Stanford, James Stanford, William Morton, the husband of Mary Stanford, John Stanford, Isaac Lamb the husband of Jennett Stanford, Daniel Malloy, the husband of Martha Stanford, John Bennett the husband of Peggy Stanford, all of the county and state aforesaid do by these present appoint Thomas Stanford Junior of the same county and state, our lawful attorney in fact for us and in our names to use all lawful means for the purpose of collecting by law or otherwise all monies and personal or real estate to which we may be entitled as the lawful heirs of George Brown, late of Chester District, in the state of South Carolina, deceased, in whose estate we the said...became interested by our Mother Martha Stanford, formerly Martha Brown sister of the full blood to the said George Brown and we, the said William Stanford....do by these present ratify and confirm the acts of our said Attorney lawfully done by Virtue of these presents they are hereby declared to be as lawful obligatory and conclusive as if such acts had been performed by ourselves in person.

Witness our hands and seals this 30th day of August, 1821.

William Stanford	Seal
George Stanford	Seal
James Stanford	Seal
John Stanford	Seal

William Morton, husband of Mary Stanford   Seal
Isaac Lamb, husband of Jennet Stanford   Seal
Daniel Malloy, husband of Martha Stanford   Seal
John Bennett, husband of Peggy Stanford   Seal

Source: Page 117, *The Revolutionary Soldiers of Catholic Presbyterian Church Chester County, South Carolina* by Mary Wylie Strange (Mrs. R. M. Strange) Historian of the Catholic Memorial Association 1946.

Thomas Stanford

Dedication to Thomas Stanford, Revolutionary War Veteran

On Sunday, April 24th, 1994 at 2:00 p. m., a tribute to the Revolutionary War veteran, Thomas Stanford, was held at the Old Nebo Cemetery off Highway 18 west of Vernon in Lamar County, Alabama.

Descendants, DAR members and the general public attended the dedication. Several members of the MSSDAR Cotton Gin Port Chapter, Amory, are direct descendants of Thomas Stanford. Many of his descendants live in Monroe County, Mississippi.

Thomas Stanford, who lived from 1756 to 1843, came to Marion County, Ala., about 1820 and homesteaded land there. He lived in Marion and Fayette counties for the remainder of his life. Lamar County, where the dedication was held, was at that time a part of Marion County.

William Stanford, father of Thomas Stanford, came from Ireland and settled in Virginia near the Potomac River where Thomas was born in 1756. A few years later, William moved to Chester District S.C., where Thomas grew up. In February 1776, Thomas enlisted in the South Carolina military forces and served in a number of engagements against the British.

One writer said of him, "Thomas Stanford came alone in the dead of night to (General) Tarleton's encampment on the creek and picked off some sentinels as they passed from point to point, being so well acquainted with the ground that he easily avoided reconnoitering parties."

In his pension application Thomas stated he was almost continually engaged in the service of the United States from the time he entered in 1776 until the end of the war.

Thomas Stanford married Martha Brown in South Carolina and reared a large family. As land to the west became open for homesteading, he moved his family first to Giles County, Tenn., and about 1820 to Marion County, Ala., where he and some of his sons homesteaded land.

In 1834, while a resident of Marion County, he went to Fayette County and applied for his Revolutionary War Pension through the Probate Court.

He stated he came to Fayette County to file his claim as he needed to get statements from men who had served with him and there were two then living in Fayette County.

Thomas Stanford was awarded pension at the rate of $50 per year beginning in 1832, the year Congress passed the pension law. His last pension payment was in September 1843 through the paying agent in Tuscaloosa.

His exact date of death is not known but it was before the next semi-annual pension payment in March 1844.

The exact burial site for Thomas Stanford is not known, but census records indicate he lived at one time with his daughter Martha who married Daniel Malloy. Both Martha and Daniel Malloy are buried in the Old Nebo Cemetery in marked graves. The Ozark, Alabama Chapter DAR, which has a number of members who are descendants of Thomas Stanford, is sponsoring the dedication. Invitations were sent to DAR chapters in North Alabama and East Mississippi to join in the dedication. Source: Written by Alfred "Bill" Tate (now deceased)

William Stanford Estate

This court document has death of William Stanford AD 1861, no month or day listed, place of death as "said county"; Sanford County was not formed until 1868, therefore the county would have been either Marion or Fayette.

Heirs or distributes of said deceased are as follows: James Stanford who is over 21 years of age and of sound mind and resides in Sanford County Alabama; Polly Carruth who is over 21 years of age and of sound mind and resides in Sanford County Alabama, wife of Thomas Carruth; Adeline Alexander who is over 21 years of age and of sound mind and resides in Alabama P. O. address Buckhorn County not known, wife of William Alexander; Jesse Stanford who is over 21 years of age and of sound mind and resides in Franklin County, Alabama P. O. Buzzards Roost; John Stanford who is over 21 years of age and of sound mind and resides in Tippah County, Mississippi P. O. Box unknown. That the decedent at the time of his death was an inhabitant of this State and he left property to be administered in this County. Your petitioner prays to have letters of administration granted to Jason Guin General Administrator of Sanford County as no person entitled to such Administration has applied for letters on the estate and your petitioner is a condition of said estate and one of the heirs and distributes of said estate." Signed James P. Stanford and W. H.

DeRochmond, attorney for petitioner. Dated November 19, 1873. Source: *Sanford County Alabama Order Book 2* Pages 41, 42. Lamar County Courthouse Vernon, Alabama

Commissioner Stone

Commissioner Stone who served on the grand jury last week procured a leave of absence to go home and see a little Miss who had made her advent during his absence. He found the mother and child doing well, whereupon he filled is saddle-bags with apples and returned to the jury room. Source: *The Vernon Pioneer,* February 6, 1878.

Sabra Newell Sudberry

Sabra Newell Sudberry, age 41 died March 3, 2004. She battled cancer for years. At a young age she became interested in local history and family genealogies. She was a huge contributor to the preservation of the history of Lamar County and surrounding counties. Throughout her fight with cancer, she still researched, preserved, seeming to never take a break. Many lives have been touched through her work.

I received this note from Sabra on December 6, 2003, not many weeks before her death: "I am home now until January, then I have to return to Mexico. While I am here, I am going to start transcribing the Order books at the Vernon courthouse, which are the next books following the Estate book or books that I already transcribed. I am also going to be working on Judge John Dabney Terrell's (Sr.) papers that will be posted to both Lamar and Marion county websites. These papers contain information from his daily business dealings (from the early 1800s, and contain some marriages from the 1830s (at least-so far, I have not read through all of them- thousands of pages) from Marion County, that were of course burned up when the courthouse burned. They would include people living in what covers the northern part of Lamar County."

Alfred William Tate

In Honor Of Bill Tate On His 92nd Birthday

Alfred William (Bill) Tate was born December 16, 1912, Newton, Dale Co., Alabama, son and tenth child of twelve born to Augustus Walter Tate and Florence Victoria Stanford. Bill retired in 1976 as Director of VA Regional Office, Atlanta, Georgia. He met his wife, Edna Thagard in Ozark, Alabama where he was teaching school after college graduation. They married in 1936 and had two daughters, Martha and Carol, five grandchildren and ten great- grandchildren. Bill and Edna moved to Ozark and were residents for many years. They were members of Center Ridge Baptist Church where Bill is still a member.

Bill is a seventh generation descendant of William Stanford of North Ireland whose son, Thomas Stanford served in the Revolutionary War. Thomas, born 1756 in Virginia, married Martha Brown, born 1760, also in Virginia. In 1983 Bill bought a copy of "Scotch-Irish Forever! The Stanfords", book which peaked his interests in his family becoming members of the DAR, SAR and CAR. Bill then set out to aid his family and other descendants in filing their applications for membership.

Years ago, the graves of Martha Molloy (daughter of Thomas Stanford) and her husband, Daniel Molloy, were discovered at an old, almost abandoned cemetery called Nebo, located near Vernon, Alabama. Bill became very interested and had this old cemetery cleared. He later wrote letters to descendants and asked for donations for further work. After the Lamar Co. Genealogical Society was formed and later gained ownership of the cemetery, they oversee it's upkeep. After it was fairly well established that Thomas Stanford was buried here, Bill took on the task of beautifying the graves as they appear and had DAR and VA markers erected.

On April 24, 1994, a well-organized dedication ceremony was held with over 100 attending. It was beautiful and enjoyed by all. Many friends met that day for the first time. The program ended with taps. What a wonderful tribute to our ancestor!

Bill lost his beloved wife, Edna, on January 14, 2001 and lived on in Ozark until January 31, 2003 when he moved to Eatonton, Georgia to be near his daughter Martha. Bill is still very active, still drives, walks three miles a day, goes to church and meetings, buys groceries and works at home, keeps house, reads the newspaper, watches tv, works on his computer and says he is content.

In October 2003, Bill lost his brother, Jack, making Bill the last living sibling of twelve. Is it sunset? Not yet! Bill says he would not mind living to 100 years if he could have good health.

God bless you, Bill. May your life continue to be long and happy! Source: Mrs. Laverne Stanford (now deceased)

Jesse Taylor

At the Old Pioneer Office will be found a full line of Dry goods, boots, hoes, hats, Glassware, Woodenware, tinware, Family Staple and Fancy Groceries. I have resumed business at my old stand and will be pleased to have customers to call and price goods before buying elsewhere. I sell at bottom prices for cash. Jesse Taylor, Vernon. Source: The Vernon Pioneer June 28, 1878.

Mr. Jesse Taylor showed us a 12 ½ cent piece in silver the other day that was coined in 1776, but it was badly worn and abused that nothing else could be deciphered except the date. Source: *The Vernon Pioneer*, February 6, 1878.

A petition containing a number of names was presented to the court asking appropriations for several aged and indigent people, and that they be allowed to remain with their relatives and friends. It was said that one object of the was to have the court go on records as to how they stood on this kind of a measure. It developed that the petition was without the knowledge and consent of the relatives of "Uncle" Jesse Taylor and Mr. Norton, a relative, asked that his name be stricken from the list as he would look after M. Taylor himself. The brought the question of boarding folks with their relatives square up and an order was made that it is the judgment of this court that the law does not authorize expenditures for the maintenance of poor people not under the control and charge of the county, and that no further appropriations will be made to support persons who resides with their relatives. There were three in favor of the order and commissioner Jackson dissented. Several persons refused to sign the petition believing that sworn officers who had the responsibility to bear and would leave the mater to their judgment. The law and Christianity requires of every man to support his dependant relative. Whenever a court goes out of the strict letter of the law embarrassment soon follows. Source: *The Vernon Courier* - May 14, 1896.

John D. Terrell Jr.

The land sold by the sheriff on last Monday morning as the estate of Jno. D. Terrell was bid in by Hon. T. B. Nesmith at $600, he being the highest bidder. Source *The Lamar News* January 10, 1884

Mrs. S. M. Terrell

It was the pleasure of the writer to be present at a very enjoyable picnic at the Chalybeate-spring of Mrs. S. M. Terrell on the 4th inst.

The crowd began to assemble early in the day and vehicles came from almost every direction bringing their quota of passengers and viands. When the Iron Horse came snorting down the track about 11 a.m. and pranced impatiently on the switch for its load to be diminished.

With this reinforcement the crowd was estimated at not less than a round thousand. As is usual on such occasions there was a goodly number of Candidates on hand all smiles.

In addition to a bountiful supply of excellent mineral water there was a bountiful supply of ice lemonade and cider. About noon a bountiful repast was furnished and was heartily enjoyed by those who partook of it.

After dinner speeches were made by Capt. McCluskey, Mr. Alexander and Dr. Bradley and it has been remarked by competent judges that he speeches were all good and reflected credit on the speakers.

Altogether it was one of the most pleasant social gatherings it has been my lot to participate in for a long time, and all present went away well pleased with the hospitality and social entertainment furnished by the citizens of Beaverton and the surrounding communities.

x x, Vernon, July 5th., 1888   Source *The Vernon Courier*, July 6, 1888

Thomas Family Reunion

A Thomas Family Reunion is planned Saturday June 03, 2006, at the new Lamar County High School Cafeteria, Highway 18 west, Vernon, Alabama , for the descendants of John Tapley Thomas and Sarah Key/Thomas, who moved from Georgia to Lamar County, Alabama sometime in the 1860's. Our first documentation of that date is when he donated land for the Emmaus Church on July 21, 1868. His parents are believed to be Beasley/Bradley Thomas and Martha a/k/a Patty Key.

Children of John Tapley and Sarah Thomas are; Virginia "Jennie" married to Sherwood Reddrick Holley; Simeon Brantley married to Nancy Copelin/Copeland and Margaret J. Graves ; George Key Married to Rebecca Copelin/Copeland, William H. married Unknown, John Christopher Columbus "Lum" married Martha E. Jackson and Georgia Baker; Mary Jane married James Benjamin Chandler; Elizabeth "Lethia"married Thomas Harvey "Tom" Finch; Franklin Pierce married to Molly Riley.

Please bring information from Family Bibles, or other information on your family and a copy of any photos that you are willing to share.

A luncheon is planned for 12:00 noon. at Lamar County High School Cafeteria, Vernon, Lamar County, Alabama. Please bring a covered dish/beverage. Eating utensils and ice will be furnished.

William Murray Thomas

William Murray Thomas was born in the Bluff community on June 05, 1889, died December 01,1981 and is buried in the Fellowship Cemetery in Lamar County, Alabama with many of my other ancestors. His mother was Mary Francis Morrison who married George Franklin Thomas. I am trying to find out more about her parents Noah Morrison and Malinda Stone. M.W. Stone and N.J. Morrison both show on the 1870 census for Sanford County, now Lamar County. Noah J. Morrison bought 79.58 acres on 07/02/1860. Noah Jefferson Morrison's death was 02/06/1901; his birth was abt 1828 in Tennessee. Malinda P. Stone was born abt 1836 and they married in 1857.

At one time, William Murray Thomas lived by the Sandlin Cemetery outside of Sulligent, Alabama near the Buttahatchee River. He lived near Sulligent from at least the 1920's. My father was James Sandlin Thomas. Written and submitted by Bob Thomas.

Annie Belle Flynn Thornton

The storm of April 16, 1921 is when my mother's home in Wofford community (Lamar County, Alabama) was destroyed. The Red Cross helped with food, water and shelter. Mother and her family lived in an army tent that the Red Cross furnished until they could rebuild.

It was the time of year when farmers had to prepare the land to plant crops for food, cash crops and to feed livestock. It was difficult to think about planting crops when your home and all possessions were destroyed and no money and no insurance to help replace anything. They had very little left.

Grandpaw and grandmother Flynn were injured during in the storm trying to protect their children. Everyone in the Stonewall Jackson and Henrietta Hardin Flynn family were alive but not in good shape, but they did survive.

My mother, Annie Belle Flynn, was 3 1/2 years old. Later just 73 days after the storm, her mother, Henrietta H. Flynn died on June 28, 1921. She was buried At Wofford Cemetery in Lamar County, Alabama.

According to National Weather Service records this was a F2 Tornado - 15 miles in length x 500 yards wide path with 4 fatalities & 30 injuries, at least 20 houses were destroyed. The tornado hit Lamar County about midnight.

Three cooking utensils were all that my grandparents had left to use to cook food for the family after the storm. My mother always said she kept these old broken utensils to remind her just how bad times could be. She also said "But if one tries they will make it through the bad times to the good."

The Lamar Democrat April 20, 1921
Tornado Plays Havock in Lamar County

Last Friday night about midnight a tornado struck Lamar county just above Steens, Miss., and plowed its way through the county, striking a few miles west of town and running thru to the Marion county line. Just how many houses were blown down we have not been able to find out, but there were only 3 or 4 deaths reported, those were negroes near Sulligent.

After leaving Steens where several deaths were reported, it seems that Mr. Cap Loftis was the first to feel the heavy hand of the storm. Messrs Joe and Claude Odom and J. A. Ayers together with several others whose names we have been unable to get also lost their homes, and we suppose everything they had in the house. Next it struck west of town about the Woodmen Hall three miles from town, demolishing houses and timber as it came to them. The Woodmen Hall is a total wreck as was several residences in that immediate section. Messrs Morris, John Turner and Nat Edgeworth were heavy losers, but fortunately there was no one killed other than the negroes near Sulligent. Messrs Tom Woods on Vernon pike and Lamar Henson on pike near Sulligent, were hit hard. Mr. Woods lot building were blown down, while Mr. Henson's out buildings and tenant houses were totally demolished, his fine two story residence was not blown down but damaged in such a way as to be almost worthless. All our people who could left Monday for the storm district to help the sufferers to rebuild. Submitted and written by Carl Thornton.

Ruby Todd

Ruby Todd

02-09-2004

During Black History Month it is fitting to remember a woman that came to Lamar County in the 1920's and even though she is deceased, her works still live. Many, many were touched by her life not only "her people" as she called African Americans of Lamar County, but other residents as well. She touched my life when I worked in Vernon at the local farm office in the late 1960's and 70's just by hearing other individuals tell of her. When I met her, I found Miss. Ruby Todd to be a gracious woman and I immediately knew why "her people" and others respected her.

Miss. Ruby Todd came to Lamar County, Alabama from Selma, Alabama and began her work as Supervisor of Negro Schools on September 19, 1928. She was told, by Superintendent G. S. Smith, to do whatever she saw to do to help "her" people. She was well educated, having attended schools in Selma and Montgomery in Alabama and Hampton, Virginia. She found 22 Negro schools, having only one teacher at each school.

She arrived in the county driving a shiny black car. There were not many cars in the county back then, and probably no Black women owning or driving a car. Mrs. Todd once said that she found a town like Dodge City and very poor conditions existed among the black people. Shacks were being used for schools and church buildings. Having her work cut out for her, she began a life's work, a work that would consume her, yet put her in the hearts of countless people. The Lamar County Training School was one fruit of her labor. She told how the people would have "possum suppers." The women would cook possums killed by the men. Miss. Ruby, not timid, asked for donations and planned events to make money for her dream, a school for "her people."

After the Lamar County Training school was a reality, Mrs. Todd's sister, Zephrus, later known as Miss Z, joined her and became principal of the school. The two sisters had a dairy that brought in some money and they boarded teachers who would pay a small amount to stay during the week. Miss Ruby kept close watch over her teachers.

Ruby Todd saw the need of children to be educated, and she did more than was expected of an educator. If a child or children had no shoes to wear to school, Miss Todd bought them shoes. Whatever the need, Miss Todd tried and usually provided so the children could be in school. She did this not for recognition, because she did not want people to know what she did. She provided these necessary things so the children could be in school and get an education. She would drive miles to visit with parents to see why a child was not in school.

People were encouraged by Miss Todd to raise food and can it at a canning plant located in Vernon. She began a Community Singing so that each church could raise money to improve church facilities. Miss Todd was a contributor to each church. She was always thinking of ways people could help improve the schools and community. She never asked anyone to do anything that she would not do herself. She was not always popular for her ethics and discipline came hard to some, but I think she always had respect of everyone who knew her even if they did not agree with her at the time.

Miss Todd provided a home for several children and helped educate them. They would not have had an opportunity for an education if not for Miss Ruby and Miss Z.

An amusing story about Miss Todd, was that she would trade cars about every two or three years. She would buy from the same dealer and tried to get the same color each time, she said "So that the people will not think I am rich or better than they are." I remember Miss Ruby's shiny car, I do not remember seeing it dirty.

Miss Ruby was witty and loved telling tales. I have heard that she would have fun with newcomers when she would tell them "I have been to Hell and back". They would look puzzled and she would laugh and tell them there was a creek nearby called "Hell's Creek".

A newly built Todd High School for Blacks named for Miss Ruby Todd and her sister, another dream that came true. This school became vacant, when schools in the county were integrated. Later it was sold, and turned into a nursing home for the elderly or disabled.

Miss Ruby Todd died January 17, 1985. Lamar County is a better place to live because of a little black woman, driving down a country road in 1928, accepted a challenge…..a challenge to do all she could for "her people".

J. M. Trim

On the 8th inst., near Webster, J. M. Trim slipped his gun out and went about two hundred yards from his house and shot himself, and died in about four hours. Cause, insanity. Source: *The Vernon Clipper*, January 16, 1880.

Eunice Trimm and Willie Mae Trimm Hamm

A Birthday Celebration To Remember

After lunch on Saturday afternoon , June 25, 2016, automobiles began arriving in the quiet Oak Hill Community to Oak Hill United Methodist Church , filling the parking area to capacity. This occasion was quite remarkable as the church fellowship were hosting a birthday celebration for Miss Eunice Trimm, who was 104 on June 19th and Mrs. Willie Mae Trimm Hamm, who will be 100 on July 1, 2016.

The birthday celebration began at 2:00 p. m. with Pastor Greg Cook opening with prayer. Over 100 guests stood singing "Happy Birthday" to the lovely ladies, as the church building was filled with family, former students and friends.

Probate Judge Johnny Rogers presented both ladies with a *"Letter of Proclamation"* from Lamar County.

Pastor Greg Cook presented *"Certificates of Recognition"* from Governor Robert Bentley.

Dwight Gentry presented *"Letters of Recognition"* from Senator Richard Shelby.

Mayor Scott Boman presented *"Grateful Celebration and Honor"* plagues from the Town of Sulligent.

Larry Hall presented a *"Recognition"* plaque to Ms. Trimm from Oak Hill Methodist Church.

Ray Thompson presented a *"Recognition"* plaque to Ms. Willie Mae Hamm from Oak Hill Methodist Church.

Between the two ladies, they received 134 birthday cards. Guests came as far away as Huntsville, Cullman, Birmingham and Tuscaloosa to celebrate and honor these two, with love and affection.

After the ceremony, guests enjoyed visiting with Mrs. Hamm and Miss Trimm, while enjoying delicious refreshments provided by Oak Hill Church fellowship. Source: Submitted and written by Pat Reeves of Sulligent

Joe & Sibbie Turner

"Joe Turner was born December 1, 1883. He celebrated his 102nd birthday on December 1, 1985. He was the son of Mary and Nelson Truelove. *(I believe this is a misprint and should be Turner not Truelove, but I did not change from original printing.)* Joe Turner was born in Lamar County. Also, Mr. and Mrs. Joe Turner have lived in the Detroit, Alabama area many years and reared a family that believed in work.

It isn't often that you meet someone who has lived to reach 100 years of age. and even more unusual to see someone who has lived to be 102 years of age. Well, Joe Turner of Detroit, Alabama, has been blessed to reach 102. Whew 102 that's old, Right? Well, Mr. Turner doesn't seem to think that's so old. As a matter-of-fact, he says that he had an aunt who lived to reach 124 years of age and that he does not expect anything less.

When asked the secret of his long living, Mr. Turner's reply is simply, 'Good clean living,' He has lived to see three generations after him, and has always expressed the pride he has for his children, grandchildren, and great-grandchildren.

It is no secret that the Turner family is small in number and close in unity. As the saying goes, 'All for one, and one for all.' Mr. Turner says that he never really had the opportunity to be close to his family when he was growing up, so he has always taught his own offspring to be close to one another. Any one of his 14 grandchildren will quickly tell you that their grandfather and grandmother have always been proud and dignified people.

This Thanksgiving, Mr. Turner was hospitalized for the second time in his life. His family rushed to his side, fearing the worse. Nurses gathered around, saying that, they had heard of this man who had lived for so long and were honored to have the opportunity to finally meet him They were eager to make him feel as comfortable as possible, telling him to lie back, but he politely refused, saying he'd just as soon sit, if they didn't mind. He never was one who cared for (as he so often put it), 'A big rig-a-ma-roo.'

Family members gravely awaited the Doctor's results, but, it seems that the Doctor's only diagnosis was that he had a slight cold, which congested his lungs The Doctor also said, 'he's out lived everything that can kill him,' For his age. 'I'd say he's doing a hundred'. When the nurse asked for his height, someone said 5'8" but Mr. Turner quickly intervened saying 6'2". He doesn't appear to be as tall as he once was but it only takes one glance to tell that he is every bit as proud, and as dignified.

This article is a special 'tribute to Mr. Turner from his grandchildren and great grandchildren who wish to say, 'Grandpa, we hope you live forever, and as far as we are concerned, you will!' Love, Your Grandchildren and Great-Grandchildren"

October 27, 2004

Joe Turner married Sibbie Metcalf, who was born August 12, 1887. Her parents were Mr. and Mrs. Sam Metcalf. I tried to find out Mrs. Sam Metcalfe's maiden name, but have not, if you have information, please contact me. She died February 9, 1992. Joe and Sibbie Turner had seven children: Beatrice, Victor, L. C., Robert, Jewell, Mildred and Vernon. All are deceased today except Mildred. Joe and Sibbie, both, were buried in the Allmon Cemetery near Detroit, AL.

Mrs. Sibbie Metcalf Turner professed a hope in Christ at an early age and later united with the Freewill Baptist Church, where she remained a faithful member, and served as "Mother of the Church" until her death. At her death, she was survived by two daughters; Jewell Turner of Detroit, AL and Mildred Truelove of Vernon, AL; one son, Vernon Turner of Hamilton, AL; one sister, Quiller Watkins of Hamilton, AL; one brother, Clay Metcalf of Memphis, TN; 14 grandchildren, 21 great-grandchildren, one great-great-grandchild, three daughters-in-law, and a host of nieces, nephews and other relatives and friends.

Source: *The Lamar Democrat and Sulligent News* Wednesday, January 22, 1986.and obituary for Sibbie Turner.

Jeremiah and John Michael Vail

History is recorded by someone who is literate and dedicated enough to write it down or by word of mouth from one generation to another. Most of our ancestry information is recorded by word of mouth. This Vail narrative is from a book researched by Andrew Jackson Vail (born 1907 and died 1990 over a twenty year period. His relatives complied the book from his many notes. This book is titled *Descendants of William Vale/Vail and his twin sons, Jeremiah and John Michael*.

Lida E. Logan has researched a book by the title of *Three Vail Brothers and their Descendants*. MS. Logan's book is not as extensive as Mr. Vail's book. Both books can be found in the Mary Wallace Cobb Library in Vernon, Alabama.

Other contributors to this narrative are my sister Ada Faye Bryant and many relatives who have been patient enough to help me dig for pictures and answer my many questions on relatives that they have in their memories.

The story goes that an immigrant by the name of Wilmot came from Ireland after returning home from the Seven Year War to find his wife with a child not his own. Wilmot married an Elizabeth. The hearsay is uncertain whether Wilmot was a Vale/Vail Faille or whether this was Elizabeth's last name. There seems to be controversary whether the last name was actually Vale/Vail/Faille. The consensus seems to be that there was only one child from this union William Vail.

Married Indian Girls Of The Catawba Tribe

Supposedly, William Vail was abducted by Indians as a small child. This hearsay has been handed down to the generations by almost every segment of the family. It was said that William married a daughter of King Haigler of the Catawba tribe in the Lancaster District of South Carolina. William had twin sons with the Indian wife. During Indian strife after the death of King Haigler, he and the twin boys escaped and went to the home of his mother Elizabeth Vale/Vail/Faille. He, a wife and the boys were listed in the 1790 census. William and twin boys, Jeremiah and John Michael, and other children were listed in the home of Elizabeth Vale in the 1800 census. The consensus is that the William Vail family moved back and forth between the Indian camp and Elizabeth's home.

There is a story that Jeremiah also married Indian girls and had a child. The Indian wife was drowned in a river. He then married Mary Funderburk. In the 1820 and 1830 census, Jeremiah is listed as head of the household with wife Mary and seven children.

John Michael Vail married Rachael Funderburk, sister to Mary. He is listed in the 1820 Pickens County, Alabama census with wife, Rachael and three sons. A later Pickens County, Alabama census lists John Michael and Rachael's children as Jacob Hiram, William Melton, Joshua V, Jeremiah, John M., Irvin A. Nathaniel, Henry, Jonas H. and Mary A.

There is record of John Michael purchasing and selling land in Lancaster County, SC.

Fist Cuffs and Court Appearances Left for Alabama

Supposedly John Michael and Jeremiah both had some controversaries with neighbors which led to fist cuffs and court appearances. Sometime after that the twins and their families, perhaps some brothers, along with the Funderburks and others left South Carolina. Note of interest is the twins were in their forties when they made the trip to Alabama. The move probably took place around 1836. John Michael and family appeared in the 1840 Pickens County, Alabama census. Both Vail brothers, their children and the Funderburks purchased land in what is today upper Pickens County and lower Lamar County, Alabama. Many of these lands are still owned by the twin's descendants.

The children of the twins seem to have migrated to Mississippi, Louisiana, Arkansas and Oklahoma. This migration was probably caused by lands being freed up further west they went. During the early 1800's Alabama seems to have been a stopping place for many families from the Carolina's.

There has been confusion as to how many Jacob Hiram Vails existed. Some say two and some say three. If there was a third, he was probably a child of one of the twin's children. My grandfather and brothers said that their great-great grandfather was John Michael Vail.

My line comes from John Michael consequently so the rest of this narrative will be about his descendants. John Michael Vail disappeared from the Pickens County, Alabama sometime between the 1840 and 1950 census. The story is that he left to go to Chicago, reason unknown and never returned. This trip remains a mystery today. John Michael would have been between 50 and 60 years of age. In the Pickens County, Alabama census, wife Rachael is listed with three children.

Jacob Hiram Vail Esquire

John Michael's oldest son, Jacob Hiram Vail Esquire married Sara Marilza Coleman. He was my great great grandfather. Not a lot is known about him except he did own lots of land and was reputed to be a money lender. The Esquire attached to his name tends to lead one to believe that he was considered to be affluent. The children of Jacob Hiram and Sarah M. are William M., Jesse Malcomb, Andrew Jackson, Francis Marion (Frank), Mary F., and Jacob Hiram (Jake), Burrell B., Rachel Jane, Thomas, Thomas G., and Faith M. E. Some of their children stayed in the now Pickens and Lamar Counties and some left and went to Louisiana and Arkansas.

Jacob Hiram Vail, known as Jake, was my great-grandfather. He owned property about a mile east of the Springhill Church in lower Lamar County, Alabama. Jake married Henrietta Caldwell.

Old Man, Long Hair, Long White Beard Sat on Porch

Jake was a farmer as well as I have been able to determine. I remember him as an old man who sat on his front porch with long white hair and a very long white beard. I was only two years old when he died. My mother said I could not remember him. I conceded that was a young age for such a memory, so who was this old man? She relented that it must have been grandpa.

I remember my great grandma Henrietta, only as a very old lady, who was at the family's home place and also at her son's, my great uncle Lee Vail. I do not think they were very well off.

She Asked Grandma if She had Seen Anyone Milking Her Cow

There is a story about Henrietta and my great grandma Sophia Dawkins. Sophia's cow kept not giving milk. She knew the cow had milk, because she could see the bag as it filled. When she would go in the evening to milk, there was very little milk. She asked Grandma Henrietta if she had seen anyone milking her cow. Grandma Henrietta confessed she had been milking the cow because her cow was dry and she needed milk for her babies. They shared the cow until Grandma Henrietta's cow came in. Interesting to note, Sophia was a young widow with five children.

Jake and Henrietta had ten children. They were: Bessie Beatrice, William Walton, Frances Elmo, Jacob Lee, Henry Glenn, Annie Marilza, Jesse Lewis, George Washington, Velma and Mary Etta.

Bessie Vail Went to Bed and Died

Bessie Vail married Oscar (Bud) Ponds when she was fairly young. She and Uncle Bud had five children. During a bad flu epidemic she nursed everyone in the family as they came down with the flu. When she had the last one on their feet, she went to bed and died. Her children were partially raised by Jake and Henrietta.

William Walton Vail was my granddaddy. He married Ada Octavia Dawkins. The interesting story about their courtship is they both stayed home with their parents and helped raise their siblings before they married. They were in their early thirties when they married. They had one child, my mother, Nell Vail who married Manly Thomas Bryant.

There are other stories from Walton, Ada, Nell and Manly. These stories are for another day. This narrative was intended to give a small synopsis of Jeremiah and John Michael Vail and their descendants. Written in 2004 and submitted by Flora Bryant McCool.

Laura Veal

Girl Found Mysteriously Killed Near Sulligent Past Week
Murder is Suspected.

A young girl, Laura Veal, was found strangely killed about three miles from Sulligent, between, Sulligent and Gattman, late last Tuesday afternoon.

The girl's body was found dangling from a tree just back of the barn owned by Mr. Willy Karr. A plow line had been tied around her throat and tied to a small branch of a tree, where her feet were just off the ground. She was probably killed in some mysterious way, or strangled and tied to the tree.

The girl had been missing since last Thursday, almost a week ago. Her body was found frozen stiff, where it had been hanging for probably five days. The body was found about 200 yards from the home of Mr. Karr, where she was living at the time of her death.

Miss Veal came to Alabama about a year ago and resided with her brother in Pine Springs community. She had been living at the Karr place almost 60 days before her body was found by one of the members of the Karr family.

She is reported to have been rather moody and left the Karr home early last Thursday after some disagreement. When her body was found last week, it was hanging from a small branch, by an old, worn out plow line and branches were broken off as evidence that the girl climbed up the tree and jumped.

An investigation was made by the officers but they were uncertain as whether she had been murdered or had committed suicide. Several answers that the officers received during the investigation were confusing."

Source: *The Amory Advertiser*, Amory, Mississippi, January 30, 1936

Edmond W. Vernon

It seems the search for information on the late Edmond W. Vernon,

(1825-1897) the Englishman for whom the town of Vernon, Alabama is named, and Vernon's first mayor was slow to come. The town of Vernon was first called Swayne or Swaynesville. It has been 109 years since the death of Edmond W. Vernon, who is buried in Fayette County in the Bluff community at Bethel Baptist Cemetery.

He settled land in Lamar County just west of Hightogy off of Highway 17, between Millport and Vernon. It was strickly by accident that we found his burial spot. A confederate foot marker with his name and company was dropped off at Walnut Grove Cemetery next to Ida Vernon Cole's headstone, who is my grandmother. We didn't even know her father's name at the time that was found, so this made us wonder. So, the search began with help from Howard Rector, formerly of Lamar County.

Edmond Vernon was married to Amy Hartin. Their union produced three children. Then Amy died. Edmond then married Elizabeth Corbett, whose husband died after they had three children together. Elizabeth and Edmond had four children together. Elizabeth is buried with him at Bethel. Amy's burial place is unknown at the present time. My grandmother was the third child of Amy and Edmond. There are many descendants of the Vernon: locally the Crawfords, Corbetts, Duboses, Moores, Wheelers and Coles to name a few.

One of the biggest surprises came when Lowell Wheeler responded to my invitation to attend the monthly meeting in Vernon of the Lamar County Genealogical & Historical Society. He brought a large fine, family heirloom picture of Edmond W. Vernon. In addition to his serving as Vernon's first mayor, Edmond also served as a U. S. mail carrier.

This is where we are todate (2006). If anyone has any further information, please pass it along. Submitted by Jake Cole, great grandson of Edmond W. Vernon 742 Narrows Point Circle, Birmingham, AL 35242

W. W. Waldrop

W. W. Waldrop in Millport

W. W. Waldrop, a man who meant much to Millport, Alabama , serving on the town council for 28 years. He was elected by write in votes, when he was away from Millport. He was known to be a "workhorse" for the town. He also worked for the county and his friends. Productive was a word which described him.

Mr. Waldrop built the first electric light plant in Millport and was a Ford dealer there from 1916 until 1942. He also served one term in the Alabama Legislature. He was a Justice of the Peace, and Notary Public. He handled Millport Trade Day Promotions for 63 consecutive weeks, was a Democrat and served on the Democratic Executive committee 20 years.

Mr. Waldrop was married to the former Bertha Conner of Millport. .Baseball was his hobby and he played on and managed semi-pro teams all over northwest Alabama. Source: *Alabama Municipal Journal* October, 1962.

A. A. Wall

Mr. A. A. Wall, formerly of the Courier was in town Saturday. Mr. Wall is now engaged in the mercantile business at Sulligent with the reliable firm of Rush & Clearman. This firm has just laid in a full stock for the fall trade and when you want to by the best goods for the least money, call on Mr.

Wall, who will wait on you to his usual pleasing and affable manner. Source: *The Vernon Courier*, September 28, 1888

Wall – Summers Wedding

Knowing the "Local's" constitutional modesty and that his many anxious friends abroad, would go uninformed of the auspicious pageant foretelling we hope a long sunlit summer of happy fortunes, unless some looker-on recorded it, we take upon ourselves the office of informing al and singular that the lucky Alex. A. Wall has drawn one of the richest prizes in the lottery of life in binding himself in the golden chains of wedlock, with one of Alabama's fairest daughters, Miss Aggie Summers. Wednesday evening, Nov. 12th, was one long to be remembered in the annuals of Vernon romances. The consummation of the hopes, and the hapy reward of the loyalty and love of manly excellence and womanly loveliness. The day which had wailed itself away in lowering clouds and fitful showers, gave place to the mild radiance of a serence night, while in the azure expanse of the heavens, the stars smiled knindly down upon the "beauty and the chivalry" of Vernon assembled at the Home of Mr. A. A. Summers to witness the espousals of the happy pair. At early candle light groups of guests could be seen flitting here and there through the illuminated mansion awaiting with eager expectancy the approaching ceremony. At 8 o'clock the buzz of voices ceased and the groups condensed themselves into a silent mass as the bride and groom were ushered into the parlor. Each attired in simple elegance of costume, each calm and self-possessed. The marriage ritual of the Methodist Church was performed by the Rev. Mr. Miller in a solemn and impressive manner. Then swelled the `chorus of congratulations. The hearty hand shaking of manly friends. The bubbling mellifluous kisses rained upon the radiant face of the bride by her fair friends while youthful gallants looked on longingly and said mentally while every kiss was delivered: "Oh, that a few could be invested with us, for it is the exercise we are pining for!" For some time the hum of conversation and silvery peals of youthful mirth swelled upon the night, but a hush again fell upon the crowd when the doors of the banqueting hall were thrown open and a display of artistic elegance blazed upon the entranced vision of the beholders! Lucullus or Apicius would have gone into raptures over the scene. The long table groaning beneath the weight of choicest viands, so plentifully yet so tastefully spread demonstrated the magic touches of woman's beautifying hands. The seductive array of the most elegant and delicious cakes that culinary ingenuity could devise; some gleaming in their snowy coats of icing, some gay in tasteful devices and figures of confectionery, garnished with such domestiables as salads of different varieties, creams, and ambrosia that would have delighted a sociable of Olympian deities formed both a scene of beauty to the aesthetical mind and none of Paradise to the epicure. Above all and greatly enhancing the joy of all, the presiding deities of this festive Elysium shone prominent. The dignified courtesy of the lady hostess, the genial manners of the hose, and the ready wit, engaging manners and sprightly vivacity of their fair daughter, Miss Donnie, who applied herself to the wants of the guests with the grace and airiness of Hebe herself, will long remembered by those who shared the festivities of that happy night. "But all that is bright must fade." after a merry round of sprightly games the entertainment closed and as the "state dials pointed to morn" all wended their way homeward, sated and happy souls. - A Friend Source: *The Vernon Clipper*, November 14, 1879.

Ward Family

Died of pneumonia last week, Mr. Robt Ward and Friday night his son S. W. Ward. The above deceased leaves widows and orphrans to mourn their departure. Source *The Lamar News* January 10, 1884

Dumas Webb

Sulligent Al, March 7 (Abt 1891)
News reached this place today of the killing of Dumas Webb by his brother Jack Webb, five miles from here. The circumstances of the killing as gathered by your correspondent are as follows: The farm on whom Jack was living and which belongs to his father was cultivated last year by Dumas. When Dumas moved off the place he put the rent corn into the crib and left it there for his father, who resides in Itawamba County, MS. In passing the place now and then, he noticed that the corn was being taken by someone and he nailed the door up hard and fast. Yesterday morning he went over again and on arriving found his brother Jack and (Jack's) wife in the crib Shelling Corn. This led to a quarrel between the two, when Jack went to the house got his Winchester rifle and taking diliberate aim at Dumas shot him through the heart. Mr. Joseph Bilbo Webb, grandson of Dumas, relates that during the argument, Jack's wife tried to keep Dumas from chasing Jack into the house and was tugging at him by his coat

sleeves. This sufficiently slowed him down to allow Jack to return from the house with his rifle. Dumas came up the porch and Jack lowered the gun. Dumas told him, "Shoot or be damned!" Jack shot, and the rest of the story follows. No one was present but the two brothers and Jack's wife, who told this story to some person. Jack and wife bundled up their traps and left the country at once. They told to some of the neighbors on the road what had happened and claimed Dumas was rushing him with an open knife when he shot him. A crowd of neighbors went to the scene of the tragedy and found Dumas' dead body which had been lying there since early in the morning until 2 o'clock p.m. Dumas Webb was a quiet personable citizen while his brother Jack has a character not to be envied. He had been living in Indian nation for the last year and had just moved back a short time ago. Source: Birmingham Age Herald date unknown (Incident happened in Lost Creek Community near Sulligent.)

Jack Webb

Jack Webb an old bachelor miser, died near Sulligent, Ala., the other day. He left a will directing that the money which he left, four thousand dollars, should be expended in keeping fresh the grave of Frances Stewart, his sweetheart, who died fifty years ago upon the eve of their wedding day. There is an instance of true love such as is very rare in this age. Source: November 2, 1895, *Bay City Times* (Bay City, Michigan)

Joseph and Lucinda Emiline Evans Webb

Lucinda Emiline Evans, known as Emiline, was born in Marion County, Alabama, on November 9, 1836. She was the oldest child of Thomas Evans' second marriage. She had older half-siblings, but she was the oldest of the ten children of Thomas and Lucinda Webb Evans. The family grew up in what is today Lamar County, Alabama, in the Pine Springs and Lost Creek communities just northwest of the town of Sulligent.

In about 1858, she married Joseph Webb (at least one descendant says his full name was Joseph Henry Webb, but we have not been able to confirm this yet).

At about the same time they married or just before the marriage, Joseph bought 198 acres of land north of the Evans Cemetery on a branch of the Lost Creek. This land lies on Chapel Road today. In 1860 Joseph and

Emiline bought 119 more acres adjoining their land. By then, they had their first child, Mary Lucinda, born in 1859 and their second, Martha Jane, just before the Civil War, in 1860. From the 1860 census, it appears that Joseph and Emaline were raising her younger siblings. We know that Thomas Evans died in 1856, and Lucinda Webb Evans must have died too or she would have her children with her at that young age.

During the war, Joseph served in 2 Miss CAV CSA. Emiline and Joseph had Will Tom Webb born during the war, in 1863, and then Hiram Dave Webb born right after the war in 1865. Then Henry Ben Webb born in 1867; Jeptha K born in 1868 or 1870; Green Wesley Webb born in either 1870 or 1871; John L. Webb born in 1877, and Ardavilla Clementine Webb in 1878.

In a local paper from 1879, we have been told that Joseph, who supposedly had a new team of horses which ran away with him, wrecked his wagon and was killed in the accident. This information is from a newspaper article in the Vernon Clipper 1879-1880 which states that Joseph Webb died in an accident with a wagon and team on Nov. 21, 1879. He was from the Pine Springs area and is buried in the Evans Cemetery in the Lost Creek Community.

Immediately after Joseph's death, Emiline is listed as the household head in 1880 census. After this, it seems that Emiline moved to Oklahoma with her family. Apparently all her children went to Oklahoma with her, though we do not know for sure. We do not think Emiline married again. She died in Southeastern Oklahoma on October 21, 1913. Source: Research of Dave Webb and Barb Carruth

Weeks

A white man named Weeks was committed to jail by Justice Stanford at Brown's Beat, last week on the charge of bringing stolen property in to the State. The property was a mule which was identified and claimed by Mr. Medford, of Corrinth, Miss. The grand jury returned an indictment accordingly and Mr. Weeks was brought before Judge Sprott Saturday to have a day set for trial, but he was not ready for trial this term, so his case was set for the second day of the next term, and he was released under $250 bond. Source: *The Vernon Courier*, September 28, 1888

Dug Wells

Sulligent, Alabama, February 7. Dug Wells, a Negro, who lived about 3 miles from this place, was killed yesterday evening, about night, by Marion Bankhead another Negro. Bankhead went to Wells house and called him out to the gate, where he raised a quarrel with him and after bandying a few words he drew his knife and stabbed Wells in the neck killing him in a few minutes. Bankhead has not been captured. Well's relatives have put out a reward of $50 for his arrest. Source: *The Vernon Courier*, February 10, 1898

Susie Davis Wells

On Tuesday, October 7, Susie Wells would have turned 78 years of age. Born in Sulligent, she was the last surviving child and youngest of the ten children born to Tob and Hattie Davis, who, also had been farmers. Mrs. Wells died on Monday, September 1st in Shadescrest Healthcare Center, Jasper. She had been in declining health for some years following a series of strokes.

Born Susie Louise Davis, on October 7, 1925, she and her nine siblings were born to sharecroppers, who later purchased 80 acres of farmland in Sulligent. She was the fifth daughter and youngest of the ten children, in addition to her five sibling brothers. Her predeceased brothers were Leroy, Grafton, Chorch, William Gannor, and Joseph Oliver. All except Grafton lived and resided in Cleveland, Ohio, who lived in Brighton, Alabama with his family. Her predeceased sisters were Growdie Davis and Mistory Darnell of Detroit, Michigan and Estelle Gainey, Annie Lee Kennedy of Brighton.

As a young woman, she married Kelsie Wells in 1947. She was twenty-two years of age. He was a WWII veteran. She became a step-mother to his children. O'Clay, who remarked at her funeral held on Thursday, September 11, that throughout her childhood she knew that on her birthday, she would always be remembered with something thoughtful from her step-mother.

Her brother Grafton had seven children. Two of his sons, Leon and Lee Ander, often spent their childhood summers with their maternal grandparents Houston and Ada Thompson. They often visited their Aunt Susie who was noted for her cooking.

During their thirty-three years of marriage Susie and her husband Kelsie were active members of Powell Chapel C.M.E. Church. They were also active participants in the West Alabama Union Singing Convention. They kept and nurtured a nephew in their home, Mr. William Darnell.

According to family lore, her father, Tob was one of the few literate men in the late 1800's and passed on the thirst for knowledge to his children, who in turn passed it onto the next generation. As a share cropper, he had two children in college. He made ends meet by cutting cross ties for the railroad. Two of the children attended college, with Leroy attending Miles College in Birmingham and Mistory a woman's college.

During the Depression, Tob Davis passed away and it was Grafton, the second of five sons, who with the assistance of their maternal grandmother, Fannie Johnson, purchased the family land, where Susie grew up. It is still in the family.

His mantra of "get an education, so you can prosper" came true with their sacrifices for the 4th and 5th generation, Today those children are graduates of such colleges as Miles, Johnson C. Smith University, Clark Atlanta University, Spelman College, Quinnipiac University, Houston Tillison University and University of Alabama. In. addition, to her stepchildren and ward, Susie is survived by seven nephews and nieces, respectively, along with several great nieces and nephews. She was a lady who had a marvelous laugh and a sense of wonder.

During a span of her illness, Mrs. Wells lived in the home and on the home place Wells estate with her nephew, Mr. William Darnell, Sulligent, AL. Source: *The Lamar Democrat*, October 8, 2003.

A. J. Wheeler

As an evidence of the rapid advance of real estate in Vernon, Mr. A. J. Wheeler has refused an offer of $500 for a two-acre lot lying southeast of the court house, through which the survey of the Tombigbee road runs. He holds it at $700. Source: *The Lamar News*, May 5, 1887.

Andy Wheeler

Uncle Andy Wheeler proposes to drink his own water. Source: *The Vernon Pioneer* July 19, 1878.

Uncle Andy Wheeler has quit the "mill business" and gone into the "poultry business". He had such good success with his chickens in Columbus last week that he has gone again this. Those who have chickens to dispose of can find ready market for same by applying to A. J. Wheeler. Source: *The Lamar News*, September 23, 1886.

William Chester Wheeler

The Journey To Find My 2x Great Grandfather's Photograph

I have some very exciting news! Like many times before, I was at my 91 year old grandmother Charlene Wheeler's house. I decided to go through every one of her photo albums to make digital copies of any photo that she had and could remember who was in the photos so that those photos would not be lost to memory once she was gone. I made over 200 digital images of her photos. Some, she could not remember who was in the photos and some were labeled, which helped. Sometimes she is forgetful in her young age of 91 however; that night something triggered in her and her memory was awesome! She and I sat from 4 p.m. till around 2 a.m. going through her old albums. I could tell she really enjoyed herself. I know I enjoyed myself.

The highlight of that day for me (besides spending quality time with her) was turning the page to find an old tintype with a label underneath the photo that said "Check's grandfather, Grandfather Wheeler." Check is what they called my grandfather, William Chester Wheeler. I knew right away what I was looking at because I have searched for many years in hopes to find a photo of this man, my 2 times Great-Grandfather. I was looking at a tintype photo of Jesse Wheeler and his wife E.C. Wheeler and their child.

A little back story if you will......... When I first started in my family research there was one name that really stuck out to me. Jesse Wheeler, from Hall County, Ga. Jesse was born in Hall County, Ga. but moved to Lamar County in the 1850s. His headstone says that he was in Company D of the 26th Alabama Infantry during what many now refer to as the Civil War. Jesse is buried at Mt. Zion in Lamar County. The first time I visited his grave was a very emotional day for me. I was standing at his grave in amazement that so many years after he was laid to rest I was meeting him (so to speak) for the first time! I envisioned him going to church there a few feet away from his grave in the little church building. I   envisioned so many things that he would have lived through in the 1800s. I thought about what he may have looked like. I could just see these things in my mind and felt compelled to learn more about him and also the 26th Alabama Infantry.

As it would turn out information on him was limited. I searched everywhere for a photo of him but could not find one anywhere that I looked. A local book about the first settlers had his parents wrong and sent me on a 3 year wild goose chase. I eventually figured out that the book had his parents listed wrongly and once I figured that out many doors started to open. I was able to track him back to Hall County, Ga. and found photos of some of this brothers but never much on him.

Over the years of researching my family and obsessing with Jesse and also the 26 Alabama Infantry I started to realize that I had a rather large collection of photos and documents from the 26th Alabama. I started a facebook page dedicated to the men of the 26th in hopes that I could help others find photos or documents on their ancestor, and admittedly, I hoped one day someone would come to my page and have a photo of my ancestor. I can tell you that I feel a great deal of joy when someone comes to my page and tells me that because of my page they have seen a photo of their ancestor for the first time or the final resting place of their ancestor.

For years I have added things to that page as I found them and have tons more to add from my records as I have time but I was starting to think that I would never find a photo of my ancestor, Jesse Wheeler. Maybe a photo of him didn't exist. Maybe it did, but was not labeled and I would never have a way of knowing. I won't say I was losing hope but I will say that I felt like my chances were slim. My only hope was the advances in technology on the internet with websites such as ancestry.com and other sites where users are always adding new photos and information.

Now, here I was this weekend with my eyes and mouth wide open! Looking face to face with a man I have researched for many, many hours. I was in amazement all over again even more than when I stood at his grave. I found it! There he was with his wife and child!

I will say here that I was beyond happy that the photo was labeled underneath it because right away I had a question about the child. The child appeared to be in a dress of some sort. The child's age was too young to be the last girl child of Jesse. I had heard about boys wearing "dresses" or "gowns" back in the old days. I even have a photo from the 1920's of my grandfather on my mom's side wearing what appears to be a gown of some type. I guess this was common practice among young children due to an ease of changing them. That said, I wanted to be sure so I sent copies of the photo to three different people whom I consider experts in styles of the day, photos of the day and just experts in general when it comes to old photographs such as this. I did not give them any information on the photo and all three came back and dated the photo as being late 1860s through very early 1870s. That fit in perfect with the age of the man in the photo along with when he died, around 1871.

What about the child? ....Well all three said they felt it was a boy. One said the boots appeared to be that of a girl but still felt it was a boy due to a side part in the hair rather than a middle part which was common in girls of the day and which can also be seen on the woman in the photo. I was also told that poor families would use hand me downs and that the boots the child were wearing could quite possibly be left over from the child's sister a few years earlier.

With everything checking out with the photo I was very happy. I just wanted to be sure, even though it was labeled.

On top of all of that, my grandmother saw the excitement that I had when finding the old tintype so she told me I could have it. It is now one of my most prized possessions. I will cherish it from now till my dying day.

Thank you Maw, Love You!

If you made it to the end of this long post I want to thank you. I had to share my joy and excitement and let it also be known that if you are looking for something on an ancestor to NEVER give up that search. You may find what you are looking for and it may be right under your nose somewhere like this photo. Submitted and written by Joe Wheeler. http://joewheelers.blogspot.com/

White

Buck White will resume his school at Pine Springs on Monday the 20th instant. Source: *The Vernon Pioneer*, May 26, 1876.

Professor James F. White has a fine school at Bexar, Marion Co. His Vernon friends will ever rejoice in his prosperity .Source: *The Vernon Pioneer* May 26, 1876

J. E. A & Rody Pennington Wilson

J. E. A. Wilson married Rody Pennington Wilson. He was born January, 1861 in Fayette County, Alabama. J. E. A. and Rody were married July 1884 at Furnace Church in Vernon, Alabama by Rev. I. N. Kemp.

Rody was the daughter of Rena Pennington. Rena was a slave and it is said that her father was a white man.

We have no information on J. E. A. Wilson before their marriage in 1884 in Lamar County.

J. E. A. Wilson and Rody Wilson

L. M. Wimberly

Rev. L. M. Wimberly, Primitive Baptist minister, grandfather of Maggie Lee Hayes, owned and operated the first hotel in Vernon, Alabama about 1870. Stagecoaches on their way to Mobile, Alabama from Nashville, Tennessee stopped overnight at the inn. Charges were 25 cents for overnight plus supper and breakfast. Fifteen cents to lodge and fee your horse. Source: *History of Lamar County Alabama* written by Joe Acee, 4th Revised Edition, published by The Lamar Democrat Vernon, Alabama

Jessie Woolbright Woods

My Sister – My Friend

I'm missing my sister Jessie, I have wanted to call her many, many times to tell her something........then I remember....... She had a personal relationship with Jesus, we often discussed our faith, how our faith gets us through all the things we are faced with while living our lives. We both questioned how a person makes it without Jesus.

She took treatments because she wanted to live as long as she could. She loved her family, loved watching the grands and great grands grow into young adults. But after her last chemo and all the complications started....she changed her mind. About two weeks ago, she prayed, asking God, that if she could not be able take care of herself, would He please take her to heaven. God honored her request, for that I am thankful.

My sister wasn't like me.....she was quiet, not outspoken at all, believed in staying at home, a wonderful homemaker, she truly knew how to make a "home". We all relied on her expertise and advice when things went wrong. After our mother died, she became my second mother.

Jessie was a true stay-at-home person, she went to church, grocery shopped and that was about it. The rest of the time she was home "working", cooking, taking care of her home, vegetable gardening, preserving those vegetables, tending to her flowers or doing crafts, such as crocheting, in the past she has created beautiful crochet pieces of art. She was a master seamstress and mender, for family, she gave many pairs of pants, new life....that otherwise would have been thrown in the garbage. My son Berney has sneaked pants out to her house, asking her to mend for him, even though I told him to not bother her.

She loved to read, her most enjoyable reading material was the Bible, her Sunday school book and magazines, always being interested in new recipes, sewing projects, natural remedies for any health problems one might have, house tips for better keeping the house. She was always quick to share these tips with all of us. I once heard her daughter, Tammy Woods, say "She's better than Google." That's true because we knew she weeded out the bad and only told us the good, which is better than Google. We all trusted and respected her....now....we didn't always do as she told us, but in most situations, we should have.

If she ever sat down, she told me, "I feel guilty, I should be doing something." I smile when I think of a few years ago when she bought an iPad and soon became addicted to Facebook! She was a silent "facebooker", but it helped her keep up with family and friends that she didn't get to see often. She loved seeing pictures people posted of their flowers and crafts too. She soon overcame that guilty feeling when she was on Facebook, enjoying it every day.

Being an older sister of almost 17 years, and because I am hyperactive, for as long as I can remember, Jessie tried to make me "sit down and be quiet," not talk so much, stay at home and do more things around the house instead of being "out and about" all the time. I have always enjoyed having an older sister, when mother was alive, I loved to introduce Jessie as "my mother" and my mother as "my grandmother", just to aggravate her. After about 64 years she finally gave up trying to change me, and began to accept me as I am. A turning point in our relationship happened on a Sunday afternoon, Mrs. Clytee Jaggers and Jessie accompanied me to accept a community service award presented by Daughters of American Revolution. I'll never forget on the way home Jessie said "Well I guess all the times you have been away from home, you have been doing good things," from that day forward, we have enjoyed each other so much.

Before then, we loved each other as sisters, but not friends, when she breathed that last breath, I lost one of my closest friends.

After her husband, William, and our mother died, I asked her to help me in my community service, she finally decided it might just be good to get away from the house and be involved in something other than home and church. I remember at the Rube Burrow Gathering in Sulligent, several years ago. I asked Jessie, Laura Trimm and Sue Norton to help us in welcoming people to the exhibits. They were all nervous about being there, but they did fine and it was a great day. Jessie became very willing to go with me and to help, when I volunteered for something, getting myself into a pinch, she was there to help me and cheer me on. She did think I needed to learn the word "no", but she helped me anyway. Like one time when I needed her to help fold our Lamar County Genealogical & Historical Society's newsletters and get them ready to mail in a very short time.

I have many memories of our times together, but this one is a favorite. About two weeks before her death, we had a scare, we thought she was going to die, there in the hospital room, after Tammy, her daughter arrived, I was going to leave to go home, when I leaned over her bed telling her good bye, she said "If I don't see you anymore here, I will see you in Heaven". As I nodded, I thought about the many times she has told me through the years "You think you know everything" (I ask you what could have made her think that, I'm not bossy, I just have better ideas), so I said to her "Jessie, you know if you get to heaven before I do…you will know something, I don't know". For a moment her face was blank, then a smile covered her face and she glowed. She said "Yes, but I won't be able to tell you about it." I replied, "I'm not sure about how everything will be in heaven, but if there is a way that you can get word back to me, will you do it?" Jessie said "I sure will." She also told me that she had always loved me…just didn't want me to know! This past Monday, when she was in end of life, lying there, with her eyes closed, and so still, I learned over her, saying "I love you" then I said "Jessie remember what we said about heaven…. if you get there first….about …..letting me know"……she heard me…she nodded yes.

Jessie was firstborn, to Jack and Lula Bell King Woolbright on December 30, 1928 in Monroe County, Mississippi "Just across the line" (Mississippi/Alabama state line) from the Shiloh North or Lost Creek Community, where she lived about 87 years. Jessie left for her eternal home on March 1, 2016.

In her young years, she experienced the birth of a sister, Sarah Kathleen, on October 28, 1932 and then the death of this little sister on June 25, 1934. Later in 1941, her mother and dad gave her a little brother, Bobby. In 1945, at a time when my mother thought her family was complete, with two children, she found she was with child. My mother was not so happy about having another child, but God doesn't make any mistakes, so I was blessed to be born into this family. My mother always told me. "I didn't want you, I didn't want another baby, I cried and cried, when I found I was going to have you." In later years, mother said "I didn't want you, but I'm so glad I have you." Even though I heard this story growing up, I never felt "not loved."

Jessie graduated from Sulligent High School in April of 1947. After high school, in June, she began studies at Draughon's Business College in Birmingham, Alabama. In 1879, Professor John F. Draughon realized the need for business-trained people. With very little capital, a horse, a wagon and the teaching materials that were available at that time, he founded Draughon's Practical Business College on wheels. He made a monthly circuit of towns in Northern Middle Tennessee and Southern Kentucky for several years before opening his permanent school in Nashville. From this humble beginning of his business college on wheels, he started one of the largest chains of business colleges in the nation. His business schools were located in practically every Southern and Western state, including the Oklahoma territory and the Indian Territory. After Professor Draughon's death in 1921, many of the business schools he established merged with other schools or went out of business. After the war, under new management, Draughon's Business College again assumed its role in the community to train secretaries, accountants and other qualified business personnel. In 1954, the School was accredited by the Accrediting Commission for Business Schools, which was recognized by the United States Office of Education as the accrediting agency for this type of school. In 1978, Draughons was accredited as a junior college of business by the Accrediting Council for Independent Colleges and Schools.

Living in Birmingham, working as a secretary, after business school, Jessie met the love of her life William Thomas Woods, who grew up near Vernon, Alabama. After serving in the United States Army, William was living there, employed as a bus operator for the city of Birmingham. They were married February 12, 1949 in Winfield, Alabama by Reverend Wallace Lovett.

Sulligent Manufacturing Company or McCoy Manufacturing Company opened in Sulligent, Alabama in May of 1953, according to a newspaper article in *The Lamar Democrat* April 23, 1953. The pants factory began operation with approximately 150 employees and manufactured youth pants. Jessie and William moved to Sulligent, not too long after the plant opening, where Jessie took a job as bookkeeper, later on she was bookkeeper at Detroit Slacks in Detroit, Alabama. After several years Jessie quit the bookkeeping job, becoming a full-time wife and mother, wearing many different hats, doing whatever needed to be done while living on a cattle farm. Jessie was a strong, independent woman, showing courage, compassion and dedication to those around her.

Having a sister almost 17 years older, proved to be a bonus, because in later years, she did become my second mother, we made each day count during those last months, taking one day at a time, loving each other.

Lula Bell King Woolbright

09-22-2004

Sunday, September 19, 2004, was a special day. My mother, Lula King Woolbright celebrated her 93rd birthday with a quiet day at home. Friends and family dropped by during the day to wish her well. My sister, Jessie Woods baked and frosted a delicious cake for her. She left it in the kitchen and we all enjoyed it, by night time it was gone.

I hesitated to write about my mother in this column, but I am reminded of my cousin Donald King's response when I asked him to do a favor for me. I said "I don't want to be any trouble, but." Donald said, "No use to have kin folks, if you can't use them." So there's no use in writing, if I can't write about my mother. She has always been there for our family, through the good times and bad. It seems as if she has lived for us. She cooked most of my meals for me for years after I married and ironed for me until she was in her eighties. We do not know how many quilts she has quilted for us, but it is many. She has taught us and is still teaching us the true meaning of love. We have seen her love for us in so many different ways. I cannot begin to list them.

A little background on mother, just in case you don't know, she was born September 19, 1911 to Willie Washington "Wash" and Sarah Telitha Evans King. She was one of 10 children. Her brothers are: (1) Clarence, (2) Claude, (3) Clyde, (4) Carl and (5) Clay King. Her sisters are: (6) Pearl, (7) Connie, (8) Ruby, (9) Louise. All are deceased except mother and Louise. Louise lives in Virginia Beach, Virginia and calls on the phone often. Mother married Hobbie Lee (Jack) Woolbright on October 23, 1927. They were married almost 62 years when he died suddenly on October 10, 1989. I have a sister Jessie and a brother Bobby. We have a sister, Kathleen, who died as a young child. Jessie married William Woods in 1949, they have been together for as long as I can remember, until he was buried last week. I am married to Dewey Carruth. Bobby is married to Bertha Merchant Cunningham. Mother's grand-children are: Phyllis Woods Lucas, Pamela Woods Reed, Tammy Woods, Terry Woods, Barry Carruth, Berney Carruth, Brad Woolbright and Beth Woolbright Hays. Great-grandchildren are: Melanie Lucas Reeves, Savanna Woods, Ty Woods, Casey Carruth,

Summer Carruth, Annia Bell Carruth, Jordan Hays and Abby Hays. Great-great grandchildren are: Dustan Reeves and Lucas Reeves.

    Mother wonders just about every day, why she has lived 93 years. She thought when she was not able to work any longer, she should die. But God is not finished with her yet. My sister, Jessie, and I have learned much sharing the responsibility of caregivers for her. Not a day goes by that I don't learn a valuable lesson from her. I have seen such determination that it amazes me. She may be weak physically but she is strong in spirit. We are blessed she is still with us. I stay with her at night, and the other night she woke me. She was talking to someone, and when I turned the light on, she said "Why did you do that? Two of the prettiest people, I have ever seen, were here with me and when you turned on the light, they left." In my spirit I know who was with her. I have never seen an angel but I believe in them and have felt their presence. I wish I had not turned on the light and spoiled it for her. I am blessed to be able to call her "Mother." She recites a little rhyme to just about anyone that visits her. It goes like this: "Pretty as a pink, Sweet as a rose, How much I love you, Nobody knows." Only God knows how much we all love her!

Ellis Northington Wright

    Ellis was married to Tess (Estus) Wright. Tess was a brother to J. C. Wright and my step-father, Doc Wright and several other siblings. She was born in the Detroit, Alabama area but lived a few miles outside of Vernon for as long as I can remember. She taught school in Lamar County in some of the more rural areas for over 25 years. If I remember correctly, she taught at Wofford and maybe at a school named Bedford. Submitted by Peggy Guin Faulkner

Robert Green Wright

A Lamar Raised Man On Top

    In 1835, there was born in an humble cottage of poor but highly respectable parents, on the banks of the Sipsey, in the county of Lamar a male child, who was christened Robert Green, and whose sir name was Wright. It was here in this quiet and unpretending home the object of this sketch grew to manhood. His early education was sadly neglected, receiving such as could be obtained at the Old Field school of that day and place. When Mr. Wright attained his majority and went out in the world to carve out his own fortune, he decided to educate himself, which he did by alternate teaching and attending school. This first great object attained he chose the high and noble profession of medicine and entered at once upon the study of the same. Mr. Wright opened an office at Pleasant Site, Franklin County, in 1860, and commenced the practice of his profession. By close attention to business, and untiring application to books he soon built up a lucrative practice. But he was not left to pursue the even tenor of his way long, for soon, ah! soon wars dread alarm was sounded. "His brethren were already in the field." He could not stand idle, so he laid aside his books, closed his office, raised a company and joined the 27th Alabama Regiment, and on it organization was chosen Major. His first service was at Ft. Donolds where the 27th was captured, the Maj. however made his escape, and returned to Alabama and raised a Battalion with which he served with distinction to the close of the war, covering himself with honors as he was covered with scars.

During the war Maj. Wright met, wooed, and married one of Alabama's most beautiful and accomplished daughters. This good lady aided him in his early struggles after the war and now enjoys with him the rich fruits of his labor.

Maj. Wright settled at Union Springs after the war where he engaged in the drug business in a small way on borrowed capital. Finding this too slow for his energies and genius, he closed out and opened a Supply House which he now operates. His sales this year will amount $25,000. He raised last year 1,000 bales of cotton on his farms, and expects to gather 1,500 this year. He is now building a large fire-proof ware house, and has a contract out for building three brick stores with city hall above. One of these stores is to be used by the Major as a Banking House. Major Wright also owns an orange farm in Florida which he is enlarging every year, and expects to realize largely from it soon.

So you see if the same success attends him for the next ten years that has for the past ten he will be worth his millions.

Our young men ought to take fresh courage when they see what one poor friendless young man has done.

May you live long Green and be happy, is the wish of one who knew you when a poor boy. J. H. B.   Source: *The Vernon Clipper* August 1, 1879

Alexander Young

Another Good Man Gone

Died suddenly on Sunday evening last, at his home eight miles west of town, Mr. Alexander Young, in this 84th year. He was born in the state of South Carolina, on the 4th of Jan. 1805, and has resided in this section for 55 years. Outside of his immediate relatives he was known by all the people of his neighborhood as "Uncle Alex" and many who have received help and encouragement from him will, no doubt, realize that they have lost one to them worthy of the kind name which they bestowed upon him. While the summons was sudden, it was no great surprise to his family, for his physicians had told, both him and family that the end was near, and liable to come at any time. On the morning before his death he expressed himself as feeling better than he had for a long while, and in the evening on going out to his horse lot and remaining some minutes longer than usual, caused his wife to go in search of him, when she found him as he had fallen, without a single sign of a struggle, dead.

A large procession gathered at the old homestead on Tuesday morning, where funeral services were held and followed his remains to the grave. He had lived to see great-grandchildren several years old and out a family of six sons, surviving all but three. His mind was bright and active, and he looked on the sunny side of life to the last. And while he seemed conscious that the end was near and had made everything ready to go at any moment, he patiently waited for the summons to come. His life has been a blessing to the community where he lived, and his example will live long after him. Source: *The Vernon Courier* – March 9, 1888

Notice To Probate A Will

The State of Alabama, Lamar County

To Ella J. Young, Jas. P. Young, R. W. Young, Mary E. Dowdle, J. T. Dowdle, Columbus Ferguson, C. H. Ferguson, J. F. Ferguson, R. L. Young, Emma J. Young, Lizzie Burns, Lonnie Burns, Dora Young, Raymond Young, Goodhugh Young, J. A. Young, And Charley Young

You will please take notice that on the 24th day of March 1888 a certain paper in writing, purporting to be the last Will and Testament of Alexander Young, and that the 12th day of May 1888 was appointed a day of hearing thereof, at which time you can appear and contest the same, if you see proper. Given under my hand, this 178th day of April 1888.

W. A. Young, Judge of Probate   Source: *The Vernon Courier* - May 4, 1888

Notice Of Application To Sell Real Estate

The State of Alabama, Lamar County
Probate Court, January 1, 1890
Estate of Alexander Young, Decs'd

This day came John A. Young, Executor of said estate and filed his application in due from and under oath, praying for an order of sale of certain lands described therein, and belonging to said estate, for the purpose of paying debts, upon the ground that the personal property is not sufficient therefore.

It is ordered that the 14th day of February 1890 be appointed a day for hearing such application, at which time all parties in interest can appear and contest the same, if they think proper.

J. S. McEachin, Special Judge of Probate   Source: *The Vernon Courier*, January 30, 1890

Alexander Young Estate- Notice To Non-Resident Heirs
State of Alabama, Lamar County, Probate Court

To Mrs. C. J. Ferguson and husband J. F. Ferguson, and Columbus Ferguson, who reside at Tennessee.

Whereas, John A. Young, Executor of the estate of Alexander Young, deceased, has filed his application in said court, for a sale of the lands described therein, belonging to the estate of said decedent, for the purpose of paying the debts of said descendent, and the 14th day of February 1890, has been appointed for the hearing of said application.

You are therefore, hereby commanded to appear before the said Court on said 14th day of February 1890, to contest said application, if you think proper. Witness, this 1st day of January 1890.

J. S. McEachin, Special Judge of Probate   Source: *The Vernon Courier*, January 30, 1890

Dora Young

Died: on the 12th at her sisters, one mile west of town, Miss Dora Young, in her eighteenth year. Miss Dora was the second daughter of Mr. and Mrs. Samuel G. Young, both of whom only a short time since have died with the same terrible disease, consumption. While Dora's friends knew that the end was near, yet the summons came sooner than was expected. With a consciousness that she was gradually passing away still she waited for the messenger, which has to the world been called the "king of terrors' as it was only a common place invitation in life. Her fortitude and patience under so great suffering is rarely, if ever equaled. Perhaps, to yield up life just on the entering and realizing of the hopes of womanhood may be no greater cross than at any other time in line; and requires a kind of heroism not general among mankind. Miss DorA was taken on Wednesday to the old burying ground of her family, at New Hope Church, and there laid to rest. Her life has been spent in the church, and by an abiding faith in her Savior she was comforted in the living hour. Friend   Source: *The Vernon Courier* June 15,1888

Eddie Young

Eddie Young seems to posses a charmed life, falling from the top of a two story building on the evening of the first inst., making a clear fall of thirty feet. His injuries were right serious but not of a dangerous character, both wrists were badly dislocated, and an ugly wound on the forehead. He is now recovering rapidly. Source: *The Lamar News* September 9, 1886

J. P. and R. W. Young

Mr. R. W. Young will take wheat at the regular market price for subscriptions to the Pioneer at the gin house of Alexander Young & Sons, Bedford, Ala. Source: *The Vernon Pioneer* - June 13, 1877.

Messrs. J. P. and R. W. Young of Bedford, who lost their mill and gin by fire last winter, have rebuilt everything a the old stand, and are better prepared now than before, to work for the public. Source: *The Vernon Courier*, September 28, 1888.

Esqr.. Jas P. Young's leather house was broken into on the night of the 19th ult; the amount of leather taken is not known. No traces left so as to identify the robbers. Source: *The Vernon Clipper* January 16, 1880.

A new post office has been established in Military Springs Beat called Bedford, with JAS. P. YOUNG postmaster. Source: The Vernon Courier, June 15, 1888.

Mrs. Judge Young

Mrs. Judge Young, who has been seriously ill during the week, is thought to be improving. Source *The Vernon Courier*, July 6, 1888

Young-Limited Partnership

The undersigned, residing in the town of Vernon, have this the 21st day of March 1888, in pursuance of the provisions in the Code of Alabama, formed a limited partnership or the transaction of a newspaper publishing and general job printing business in the town of Vernon, Ala. R. J. Young is the general partner, and Mollie C. Young is the special partner; the latter having contributed to the common stock of the firm the sum of $266.00. The business will be transacted under the name of the Courier Publishing Company. Said partnership commences on this 21st day of March 1888, and is to continue for a term of six years.

R. J. Young
Mollie C. Young
The State of Alabama, Lamar County, Probate Court
The terms of the above named co-partnership, together with the proper certificates and affidavits, have this day been duly filed and recorded in my office. It is, therefore, ordered that the above notice thereof, be published for six successive weeks in the Vernon Courier and the Marion County Herald. Given under my hand at office, this 21st day of March 1888.
W. A. Young, Judge of Probate
Source: *The Vernon Courier*, April 27, 1888

William A. Young

William A. Young

Judge William A. Young is a native of Lamar County, Ala., and was born October 22, 1857, the second in a family of ten children, born to James P. and Martha (Box) Young, natives of South Carolina and Alabama, respectively. James P. Young came to Alabama in 1836 and settled in Fayette County, where he engaged in tanning and farming. He is a prominent citizen of Lamar, and is president of the Veterans Association of that county. The paternal grandparents of William A. Young were Alexander And Esther Young of South Carolina, and his maternal grandparents were Lyles and Mary Box, of Tennessee. William A. Young was educated in the public and private schools of Lamar county, and at the Vernon Institute. At the age of twenty-three he entered the law department of the University of Alabama at Tuscaloosa, and with one exception, completed his law education in a shorter period than any other on record in that department. After graduation he opened practice at Vernon, which he successfully continued for six years, when he was appointed Probate Judge by Gov. Seay in 1887. He filled the position with punctilious attention to every detail of the business brought before him, and was on the first day of August 1892, by a handsome majority, elected to the same office.

William A. Young

He has also served as mayor of Vernon one term and has filled the position of chairman of the county Democratic Executive Committee of Lamar. The marriage of Mr. Young took place in 1887, the bride being Miss Mary C. Crew, a native of Alabama and daughter of Titus L. Crew, of Tennessee. Two children have come to bless the household, and are named Albert and Oliver. Mr. Young is an Odd Fellow and with Mrs. Young, a member of the Methodist Episcopal Church South. His hand is always open to the demands of charity and he is a liberal contributor to all commendable enterprises. Source: *Memorial Record of Alabama* by Hannis Taylor, Brant & Fuller, Publishers, Madison, Wis. 1893. Transcribed and submitted by Veneta McKinney

ABOUT THE AUTHOR

Barb Carruth Is Author Of Two Books: *Lamar County, Alabama* Published In 2001 By Arcadia Publishing Company In Their *Images Of America Series* And *Alabama Desperado Legends Of Rube Burrow And Gang* Self-Published In 2006. She Co-Authored Along With Marion County, Alabama Historical Society, The Book *Marion County, Alabama Images Of America* Released By Arcadia Publishing April 13th, 2009. Her Historical Column *Lamar County Kin* Is Featured In The *The Lamar Leader* Newspaper, Sulligent, Alabama Periodically.

She Loves West Alabama And Its History. Her Favorite Past-Time Is "Preserving History One Piece At A Time."

Currently Serving As Vice-President Of Lamar County (Alabama) Genealogical & Historical Society.

A Researcher And Collector of Local History For Over Twenty Years.

Received Daughters Of The American Revolution D.A.R. Community Service Award In 2010:
"On Sunday, December 12, 2010, Barbara Woolbright Carruth was recognized by the National Society of the Daughters of the American Revolution for her outstanding contributions in community service to Lamar County, Alabama. Nominated by Vernon's Daring Dicey Chapter of the Alabama D.A.R., Mrs. Carruth received a certificate and a pin at the awards ceremony held in conjunction with the December D.A.R. meeting in Vernon. Several guests were present for the ceremony.

This purpose of this prestigious award is to recognize a worthy resident for voluntary achievements, and contributions to the community, in cultural, educational, humanitarian, patriotic, historical, and citizenship endeavors.

A brief list of some of Mrs. Carruth's community service activities are as follows:

Vice President of the 100+ member Lamar County Genealogical & Historical Society. Helps plan programs, does publicity, writes and publishes the quarterly "Links" newsletter, serves as webmaster.

Instrumental in setting up the Genealogy & History Room at the Vernon City Complex and serves as volunteer there to help people doing family research.

Periodically wrote a newspaper column, "Lamar County Kin," which dealt with County history and genealogy.

Does 'Story Tellin' for local students, dressing in costume and relating tales of early Lamar County settlers.

Donna S. Thompson, Chairman of the Daring Dicey Chapter's Community Service Award Committee, stated, 'When I was appointed Chairman of this Committee, the first person I thought of was Barbara Carruth. She is a one-woman, walking, talking encyclopedia of Lamar County history and genealogy. She is passionate about preserving the landmarks and culture of the area, and she is also a community activist, always looking for ways to help those less fortunate or in need. Barbara is an asset to Lamar County and very deserving of the D.A.R. Community Service Award.'

Mrs. Carruth is a lifelong resident of Lamar County, having been born to Jack and Lula Woolbright in the Lost Creek Community, five miles northwest of Sulligent. She is retired from the U.S.D.A.'s Farm Service Agency, with 37 years of service in the Lamar County and Marion/Winston County offices. She resides in Sulligent with her husband of 47 years, Dewey Carruth."

Watch For Future Books To Be Published. *Lamar County Kin Volume Two* Is In The Works. *Rube Burrow Alabama Desperado More* Is Planned For Early Spring 2018.

Made in the USA
Middletown, DE
21 December 2018